MW00763628

Step by Step Courseware

APPROVED COURSEWARE

Microsoft
Outlook 2000
Microsoft Office Application

Core Skills Student Guide

ActiveEducation™

PUBLISHED BY
Microsoft Press
A Division of Microsoft Corporation
One Microsoft Way
Redmond, Washington 98052-6399

Library of Congress Cataloging-in-Publication Data
Microsoft Outlook 2000 Step by Step Courseware Core Skills Student Guide / ActiveEducation.
    p. cm.
  Includes index.
  ISBN 0-7356-0976-4 (1 color) -- ISBN 0-7356-0706-0 (4 color)
    1. Time management--Computer programs. 2. Personal information
management--Computer programs. 3. Electronic mail systems. I. ActiveEducation
(Firm)

HD69.T54 M538   2000
005.369--dc21   99-044099

Printed and bound in the United States of America.

1 2 3 4 5 6 7 8 9   WCWC   5 4 3 2 1 0

Distributed in Canada by Penguin Books Canada Limited.

A CIP catalogue record for this book is available from the British Library.

Microsoft Press books are available through booksellers and distributors worldwide. For further information about
international editions, contact your local Microsoft Corporation office or contact Microsoft Press International directly
at fax (425) 936-7329. Visit our Web site at mspress.microsoft.com.

For ActiveEducation:
Managing Editor: Ron Pronk
Series Editor: Kate Dawson
Technical Editors: Holly Freeman, Sandra L. Knauke
Editorial Assistants: Lawrence Coles,
  Carrice L. Cudworth, Nicole French, Jennifer Jordan,
  Linda Savell
Indexer: Craig Wise

For Microsoft Press:
Acquisitions Editor: Susanne M. Forderer
Project Editor: Sandra Haynes
Proofreader: Roger LeBlanc
Production/Layout: Elizabeth Hansford
Electronic Artist: Joel Panchot

Contents

Course Overview vii

A Task-Based Approach Using Business Scenarios vii • An Integrated Approach to Training viii • Preparation for Microsoft Office User Specialist (MOUS) Certification viii • A Sound Instructional Foundation viii • Designed for Optimal Learning viii • Lesson Features x • Suggestions for Improvements xii

Conventions and Features Used in This Book xiii

Using the CD-ROM xv

System Requirements xv • If You Need to Install or Uninstall the Practice Files xvi • Using the Practice Files xv • Replying to Install Messages xviii • Copying Outlook Items to Outlook Folders xviii • If You Need Help with the Practice Files xx

MOUS Objectives xxi

Core Skills xxi

Taking a Microsoft Office User Certification Test xxiii

Preparing to Take an Exam xxiii • Test Format xxiv • Tips for Successfully Completing the Test xxv • If You Do Not Pass the Test xxvi

Lesson 1   **Introduction to Outlook** 1.1

Starting Outlook 1.2 • Navigating Within Outlook 1.3 • Using the Outlook Bar 1.6 • Using the Folder List 1.13 • Using the Office Assistant 1.14 • Lesson Wrap-Up 1.16 • Lesson Glossary 1.16 • Quick Quiz 1.17 • Putting It All Together 1.17

Lesson 2   **Using E-Mail in Outlook** 2.1

Composing, Addressing, and Sending Messages 2.2 • Attaching a File to a Message 2.5 • Checking for E-Mail Messages 2.7 • Reading Messages 2.9 • Replying to and Forwarding Messages 2.10 • Printing Messages 2.11 • Finding Messages 2.13 • Recalling Messages 2.14 • Deleting Messages 2.16 • Lesson Wrap-Up 2.17 • Lesson Glossary 2.17 • Quick Quiz 2.19 • Putting It All Together 2.19

Lesson 3   **Customizing E-Mail** 3.1

Specifying E-Mail Options 3.2 • Customizing the Appearance of E-Mail Messages 3.6 • Using Stationery 3.10 • Adding a Signature to an E-Mail Message 3.12 • Setting Viewing Options 3.14 • Sorting Messages 3.17 • Filtering a View 3.19 • Creating Folders 3.21 • Moving Messages Between Folders 3.24 • Color-Coding Message Headers 3.27 • Filtering Junk E-Mail Messages 3.29 • Archiving Messages 3.31 • Lesson Wrap-Up 3.33 • Lesson Glossary 3.33 • Quick Quiz 3.34 • Putting It All Together 3.34

Lesson 4   **Using Contacts** 4.1

Viewing Contacts 4.2 • Creating and Editing a New Contact 4.5 • Entering Multiple Contacts for the Same Company 4.8 • Using the Office Clipboard 4.8 • Deleting and Restoring Contacts 4.11 • Using Folders to Organize Contacts 4.12 • Using Views to Organize Contacts 4.13 • Using Categories to Organize Contacts 4.15 • Assigning Items to Multiple Categories 4.17 • Modifying the Outlook Master Category List 4.18 • Sorting Contacts 4.19 • Using the Address Book to Send E-Mail 4.21 • Using Contacts to Send E-Mail 4.23 • Sending Contact Information via E-Mail 4.24 • Receiving Contact Information via E-Mail 4.28 • Creating a Letter for a Contact Using the Letter Wizard 4.29 • Lesson Wrap-Up 4.33 • Lesson Glossary 4.34 • Quick Quiz 4.34 • Putting It All Together 4.35

Lesson 5   **Using the Calendar** 5.1

Navigating Within the Calendar 5.3 • Changing the Calendar View 5.5 • Scheduling Appointments and Events 5.8 • Creating Recurring Appointments 5.11 • Setting Reminders 5.13 • Editing Appointments 5.14 • Deleting Appointments 5.16 •Organizing Appointments by Using Categories 5.17 • Organizing Appointments by Using Views 5.18 • Planning Meetings 5.19 • Printing Calendars 5.22 • Saving a Calendar as a Web Page 5.23 • Integrating the Calendar with Other Outlook Components 5.25 • Lesson Wrap-Up 5.27 • Lesson Glossary 5.27 • Quick Quiz 5.28 • Putting It All Together 5.28

Lesson 6   **Using Tasks** 6.1

Creating Tasks 6.2 • Adding Task Details 6.4 • Sorting Tasks 6.6 • Organizing Tasks by Using Folders 6.8 • Organizing Tasks by Using Categories 6.10 • Assigning Tasks to Others 6.11 • Accepting or Declining Tasks 6.13 • Marking Tasks as Complete 6.15 • Manually Recording a Task in the Journal 6.16 • Deleting Tasks 6.19 • Lesson Wrap-Up 6.19 • Lesson Glossary 6.20 • Quick Quiz 6.20 • Putting It All Together 6.21

Lesson 7   Using Notes 7.1

Creating Notes 7.2 • Editing Notes 7.4 • Copying Notes 7.5 • Forwarding Notes 7.6 • Organizing Notes 7.7 • Deleting Notes 7.11 • Lesson Wrap-Up 7.12 • Lesson Glossary 7.12 • Quick Quiz 7.12 • Putting It All Together 7.12

Appendix   Setting Up Outlook A.1

Using the Outlook 2000 Startup Wizard A.1 • Creating a User Profile A.5 • Understanding, Adding, Changing, and Removing Information Services A.8 • Selecting a User Profile When Outlook Starts A.10 • Glossary A.10

Quick Reference C.1

Index C.21

Course Overview

Welcome to the *Step by Step Courseware* series for Microsoft Office 2000 and Microsoft Windows 2000 Professional. This series facilitates classroom learning, letting you develop competence and confidence in using an Office application or operating system software. In completing courses taught with *Step by Step Courseware*, you learn to use the software productively and discover how to make the software work for you. This series addresses core-level and expert-level skills in Microsoft Word 2000, Microsoft Excel 2000, Microsoft Access 2000, Microsoft Outlook 2000, Microsoft FrontPage 2000, and Microsoft Windows 2000 Professional.

The *Step by Step Courseware* series provides:

- A time-tested, integrated approach to learning.
- Task-based, results-oriented learning strategies.
- Exercises based on business scenarios.
- Complete preparation for Microsoft Office User Specialist (MOUS) certification.
- Attractive student guides with full-featured lessons.
- Lessons with accurate, logical, and sequential instructions.
- Comprehensive coverage of skills from the basic to the expert level.
- Review of core-level skills provided in expert-level guides.
- A CD-ROM with practice files.

A Task-Based Approach Using Business Scenarios

The *Step by Step Courseware* series builds on the strengths of the time-tested approach that Microsoft developed and refined for its Step by Step series. Even though the Step by Step series was created for self-paced training, instructors have long used it in the classroom. For the first time, this popular series has been adapted specifically for the classroom environment. By studying with a task-based approach, you learn more than just the features of the software. You learn how to accomplish real-world tasks so that you can immediately increase your productivity using the software application.

The lessons are based on tasks that you might encounter in the everyday work world. This approach allows you to quickly see the relevance of the training. The task-based focus is woven throughout the series, including lesson organization within each unit, lesson titles, and scenarios chosen for practice files.

An Integrated Approach to Training

The *Step by Step Courseware* series distinguishes itself from other series on the market with its consistent delivery and completely integrated approach to learning across a variety of print and online training media. With the addition of the *Step by Step Courseware* series, which supports classroom instruction, the *Step by Step* training suite now provides a flexible and unified training solution.

Print-Based Self-Training in the Step by Step Training Suite

The proven print-based series of stand-alone *Step by Step* books has consistently been the resource that customers choose for developing software skills on their own.

Online Training in the Step by Step Training Suite

For those who prefer online training, the *Step by Step Interactive* products offer highly interactive online training in a simulated work environment, complete with graphics, sound, video, and animation delivered to a single station (self-contained installation), local area network (LAN), or intranet. *Step by Step Interactive* has a network administration module that allows a training manager to track the progress and quiz results for students using the training. For more information, see *mspress.microsoft.com*.

Preparation for Microsoft Office User Specialist (MOUS) Certification

This series has been certified as approved courseware for the Microsoft Office User Specialist certification program. Students who have completed this training are prepared to take the related MOUS exam. By passing the exam for a particular Office application, students demonstrate proficiency in that application to their employers or prospective employers. Exams are offered at participating test centers. For more information, see *www.mous.net*.

A Sound Instructional Foundation

All products in the *Step by Step Courseware* series apply the same instructional strategies, closely adhering to adult instructional techniques and reliable adult learning principles. Lessons in the *Step by Step Courseware* series are presented in a logical, easy-to-follow format, helping you find information quickly and learn as efficiently as possible. To facilitate the learning process, each lesson follows a consistent structure.

Designed for Optimal Learning

The following "Lesson Features" section shows how the colorful and highly visual series design makes it easy for you to see what to read and what to do when practicing new skills.

Lessons break training into easily assimilated sessions. Each lesson is self-contained, and lessons can be completed in sequences other than the one presented in the table of contents. Sample files for the lessons don't depend on completion of other lessons. Sample files within a lesson assume only that you are working sequentially through a complete lesson.

The *Step by Step Courseware* series features:

- **Lesson objectives.** Objectives clearly state the instructional goals for each lesson so that you understand what skills you will master. Each lesson objective is covered in its own section, and each section or topic in the lesson is covered in a consistent way. Lesson objectives preview the lesson structure, helping you grasp key information and prepare for learning skills.

- **Informational text for each topic.** For each objective, the lesson provides easy-to-read, technique-focused information.

- **Hands-on practice.** Numbered steps give detailed, step-by-step instructions to help you learn skills. The steps also show results and screen images to match what you should see on your computer screen. The accompanying CD contains sample files used for each lesson.

- **Full-color illustrations in color student guides.** Illustrated screen images give visual feedback as you work through exercises. The images reinforce key concepts, provide visual clues about the steps, and give you something to check your progress against.

- **MOUS icon.** Each section or sidebar that covers a MOUS certification objective has a MOUS icon in the margin at the beginning of the section. The number of the certification objective is also listed.

- **Tips.** Helpful hints and alternate ways to accomplish tasks are located throughout the lesson text.

- **Important.** If there is something to watch out for or something to avoid, this information is added to the lesson and indicated with this heading.

- **Sidebars.** Sidebars contain parenthetical topics or additional information that you might find interesting.

- **Margin notes** Margin notes provide additional related or background information that adds value to the lesson.

- **Button images in the margin.** When the text instructs you to click a particular button, an image of the button and its label appear in the margin.

- **Lesson Glossary.** Terms with which you might not be familiar are defined in the glossary. Terms in the glossary appear in boldface type within the lesson and are defined upon their first use within lessons.

- **Quick Quiz.** You can use the short-answer Quick Quiz questions to test or reinforce your understanding of key topics within the lesson.

Lesson Features

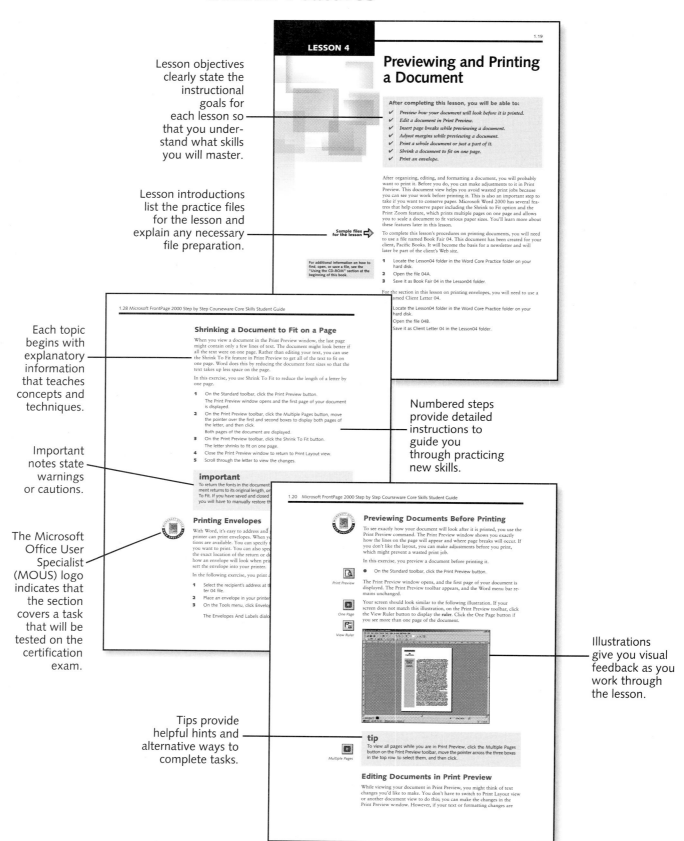

Lesson objectives clearly state the instructional goals for each lesson so that you understand what skills you will master.

Lesson introductions list the practice files for the lesson and explain any necessary file preparation.

Each topic begins with explanatory information that teaches concepts and techniques.

Important notes state warnings or cautions.

The Microsoft Office User Specialist (MOUS) logo indicates that the section covers a task that will be tested on the certification exam.

Numbered steps provide detailed instructions to guide you through practicing new skills.

Illustrations give you visual feedback as you work through the lesson.

Tips provide helpful hints and alternative ways to complete tasks.

Margin notes provide additional information.

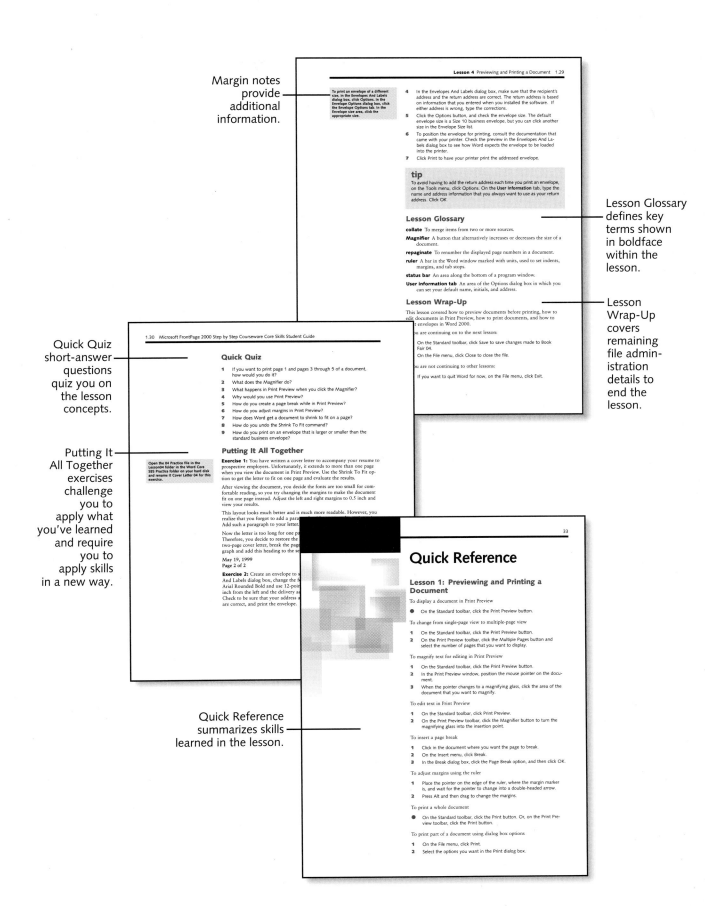

Lesson Glossary defines key terms shown in boldface within the lesson.

Lesson Wrap-Up covers remaining file admin-istration details to end the lesson.

Quick Quiz short-answer questions quiz you on the lesson concepts.

Putting It All Together exercises challenge you to apply what you've learned and require you to apply skills in a new way.

Quick Reference summarizes skills learned in the lesson.

■ **Putting It All Together exercises.** These exercises give you another opportunity to practice skills that you learned in the lesson. Completing these exercises helps you to verify whether you understand the lesson, to reinforce your learning, and to retain what you have learned by applying what you have learned in a different way.

■ **Quick Reference.** A complete summary of steps for tasks taught in each lesson is available in the back of the guide. This is often the feature that people find most useful when they return to their workplaces. The expert-level guides include the references from the core-level guides so that you can review or refresh basic and advanced skills on your own whenever necessary.

■ **Index.** Student guides are completely indexed. All glossary terms and application features appear in the index.

Suggestions for Improvements

Microsoft welcomes your feedback on the *Step by Step Courseware* series. Your comments and suggestions will help us to improve future versions of this product. Please send your feedback to SBSCfdbk@microsoft.com.

Support requests for Microsoft products should not be directed to this alias. Please see "Using the CD-ROM" for information on support contacts.

Conventions and Features Used in This Book

This book uses special fonts, symbols, and heading conventions to highlight important information or to call your attention to special steps. For more information about the features available in each lesson, refer to the "Course Overview" section on page vii.

Convention	Meaning
Practice files for the lesson	This icon identifies the section that lists the files that the lesson will use and explains any file preparation that you need to take care of before starting the lesson.
You can also create a new appointment by pressing Ctrl+N.	Notes in the margin area are pointers to information provided elsewhere in the workbook or provide brief notes related to the text or procedures.
2000 New!	This icon indicates a new or greatly improved feature in this version of the software product and includes a short description of what is new.
OL2000.3.17	This icon indicates that the section where this icon appears covers a Microsoft Office User Specialist (MOUS) exam objective. The number below the icon is the MOUS objective number. For a complete list of the MOUS objectives, see the "MOUS Objectives" section on page xxi.
tip	Tips provide helpful hints or alternative procedures related to particular tasks.
important	Importants provide warnings or cautions that are critical to exercises.
Save	When a toolbar button is referenced in the lesson, the button's picture and label are shown in the margin.
Alt+Tab	A plus sign (+) between two key names means that you must press those keys at the same time. For example, "Press Alt+Tab" means that you hold down the Alt key while you press Tab.
Boldface type	This formatting indicates text that you need to type Or It indicates a glossary entry that is defined at the end of the lesson.

Using the CD-ROM

The CD-ROM included with this student guide contains the practice files that you'll use as you perform the exercises in the book. By using the practice files, you won't waste time creating the samples used in the lessons, and you can concentrate on learning how to use Microsoft Outlook 2000. With the files and the step-by-step instructions in the lessons, you'll also learn by doing, which is an easy and effective way to acquire and remember new skills.

The CD-ROM also includes a Microsoft Word file called Testbank.doc, which provides multiple-choice and true/false questions that you can use to test your knowledge following the completion of each lesson or the completion of the *Microsoft Outlook 2000 Step by Step Courseware Core Skills* course.

System Requirements

Your computer system must meet the following minimum requirements for you to install the practice files from the CD-ROM and to run Microsoft Outlook 2000.

important

The Outlook 2000 software is not provided on the companion CD-ROM at the back of this book. This course assumes that you have already purchased and installed Outlook 2000.

- A personal computer running Microsoft Outlook 2000 on a Pentium 75-megahertz (MHz) or higher processor with the Microsoft Windows 95 or later operating system with 24 MB of RAM, or the Microsoft Windows NT Workstation version 4.0 operating system with Service Pack 3 and 40 MB of RAM.

- Internet Explorer 4 or later (Lesson 2 and Lesson 5 only).

- Microsoft Word 97 or later (Lesson 2 and Lesson 4 only).

- At least 2 MB of available disk space (after installing Outlook 2000 or Microsoft Office 2000).

- A CD-ROM drive.

- A monitor with VGA or higher resolution (Super VGA recommended; 15-inch monitor or larger recommended).

- A Microsoft mouse, a Microsoft IntelliMouse, or other compatible pointing device.

■   An Internet or network connection.

■   An Internet e-mail account or an e-mail account on a network. For information on how to set up an Internet e-mail account, see the appendix, "Setting Up Outlook."

If You Need to Install or Uninstall the Practice Files

Your instructor might already have installed the practice files before you arrive in class. However, your instructor might ask you to install the practice files on your own at the start of class. Also, if you want to work through any of the exercises in this book on your own at home or at your place of business after class, you will need to first install the practice files.

To install the practice files:

1   Insert the CD-ROM in the CD-ROM drive of your computer.

A menu screen appears.

important

If the menu screen does not appear, start Windows Explorer. In the left pane, locate the icon for your CD-ROM, and click this icon. In the right pane, double-click the file StartCD.

2   Click Install Practice Files, and follow the instructions on the screen.

The recommended options are preselected for you.

3   After the files have been installed, click Exit.

A folder called Outlook Core Practice has been created on your hard disk, the practice files have been placed in that folder, and a shortcut to the Microsoft Press Web site has been added to your desktop.

4   Remove the CD-ROM from the CD-ROM drive.

Use the following steps when you want to delete the lesson practice files from your hard disk. Your instructor might ask you to perform these steps at the end of class. Also, you should perform these steps if you have worked through the exercises at home or at your place of business and want to work through the exercises again. Deleting the practice files and then reinstalling them ensures that all files and folders are in their original condition if you decide to work through the exercises again.

To uninstall the practice files:

1   On the Windows taskbar, click the Start button, point to Settings, and then click Control Panel.

2   Double-click the Add/Remove icon.

3   Click Outlook Core Practice in the list, and click Add/Remove. (If your computer has Windows 2000 Professional installed, click the Remove or the Change/Remove button.)

4   Click Yes when the confirmation dialog box appears.

The steps on the previous page will not delete any of the Outlook items or folders that you create during this course. You will need to delete those items manually.

Using the Practice Files

Each lesson in this book explains when and how to use any practice files for that lesson. The lessons are built around scenarios that simulate a real work environment, so you can easily apply the skills you learn to your own work. The scenarios in the lessons use the context of the fictitious Lakewood Mountains Resort, a hotel and convention center located in the mountains of California.

The following is a list of all files and folders used in the lessons.

File Name	Description
Contact Records - folder Darlene Rudd Fabrikam Inc. Fukiko Ogisu John Rodman Pat Kirkland Scott Fallon Stephanie Hooper Wingtip Toys Inc.	Folder containing the contact records listed here to work through the lessons in this book.
E-mail Messages - folder FREE cell phone!!! FW Paul Borm FW Scott Fallon Progress Meeting Vigor Airlines	Folder containing the e-mail messages listed here, which are necessary to work through the lessons in this book.
Map	Graphic file used in Lesson 2.
Syllabus	Microsoft Word file used in Lesson 2.

All the files for the lessons appear within the Outlook Core Practice folder.

On the first page of each lesson, look for the margin icon *Practice files for the lesson*. This icon points to the paragraph that explains which files you will need to work through the lesson exercises.

Configuring Mail Support

To match the exercises in this course, you should set your mail support configuration to Internet Only. To set your mail support to Internet Only:

1   Start Outlook.

2   On the Tools menu, click Options, and click the Mail Services tab. (If you do not have a Mail Services tab, but you do have a Mail Delivery tab, your mail support is already set to Internet Only.)

3   Click the Reconfigure Mail Support button.

The E-Mail Service Options dialog box appears.

4   In the E-Mail Service Options dialog box, click the Internet Only option, click the Next button, and then follow the instructions on your screen.

If Outlook does not detect a network card on your computer, it will configure mail support to Internet Only automatically.

If you are working through this course on a computer that is configured to work with Microsoft Exchange Server, you will probably notice some differences in the appearance of the Folder List and some dialog boxes. Also, the appearance of the Address Book window, which is discussed in Lesson 4, "Using Contacts" will be different.

Replying to Install Messages

When you work through some lessons, you might see a message indicating that the feature that you are trying to use is not installed. If you see this message, insert the Microsoft Outlook 2000 CD-ROM or Microsoft Office 2000 CD-ROM 1 in your CD-ROM drive, and click Yes to install the feature.

Copying Outlook Items to Outlook Folders

After you (or your instructor) have installed the practice files, all the files you need for this course will be stored in a folder named Outlook Core Practice located on your hard disk. To ensure that the lesson exercises work for you in the same way they are described in the workbook, you need to drag the Outlook items in the Contact Records folder and the E-mail Messages folder to the appropriate Outlook folders. To navigate to these folders and copy the Outlook items to Outlook folders:

1   On the Windows taskbar, click the Start button, point to Programs, and click Microsoft Outlook.

Restore

2   Click the Restore button in the top-right corner of the Outlook window.

3 On the Windows taskbar, click the Start button, point to Programs, and click Windows Explorer. (If you are running Microsoft Windows 2000 Professional, click the Start button, point to Programs, point to Accessories, and then click Windows Explorer.)

Restore

4 Click the Restore button in the top-right corner of the Windows Explorer window.

Both the Outlook window and the Windows Explorer window should be visible. If necessary, drag the windows' title bars to arrange them side-by-side.

5 In Windows Explorer, navigate to the Outlook Core Practice folder on your hard disk, and display the contents of the Contact Records folder.

6 Click the first item in the Contact Records folder, hold down Shift, and click the last item in the Contact Records folder.

7 Drag the selected items to the Contacts shortcut on the Outlook Bar or to the Contacts folder in the Outlook Folder List.

The contact records appear in the Contacts folder in Outlook.

8 In Windows Explorer, display the contents of the E-mail Messages folder.

9 Click the first item in the E-mail Messages folder, hold down Shift, and click the last item in the E-mail Messages folder.

10 Drag the selected items to the Inbox shortcut on the Outlook Bar or to the Inbox folder in the Outlook Folder List.

The e-mail messages appear in the Inbox in Outlook.

Close

11 Click the Close button in the top-right corner of the Windows Explorer window and the Outlook window.

If You Need Help with the Practice Files

If you have any problems regarding the use of this book's CD-ROM, you should first consult your instructor. If you are using the CD-ROM at home or at your place of business and need additional help with the practice files, see the Microsoft Press Support Web site at *mspress.microsoft.com/ support*.

important

Please note that support for the Outlook 2000 software product itself is not offered through the above Web site. For help using Outlook 2000, rather than this Microsoft Press book, you can visit *www.microsoft.com/support* or call Outlook 2000 Technical Support at (425) 635-7070 on weekdays between 6 A.M. and 6 P.M. Pacific Standard Time. Microsoft Product Support does not provide support for this course.

MOUS Objectives

Core Skills

Objective	Activity	Page
OL2000.1.1	Read mail	2.9
OL2000.1.2	Send mail	2.2
OL2000.1.3	Compose mail by entering text	2.2
OL2000.1.4	Print mail	2.11
OL2000.1.5	Address mail by entering text	2.2
OL2000.1.6	Use mail features (forward, reply, recall)	2.10, 2.14
OL2000.1.7	Use address book to address mail	4.21
OL2000.1.8	Flag mail messages	2.3
OL2000.1.9	Navigate within mail	2.9
OL2000.1.10	Find messages	2.13
OL2000.1.11	Configure basic mail print options	2.11
OL2000.1.12	Work with attachments	2.5
OL2000.1.13	Add a signature to mail	3.12
OL2000.1.14	Customize the look of mail	3.6
OL2000.1.15	Use mail templates to compose mail	2.5
OL2000.1.16	Integrate and use mail with other Outlook components	4.21, 4.23, 4.24
OL2000.1.17	Customize menu and task bars	5.7
OL2000.2.1	Create folders	3.21
OL2000.2.2	Sort mail	3.17
OL2000.2.3	Set viewing options	3.14
OL2000.2.4	Archive mail messages	3.31
OL2000.2.5	Filter a view	3.19
OL2000.3.1	Navigate within the Calendar	5.3
OL2000.3.2	Schedule appointments and events	5.8
OL2000.3.3	Set reminders	5.13
OL2000.3.4	Print in Calendar	5.22
OL2000.3.5	Schedule multiday events	5.11
OL2000.3.6	Configure Calendar print options	5.22
OL2000.3.7	Customize the Calendar view	5.5
OL2000.3.8	Schedule recurring appointments	5.11
OL2000.3.9	Customize menu and task bars	5.7
OL2000.3.10	Add and remove meeting attendees	5.20
OL2000.3.11	Plan meetings involving others	5.19
OL2000.3.12	Save a personal or team calendar as a Web page	5.23
OL2000.3.13	Book office resources directly (e.g., conference rooms)	5.22

Objective	Activity	Page
OL2000.3.14	Integrate Calendar with other Outlook components	5.25
OL2000.4.1	Use Outlook Help and Office Assistant	1.14
OL2000.4.2	Move items between folders	3.24
OL2000.4.3	Navigate between Outlook components	1.3, 1.6
OL2000.4.4	Modify the Outlook Master Categories List	4.18
OL2000.4.5	Assign items to a category	4.17
OL2000.4.6	Sort information using categories	4.15
OL2000.4.7	Use the Office Clipboard	4.8
OL2000.5.1	Create, edit, and delete contacts	4.5, 4.11
OL2000.5.2	Send contact information via e-mail	4.24
OL2000.5.3	Organize contacts by category	4.15
OL2000.5.4	Manually record an activity in a journal	6.16
OL2000.5.5	Link activities to a contact	4.7
OL2000.5.6	Sort contacts using fields	4.19
OL2000.6.1	Create and update one-time tasks	6.2
OL2000.6.2	Accept and decline tasks	6.13
OL2000.6.3	Organize tasks using categories	6.10
OL2000.6.4	Assign tasks to others	6.11
OL2000.6.5	Create tasks from other Outlook components	5.25
OL2000.6.6	Change the view for tasks	6.4
OL2000.7.1	Create and use Office documents inside Outlook 2000	4.29
OL2000.8.1	Create and edit notes	7.2, 7.4
OL2000.8.2	Organize and view notes	7.7
OL2000.8.3	Customize notes	7.8

Taking a Microsoft Office User Specialist Certification Test

The Microsoft Office User Specialist (MOUS) program is the only Microsoft-approved certification program designed to measure and validate your skills with the Microsoft Office suite of desktop productivity applications: Microsoft Word, Microsoft Excel, Microsoft PowerPoint, Microsoft Access, and Microsoft Outlook.

By becoming certified, you demonstrate to employers that you have achieved a predictable level of skills in the use of a particular Office application. Certification is often required by employers either as a condition of employment or as a condition of advancement within the company or other organization. The certification examinations are sponsored by Microsoft but administered through Nivo International.

For each Microsoft Office 2000 application, two levels of MOUS tests are currently or will soon be available: core and expert. For a core-level test, you demonstrate your ability to use an application knowledgeably and without assistance in a day-to-day work environment. For an expert-level test, you demonstrate that you have a thorough knowledge of the application and can effectively apply all or most of the features of the application to solve problems and complete tasks found in business.

Preparing to Take an Exam

Unless you're a very experienced user, you'll need to use a test preparation course to prepare to complete the test correctly and within the time allowed. The *Step by Step Courseware* training program is designed to prepare you for either core-level or expert-level knowledge of a particular Microsoft Office application. By the end of this course, you should have a strong knowledge of all exam topics, and with some additional review and practice on your own, you should feel confident in your ability to pass the appropriate exam.

After you decide which exam to take, review the list of objectives for the exam. This list can be found in the "MOUS Objectives" section at the front of the appropriate *Step by Step Courseware* student guide; the list of MOUS objectives for this book begins on page xxi. You can also easily identify tasks that are included in the objective list by locating the MOUS logo in the margin of the lessons in this book.

For an expert-level test, you'll need to be able to demonstrate any of the skills from the core-level objective list, too. Expect some of these core-level tasks to appear on the expert-level test. In the *Step by Step Courseware Expert Skills Student Guide*, you'll find the core skills included in the "Quick Reference" section at the back of the book.

You can also familiarize yourself with a live MOUS certification test by downloading and installing a practice MOUS certification test from *www.mous.net*.

To take the MOUS test, first see *www.mous.net* to locate your nearest testing center. Then call the testing center directly to schedule your test. The amount of advance notice you should provide will vary for different testing centers, and it typically depends on the number of computers available at the testing center, the number of other testers who have already been scheduled for the day on which you want to take the test, and the number of times per week that the testing center offers MOUS testing. In general, you should call to schedule your test at least two weeks prior to the date on which you want to take the test.

When you arrive at the testing center, you might be asked for proof of identity. A driver's license or passport is an acceptable form of identification. If you do not have either of these items of documentation, call your testing center and ask what alternative forms of identification will be accepted. If you are retaking a test, bring your MOUS identification number, which will have been given to you when you previously took the test. If you have not prepaid or if your organization has not already arranged to make payment for you, you will need to pay the test-taking fee when you arrive. The current test-taking fee is $50 (U.S.).

Test Format

All MOUS certification tests are live, performance-based tests. There are no multiple-choice, true/false, or short answer questions. Instructions are general: you are told the basic tasks to perform on the computer, but you aren't given any help in figuring out how to perform them. You are not permitted to use reference material other than the application's Help system.

As you complete the tasks stated in a particular test question, the testing software monitors your actions. An example question might be:

> Change the Calendar view to Work Week, and schedule an appointment next Tuesday at 9:00 A.M. with the subject *Department Meeting*. Set the recurrence to weekly, and set a reminder for the appointmetnt five minutes in advance of the appointment time.

The sample tests available from *www.mous.net* give you a clear idea of the type of questions that you will be asked on the actual test.

When the test administrator seats you at a computer, you'll see an online form that you use to enter information about yourself (name, address, and other information required to process your exam results). While you complete the form, the software will generate the test from a master test bank and then prompt you to continue. The first test question will appear in a window. Read the question carefully, and then perform all the tasks stated in the test question. When you have finished completing all tasks for a question, click the Next Question button.

You have 45 to 60 minutes to complete all questions, depending on the test that you are taking. The testing software assesses your results as soon as you complete the test, and the results of the test can be printed by the test administrator so that you will have a record of any tasks that you performed incorrectly. A passing grade is 75 percent or higher. If you pass, you will receive a certificate in the mail within two to four weeks. If you do not pass, you can study and practice the skills that you missed and then schedule to retake the test at a later date.

Tips for Successfully Completing the Test

The following tips and suggestions are the result of feedback received by many individuals who have taken one or more MOUS tests:

- Make sure that you are thoroughly prepared. If you have extensively used the application for which you are being tested, you might feel confident that you are prepared for the test. However, the test might include questions that involve tasks that you rarely or never perform when you use the application at your place of business, at school, or at home. You must be knowledgeable in *all* the MOUS objectives for the test that you will take.

- Read each exam question carefully. An exam question might include several tasks that you are to perform. A partially correct response to a test question is counted as an incorrect response. In the example question on the previous page, you might change the calendar view, create the appointment, and set the recurrence, but forget to set the reminder. This would count as an incorrect response and would result in a lower test score.

- You are allowed to use the application's Help system, but relying on the Help system too much will slow you down and possibly prevent you from completing the test within the allotted time. Use the Help system only when necessary.

- Keep track of your time. The test does not display the amount of time that you have left, so you need to keep track of the time yourself by monitoring your start time and the required end time on your watch or a clock in the testing center (if there is one). The test program displays the number of items that you have completed along with the total number of test items (for example, "35 of 40 items have been completed"). Use this information to gauge your pace.

- If you skip a question, you cannot return to it later. You should skip a question only if you are certain that you cannot complete the tasks correctly.

- Don't worry if the testing software crashes while you are taking the exam. The test software is set up to handle this situation. Find your test administrator and tell him or her what happened. The administrator will work through the steps required to restart the test. When the test restarts, it will allow you to continue where you left off. You will have the same amount of time remaining to complete the test as you did when the software crashed.

■ As soon as you are finished reading a question and you click in the application window, a condensed version of the instruction is displayed in a corner of the screen. If you are unsure whether you have completed all tasks stated in the test question, click the Instructions button on the test information bar at the bottom of the screen and then reread the question. Close the instruction window when you are finished. Do this as often as necessary to ensure you have read the question correctly and that you have completed all the tasks stated in the question.

If You Do Not Pass the Test

If you do not pass, you can use the assessment printout as a guide to practice the items that you missed. There is no limit to the number of times that you can retake a test; however, you must pay the fee each time that you take the test. When you retake the test, expect to see some of the same test items on the subsequent test; the test software randomly generates the test items from a master test bank before you begin the test. Also expect to see several questions that did not appear on the previous test.

LESSON 1

Introduction to Outlook

After completing this lesson, you will be able to:

✔ *Start Outlook.*

✔ *Navigate within Outlook.*

✔ *Use the Outlook Bar.*

✔ *Use the Folder List.*

✔ *Use the Office Assistant.*

Until personal computers became popular, managing work-related information meant storing paper-based information in several different places. For example, a businessperson might record appointments and meetings in a day planner, while keeping phone number and addresses in a card file. Brief reminders might be jotted down on small sticky notes, and other important business information might be stored in files and folders in a desk drawer or filing cabinet.

Although many people have grown accustomed to these organizational approaches, Microsoft Outlook provides a better way to store, track, and integrate personal information. With Outlook, you can store your important information on a personal computer and access it from within Outlook. For example, you can use Outlook's electronic calendar to record meetings and appointment dates and times. Outlook can even sound an alarm or display a reminder on your computer screen when you have an appointment. You can record brief reminders to yourself on Outlook notes, which resemble sticky notes; these notes can be displayed on your screen at any time for easy reference. You can also use Outlook to record your daily or weekly tasks, and then check them off as you complete them. Outlook has an address book in which you can record phone numbers, addresses, e-mail addresses, and other information about your business and personal contacts. You can even view Web sites directly from Outlook as well as open other Microsoft Office documents. The power of Outlook lies in knowing how to use all of its capabilities to organize information efficiently.

In this lesson, you will tour many of the elements of Outlook to become familiar with it. You will start Outlook and view different **folders**, which are containers for programs and files. You will also take a closer look at the **Outlook Bar** and the **shortcuts** that you find there. Shortcuts are icons that appear on the Outlook Bar, and that, when clicked, display the contents of the corresponding folder or file. Finally, you will learn how to use the Help system in Outlook to get answers to your questions.

Practice files for the lesson ⇨

Your Outlook folders should already contain the Outlook items (e-mail messages, contact records) that are necessary to complete the exercises in this lesson. If you need to add these items to your Outlook folders, see the "Using the CD-ROM" section at the beginning of this book.

You will learn more about the Inbox folder later in this lesson.

To close Outlook at any time, in the top-right corner of the Outlook window, click the Close button.

If you are opening Outlook for the first time, the Office Assistant (the animated paper clip character) might appear in the bottom-left corner of your screen. To close the Office Assistant, right-click the paper clip, and click Close on the shortcut menu that appears. You will learn more about the Office Assistant later in this lesson.

No practice files are required to complete the exercises in this lesson.

Starting Outlook

As with all Microsoft Office programs, there are several different ways to open Outlook. You can click the Start button on the Windows taskbar, point to Programs, and then click Microsoft Outlook. This option is always available, even if you are using another Microsoft Office program.

You can also add the Outlook icon to your desktop. When you double-click the icon, Outlook will start. This is a faster way to open Outlook than using the Start button on the Windows taskbar. To add an Outlook icon to your desktop, you click the Start button on the Windows taskbar, point to Programs, hold down the Ctrl key, and then drag the Microsoft Outlook icon onto your desktop. This process will add the icon to your desktop without removing it from the Start menu.

When you start Outlook, the Outlook window will appear with the Inbox folder visible. You use this main window to view and access all Outlook components.

In this exercise, you start Outlook.

1   On the Windows taskbar, click the Start button, point to Programs, and then click Microsoft Outlook.

Outlook starts.

2   If necessary, click the Maximize button in the top-right corner of the Outlook window.

The Outlook window expands to fill the entire screen.

Maximize

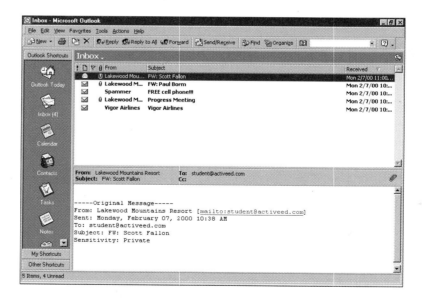

OL2000.4.3

Navigating Within Outlook

The Outlook window contains buttons, icons, menu commands, and other elements that you use to navigate within Outlook and use Outlook effectively. The contents of this window change as you click buttons and icons and choose options.

Standard toolbar   Folder Banner   Menu bar   Title bar

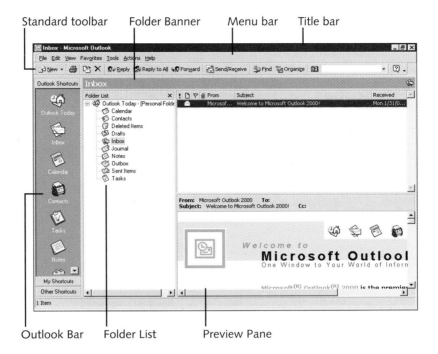

Outlook Bar   Folder List   Preview Pane

The following table describes the basic functions of the elements that appear in the Outlook window.

Element	Description
Title bar	Identifies the application being run (in this case, Outlook) and the current Outlook folder.
Menu bar	Lists the names of the menus available in the current Outlook window.
Standard toolbar	Displays buttons that allow you to quickly access commonly used features for the contents of the program window.
Outlook Bar	Displays shortcuts to the contents of different folders that are available in Outlook, such as the Inbox and Calendar. See the glossary for more information on shortcuts. The Outlook Bar is expandable and contains two or three groups of shortcuts: Outlook Shortcuts, My Shortcuts, and Other Shortcuts (also called Other). You can hide the Outlook Bar by clicking Outlook Bar on the View menu. You will learn how to use the shortcuts on the Outlook Bar later in this lesson.

(continued)

continued

Element	Description
Folder Banner	Displays the name of the open folder. For example, if you are in Contacts, the word Contacts will appear on the **Folder Banner**. When you click the folder name on the Folder Banner, a list of available folders appears.
Folder List	Displays a list of available Outlook folders. You click a folder in the list to display the folder's contents. The **Folder List** appears if you click Folder List on the View menu or click the Folder Banner. You can display the Folder List temporarily by clicking the name in the Folder Banner, or you can set up Outlook so that the Folder List is displayed each time a folder is opened. When you first use Outlook, you will have one personal folder in the Folder List for each component on the Outlook Bar. If your organization uses Microsoft Exchange Server, you might also see public folders that can be accessed by other network users. Using the Folder List, you can move items from one folder to another; create folders within folders, and much more.
Items	Information displayed in Outlook. For example, in the Inbox, each message is an item; in Contacts, the contact record (phone and address information about an individual) is an item.
Shortcut	An icon that appears on the Outlook Bar. When you click a shortcut, Outlook displays the contents of the corresponding folder or file.
Status bar	As you use the Outlook Bar or Folder List to switch to different Outlook folders, the Status bar displays the number of items that are in a specific folder. For example, when you open Contacts, the Status bar displays the number of contacts that you have in the folder.
Preview Pane	A section of the Inbox window that displays the text of the selected message. The **Preview Pane** appears by default in the Outlook window. To remove it, you click Preview Pane on the View menu.

> You can also use the Folder List to open folders on your hard disk.

Short menus show frequently used menu items.

Using Personalized Menus

Outlook has a new default feature that you can use to personalize your menus. When you first open a menu, you see a short menu that displays the commands that are most frequently used by Outlook users. You also see two small arrows at the bottom of the menu. These arrows are used to expand the menu to display more options. You can expand the menu in two ways: you can click the arrows at the bottom of the menu, or you can wait a few seconds for the menu to expand on its own. When you click a command on the expanded menu, Outlook immediately displays this command on the short menu. Over time, if you stop using this command, Outlook displays the command only on the expanded menu and removes it from the short menu.

In this exercise, you navigate through different areas of the Outlook window.

1 On the menu bar, click Tools.

The short Tools menu appears.

If you always want to see the expanded menus instead of the short menus, on the Tools menu, click Customize, click the Options tab, clear the Menus Show Recently Used Commands First check box, and then click Close.

2 Click anywhere outside the menu.

The menu closes.

3 On the menu bar, click Tools.

The short Tools menu appears.

Double Arrows

4 Click the double arrows at the bottom of the short Tools menu.

The expanded Tools menu appears.

Depending on the size of your monitor and your display settings, you might not have the up and down arrows in the Outlook Bar. If this is the case, all the Outlook shortcuts appear on the bar at one time and the arrows are not necessary.

Down Arrow

5 On the bottom-right side of the Outlook Bar, click the down arrow.

The Outlook Bar scrolls down.

Up Arrow

6 On the top-right side of the Outlook Bar, click the up arrow.

The Outlook Bar scrolls up.

The Folder List will close if you click outside the Folder List window. To keep the Folder List open, click the Push Pin button.

7   On the Folder Banner, click the folder name *Inbox*.

The Folder List appears.

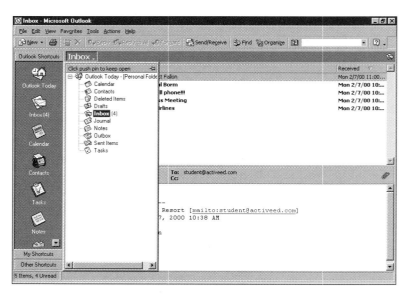

8   Click outside the Folder List.

The Folder List is no longer displayed.

OL2000.4.3

> Even though the Inbox, Contacts, Tasks, and other Outlook features are called "folders," in this book, you will sometimes see them referred to by name alone (for example, "the Inbox") rather than by name and identifier (for example, "the Inbox folder").

Using the Outlook Bar

The Outlook Bar displays the different components available in Outlook. The Outlook Bar contains shortcuts to the contents of frequently used folders, such as the Inbox, Calendar, and Contacts folders. When you click one of the shortcuts, the contents of the folder are displayed. For example, if you click the Calendar shortcut, the contents of the Calendar folder—a calendar containing your appointments—appear.

Outlook uses the term "folder" to describe how functions of Outlook and common Outlook items are divided within Outlook. For example, the Inbox folder (Inbox section of Outlook) contains e-mail messages that you've received, and you can create messages within the Inbox folder; the Tasks folder (Tasks section of Outlook) contains a list of activities that you need to perform, and you can create tasks within the Tasks folder. You cannot create a task in the Inbox folder, and you cannot create a message in the Tasks folder. When you view the folders in Outlook, you'll notice that the appearance and options differ in each folder. For that reason, you can think of each folder as a separate program within Outlook.

The Outlook Bar contains three groups (each group name is displayed on its own bar): Outlook Shortcuts, My Shortcuts, and Other Shortcuts (or simply Other). Each group contains specific shortcuts to folders.

The Outlook Shortcuts group contains eight shortcuts to the most frequently used folders in Outlook: Outlook Today, Inbox, Calendar, Contacts, Tasks, Journal, Notes, and Deleted Items. The My Shortcuts group contains at least four standard folders: Drafts, Inbox, Sent Items, and Outbox. Other folders might be displayed depending on how Outlook is set up. The Other Shortcuts (or Other) group contains folders that also appear in Windows Explorer: My Computer, My Documents, and Favorites. These folders are included so that if you're using Outlook and need to access a file, you don't have to open Windows Explorer. You can simply open the file from within Outlook.

The Outlook folders are described in the following table.

Because shortcuts can be moved from one group to another, the locations listed in the table might not be the same for your computer. If a shortcut does not appear in the group listed, look for it in another group.

Folder	Group	Description
Inbox	Outlook Shortcuts	Stores the e-mail messages that you receive
Calendar	Outlook Shortcuts	Displays an appointment book where you can keep track of your schedule
Contacts	Outlook Shortcuts	Stores the names, phone numbers, addresses, and other information of the people with whom you correspond and work
Tasks	Outlook Shortcuts	Displays a to-do list of your personal and business tasks
Notes	Outlook Shortcuts	Stores general information on electronic sticky notes, such as ideas, grocery lists, or directions
Journal	Outlook Shortcuts	Displays a history of your Microsoft Office activities in a timeline format
Deleted Items	Outlook Shortcuts	Temporarily stores the items that you delete until you permanently delete them
Drafts	My Shortcuts	Temporarily saves messages that have not been sent
Outbox	My Shortcuts	Holds e-mail messages that you send until they are delivered to recipients
Sent Items	My Shortcuts	Stores copies of the e-mail messages that you send
My Computer	Other Shortcuts	Gives access to other drives, folders, and files on your computer
My Documents	Other Shortcuts	Stores documents that you create in other programs
Favorites	Other Shortcuts	Stores shortcuts to important folders and Web addresses

In this exercise, you use the Outlook Bar to view different Outlook folders.

1   On the Outlook Bar, click the Outlook Today shortcut.

The contents of the Outlook Today folder appear.

You will learn how to use the Inbox to send and receive e-mail messages in the next lesson.

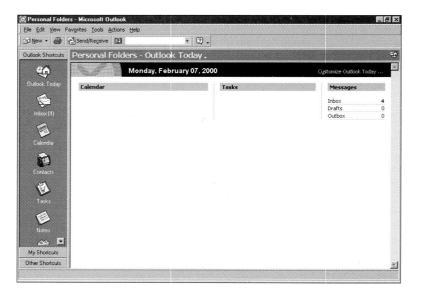

2   On the Outlook Bar, click the Calendar shortcut.

The contents of the Calendar folder appear.

You will learn how to use the Calendar in Lesson 5, "Using the Calendar."

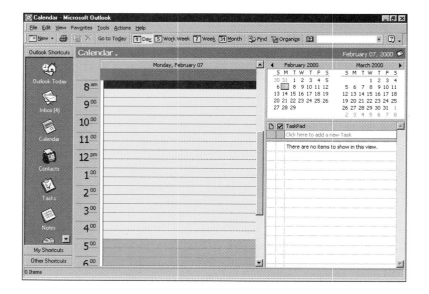

3   On the Outlook Bar, click the Contacts shortcut.

The contents of the Contacts folder appear.

You will learn how to create and edit contacts in Lesson 4, "Using Contacts."

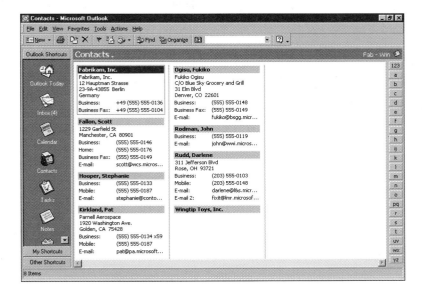

4   On the Outlook Bar, click the Tasks shortcut.

The contents of the Tasks folder appear.

You will learn how to create and edit tasks in Lesson 6, "Using Tasks."

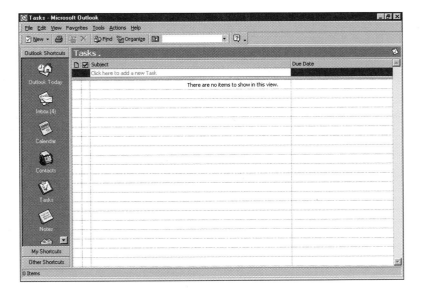

5   On the Outlook Bar, click the Notes shortcut.

The contents of the Notes folder appear.

You will learn how to create and edit Notes in Lesson 7, "Using Notes."

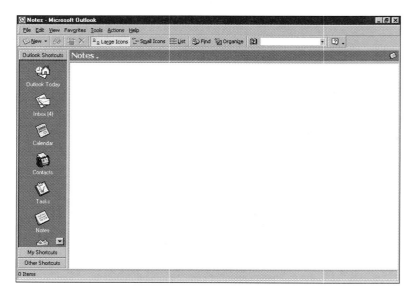

6   On the Outlook Bar, if necessary, click the down arrow, and click the Deleted Items shortcut in the Outlook Bar.

The contents of the Deleted Items folder appear. You can drag any item from any Outlook folder onto the Deleted Items shortcut on the Outlook Bar to remove the item from a folder and store it temporarily in the Deleted Items folder.

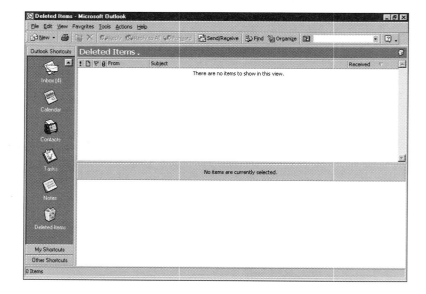

7 On the Outlook Bar, click the My Shortcuts group bar.

The shortcuts available in the My Shortcuts group are displayed.

My Shortcuts group

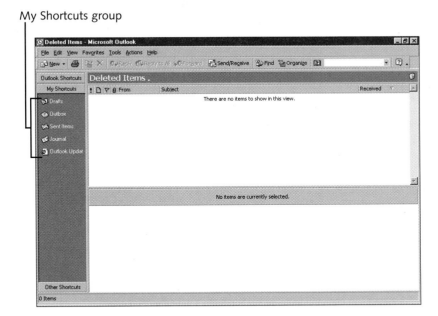

8 On the Outlook Bar, click the Other Shortcuts group bar (or Other group bar).

The shortcuts available in the Other Shortcuts (or Other) group are displayed.

Other Shortcuts group

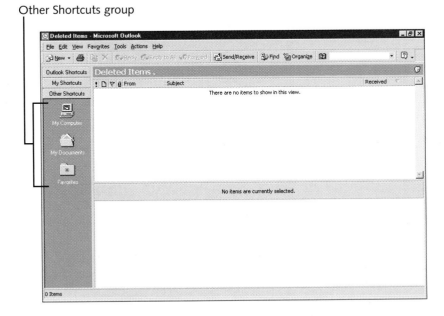

9   On the Outlook Bar, click the Outlook Shortcuts group bar.

The shortcuts available in the Outlook Shortcuts group appear again.

You can add frequently visited folders or Web sites to the Favorites folder.

Using the Favorites Folder

The Favorites folder is a shortcut to Web sites and other folders that you frequently use or don't want to forget. You find the Favorites folder in the Other Shortcuts (or Other) group.

Favorites folder

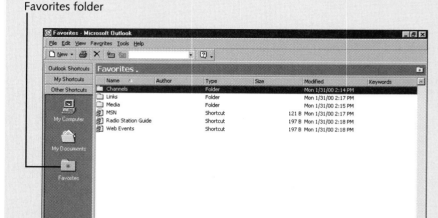

To add a Web site to the list of Favorites:

1   On the Windows taskbar, click the Start button, point to Programs, and then click Internet Explorer.

2   In the Address box, type the address of the Web site you want to add, and press Enter.

3   After the Web page appears, click Add To Favorites on the Favorites menu.

4   Click OK to accept the default title line as the name of the Favorite.

OR

Type a new name, and click OK.

To add a folder to the list of Favorites:

1   On the Windows taskbar, click the Start button, point to Programs, and then click Windows Explorer.

2   Click the folder you want to add, click Add To Favorites on the Favorites menu, and then click OK to accept the default title line as the name of the Favorite.

(continued)

continued

To access a favorite Web site or folder from Outlook:

1 On the Outlook Bar, click the Other Shortcuts group bar (or Other group bar).

2 Click the Favorites folder, and double-click the name of the Web site or folder that you want to open.

Using the Folder List

You can also view Outlook folders and their contents by using the Folder List. The Outlook Bar displays shortcuts of frequently used folders; however, not all folders are represented by these shortcuts. The Folder List displays *all* the folders available in Outlook, including the folders represented by shortcuts on the Outlook Bar.

The Folder List displays each folder as a small icon followed by the name of the folder. When you click a folder's icon, the contents of the folder will appear. For example, if you click the Contacts shortcut in the Folder List, Outlook will display the contents of the Contacts folder, where you can view contact records.

In this exercise, you use the Folder List to display many of the same folders that you displayed in the previous exercise.

1 On the Folder Banner, click the folder name *Deleted Items*.

The Folder List appears.

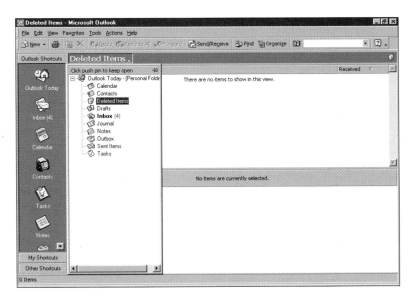

2   In the Folder List, click Inbox.

The contents of the Inbox folder appears, and the Folder List closes.

3   On the Folder Banner, click the folder name *Inbox*.

The Folder List appears.

Push Pin

4   In the top-right corner of the Folder List, click the Push Pin button.

The Push Pin button turns into a Close button. The Folder List will now remain open until you close it.

5   In the Folder List, click Tasks.

Outlook displays the contents of the Tasks folder. Note that the Folder List remains open.

Close

6   In the top-right corner of the Folder list, click the Close button.

The Folder List closes.

OL2000.4.1

Using the Office Assistant

Outlook, like all Microsoft Office applications, includes an extensive Help system that you can use to learn more about features and options available in Outlook. To get help about an Outlook topic, you can use the **Office Assistant**. The Office Assistant is an animated character that is used to ask for help on a particular topic. By default, the Office Assistant appears as an animated paper clip named Clippit; however, you can change the Office Assistant to appear as an animated dog, cat, or any one of several other characters.

To change the Office Assistant, right-click the Office Assistant, and click Choose Assistant. Click Next to view the various animations available, and click OK when you have found one that you want. Only the paper clip animation is saved onto your hard drive during installation, so if you want to change the Office Assistant, you will need to insert the Microsoft Office (or Microsoft Outlook) CD-ROM to install a new animation.

When the Office Assistant is displayed in Outlook, you can get help by clicking the Office Assistant and then typing your question in the box that appears. You can use Standard English to phrase your request—for example, "How do you send a message?" or "What is in the Journal?" Or you can simply type a few words, such as "send message" or "Journal," to get information related to those topics. The Office Assistant interprets your request and then displays topics that match one or more words in your request. You can then click the topic that most closely matches your request.

In this exercise, you display the Office Assistant, use it to get help on an Outlook topic, and then you hide the Office Assistant.

Microsoft Outlook Help

You can also display the Office Assistant by clicking Show The Office Assistant on the Help menu.

1 On the Standard toolbar, click the Microsoft Outlook Help button.

The Office Assistant appears with a yellow box, asking you what you would like to do.

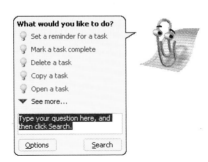

2 Type **How do I send a message?**, and click the Search button.

The Office Assistant displays Help topics that are relevant to the question you asked.

3 Click the Send Messages option.

An Outlook Help window appears, explaining how to send messages.

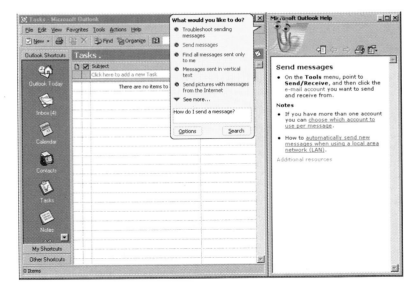

Close

4 In the top-right corner of the Help window, click the Close button.

The Outlook Help window closes.

5 Right-click the Office Assistant, and click Hide.

The Office Assistant disappears.

Lesson Wrap-Up

In this lesson, you learned how to start Outlook 2000, and how to navigate through the main Outlook window. You also learned how to use the Outlook Bar and the Folder List to display different Outlook folders. Finally, you learned how to use the Office Assistant to get more information about Outlook.

If you are continuing to the next lesson:

●   On the Outlook Bar, click the Inbox shortcut.

    The contents of the Inbox folder appear.

If you are not continuing to other lessons:

Close

●   In the top-right corner of the Outlook window, click the Close button. Outlook closes.

Lesson Glossary

folders Containers that include files and additional folders. In Outlook, folders are used to divide Outlook into different functions. For example, in the Inbox folder you can send messages, and in the Contacts folder, you can create contact records.

Folder Banner A bar that displays the name of the open Outlook folder and displays the Folder List when it is clicked.

Folder List A list of folders and subfolders used to display the contents of the folders and subfolders.

Office Assistant An animated character that you can use to get help on Microsoft Office applications.

Outlook Bar A bar located on the left side of the Outlook window that contains shortcuts to frequently used folders and files. The Outlook Bar is expandable and contains three groups: Outlook Shortcuts, My Shortcuts, and Other Shortcuts (or Other).

Preview Pane A view of the Inbox window that displays the text of a selected message.

shortcuts Icons that appear on the Outlook Bar. When you click a shortcut, Outlook displays the contents of the corresponding folder or file.

Quick Quiz

1   What is a group?

2   How do you use the Office Assistant to get help in Outlook?

3   What does the Folder Banner do?

4   What are two ways to display an expanded menu?

5   What are shortcuts?

6   List two ways to display an Outlook folder, such as the Inbox.

Putting It All Together

Exercise 1: Display the View menu, and then display the expanded View menu. When you open the expanded View menu, move your mouse pointer across different menus on the Menu bar to see what happens.

Exercise 2: Display the Folder List, and then keep it displayed. Use the Folder List to display the contents of the Contacts folder and then the Tasks folder. Then, use the Office Assistant to find out how to hide the Outlook Bar. Hide the Outlook Bar, and redisplay it. Close the Folder List.

LESSON 2

Using E-Mail in Outlook

After completing this lesson, you will be able to:

✔ *Compose, address, and send messages.*

✔ *Attach a file to a message.*

✔ *Check for e-mail messages.*

✔ *Read messages.*

✔ *Reply to and forward messages.*

✔ *Print messages.*

✔ *Find messages.*

✔ *Recall messages.*

✔ *Delete messages.*

Gone are the days when the telephone was the main way to communicate with other people immediately and postal mail was the chief way to send letters and documents to others. Today **e-mail** lets you communicate and share information with others in faster and often more versatile ways. E-mail refers to any communication that is sent or received via computers, either over the Internet or through a messaging program used with an organization's internal network or intranet.

Creating, sending, receiving, and reading e-mail messages are the activities that you will probably perform most frequently with Microsoft Outlook. E-mail provides a fast way to send and receive messages and even documents such as reports, worksheets, and pictures.

In this lesson, you will learn how to create, address, and send an e-mail **message.** You will learn how to send an e-mail message with attachments; check for and read messages; and reply to and forward messages. You will learn how to flag messages with a reminder to yourself or to the recipient to follow up on the message by a certain date. You will also learn how to print, find, and recall messages that you've sent. Finally, you will learn how to save e-mail messages that you aren't ready to send in **Drafts,** a folder that stores incomplete messages, and you will learn how to delete messages.

To complete the exercises in this lesson, you will need to use the files named Map and Syllabus in the Outlook Core Practice folder that is located on your hard disk.

Your Outlook folders should already contain the Outlook items (e-mail messages, contact records) that are necessary to complete the exercises in this lesson. If you need to add these items to your Outlook folders, see the "Using the CD-ROM" section at the beginning of this book.

Practice files for the lesson

important

To complete some of the exercises in this lesson, you will need to exchange e-mail messages with a class partner. If you don't have a class partner or are performing the exercises alone, you can enter your own e-mail addres instead of your class partner's and send the message to yourself.

OL2000.1.2
OL2000.1.3
OL2000.1.5

Composing, Addressing, and Sending Messages

If you've used other e-mail programs, you'll probably find that creating and sending messages is similar in Outlook. You create a new mail message by clicking the New Mail Message button on the Standard toolbar.

The message can be any length and can contain any information that you want. The following illustration shows the message window that you use to create an e-mail message.

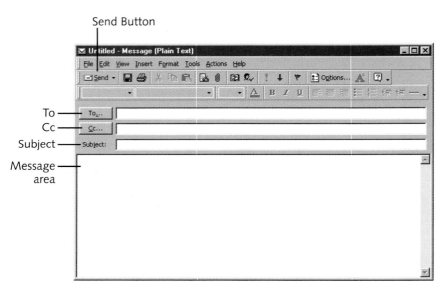

You can include a Web site address in e-mail messages that, when clicked by message recipients, automatically starts their default Web browsers and displays the Web site. Including a Web site address in the message is helpful because the recipient then does not need to go through the process of opening his or her Web browser and typing the Web site address to access the site. To include a Web site address in a message, just type it in the message. Outlook automatically formats the address (or URL, an acronym for Uniform Resource Locator) as a link to a Web page—for example, *www.microsoft.com.*

Just as you must address an envelope before mailing it, you must also provide at least one e-mail address in the To box of your message. An advantage of e-mail is that you can address a message to several recipients and send the message to all recipients simultaneously. To send a message to multiple recipients, you type a semicolon after each recipient's e-mail address or press Enter after each recipient's address. After you type one or more e-mail addresses, you enter the subject of your message, type the message, and click the Send button on the Standard toolbar in the message window. Your e-mail message arrives in recipients' Inboxes often within seconds after you send it.

Below the To button is the Cc button. Cc is an acronym for courtesy copy. Courtesy copies are complete copies of a message sent to others for information purposes only; the Cc recipients are not required to take any action. You don't have to include a courtesy copy to send a message. To send a courtesy copy message, enter the recipient's e-mail address in the Cc box. To send a courtesy copy message to multiple recipients, type a semicolon after each recipient's e-mail address. When the Cc recipient receives the message, his or her address appears in the message header as a Cc.

The subject of the message is usually a brief description of the information in the message, but it can be anything that you want. Recipients of the messages will see the subject that you type in the **message header** in their Inboxes. A message header includes the name of the sender, the subject of the message, and the date and time when the message was sent. When you include a subject, it allows recipients to quickly identify the purpose of the e-mail message without having to open the message. If you don't type a subject for a message, Outlook warns you that the message has no subject before you send it. You type the body of the e-mail message in the message area.

OL2000.1.8

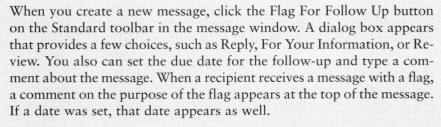

Flagging Messages

Sometimes it's necessary to remind yourself or notify recipients about the importance of a message that you are sending. Perhaps you sent a message about an event with a specific deadline or asked for input on a particular topic. You can **flag** the message to remind yourself to follow up on an issue, or you can flag an outgoing message with a request for someone else to follow up with a reply.

Flag For Follow Up

When you create a new message, click the Flag For Follow Up button on the Standard toolbar in the message window. A dialog box appears that provides a few choices, such as Reply, For Your Information, or Review. You also can set the due date for the follow-up and type a comment about the message. When a recipient receives a message with a flag, a comment on the purpose of the flag appears at the top of the message. If a date was set, that date appears as well.

The message appears in the recipient's Inbox with either a red flag, indicating that action still needs to be taken, or a gray flag, indicating that the request is complete.

In this exercise, you compose a message and send a message to your class partner.

New Mail Message

1   On the Standard toolbar, click the New Mail Message button.

A message window appears.

2   In the To box, type the e-mail address of your class partner.

> You can also display a new message window by pointing to New on the File menu and clicking Mail Message.

3   Press Tab twice.

The insertion point moves to the Subject box.

4   Type **Picnic Reminder**, and press Enter.

The subject is entered, and the insertion point moves to the message area.

5   Type **Just a reminder that our 5th annual Fun in the Sun picnic is on Saturday, June 6th.**

Your message window should now look similar to the following.

> **Your To box will contain your class partner's e-mail address.**

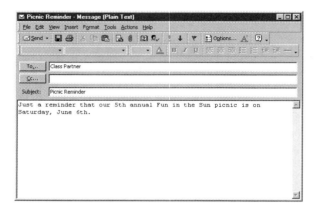

6   On the Standard toolbar in the message window, click the Send button.

The message is sent to your class partner.

> **If the server is down or if there is a problem with the connection to the Internet, messages won't be sent; instead, they'll be placed in the Outbox until a connection is reestablished.**

important

Although you clicked the Send button, the message has not necessarily been sent over the Internet (or over the intranet) yet. By default, Outlook connects to your server (Workgroup, Corporate, or Internet service provider) and sends and receives e-mail every 10 minutes. Messages that have been sent but have not made it to the server yet are stored in your **Outbox**, a folder whose shortcut is found in the My Shortcuts group on the Outlook Bar. To send and receive e-mail immediately, click the Send/Receive button. This action connects your computer to your server, sends all e-mail messages in the Outbox, and retrieves any messages that the server has for you. To avoid delays while performing the exercises in this and any other lesson in this book, whenever you click the Send button, click the Send/Receive button immediately after that.

OL2000.1.15

Using Mail Templates to Compose Mail

If you have a certain message that you send over and over again, you can save the message as a template so that it can easily be reused. For example, suppose that you want to send a weekly message to the members of your project team, and in this message, you want to include a table that lists that week's meeting agenda items. You could save the message as a template, and then use the template each week, adding current information in the appropriate places on the template. In Outlook, you can create an original message template or modify an existing message template and save the changes with a new name.

To save a message as a template:

1   Create the e-mail message that you want to use as a template.

2   In the message window, click Save As on the File menu.

3   In the Save As dialog box, click the Save As Type down arrow, click Outlook Template (.oft), and then click the Save button.

To open a template:

1   On the Tools menu, point to Forms, and click Choose Form.

2   In the Choose Form dialog box, click the Look In down arrow, click User Templates In File System, and then double-click the name of the template.

OL2000.1.12

Attaching a File to a Message

In today's fast-paced workplaces, you need to be able to get information to several people in a short amount of time. As an example, the sales manager at Lakewood Mountains Resort likes to distribute Microsoft Excel sales forecast workbooks to other managers at the resort. Rather than distributing printed copies or retyping the contents of these documents into an e-mail message, the sales manager can make the workbook file an **attachment**—an external document included as part of a message—and send the message and the attachment to all recipients at one time.

An attachment can be a **file**, a document stored on a disk, or another Outlook **item**. A file can be any type of document, such as a Microsoft Word document, an Excel spreadsheet, or a picture. An item is an Outlook object, such as a contact, task, or note. You will learn how to create and use these and other Outlook items later in this book.

The selected attachment appears in your message as an **icon**, or graphic representation of the attached file. When you send the message, the message recipient can double-click the icon to open and view the file or item.

The type of icon that appears depends on the file type of the attachment. For example, the icon for an attached Word file is the same icon that appears for Word files in Windows Explorer. The icon for an attached Excel file is the same icon that appears for Excel files in Windows Explorer.

You can also print attachments. Printing message attachments is covered later in this lesson.

To attach a file to a message, you compose the message just as you normally would and click the Insert File button on the Standard toolbar in the message window. Then you navigate to the folder that contains the file, click the file name, and then click the Insert button. You repeat this procedure to attach multiple files to a message.

To attach an Outlook item to a message, you click Item on the Insert menu to display the Insert Item dialog box. In the Look In list, click the folder name for the type of Outlook item, such as a contact, that you want to attach. In the Items list in the bottom pane, click the item that you want to attach, and then click OK.

Setting Message Priority

You can also specify the priority for a message. When you mark a message as High priority, the message header appears in the recipient's message window with a red exclamation point, indicating that you want the recipient to reply to or read the message as soon as possible. When you mark a message as Low priority, a blue, downward pointing arrow appears in the message header of the message, indicating that the recipient can reply to or read the message when convenient.

To mark a message as High or Low priority:

Importance: High

Importance: Low

- On the Standard toolbar in the message window, click the Importance: High button (indicated by a red exclamation point).

  Or

  On the Standard toolbar in the message window, click the Importance: Low button (indicated by a blue down arrow).

In this exercise, you compose a message, attach a picture to the message, and then send the message and file attachment to your class partner.

New Mail Message

1   On the Standard toolbar, click the New Mail Message button.

A message window appears.

2   In the To box, type the e-mail address of your class partner.

3   Press Tab twice, and type **Fun in the Sun Picnic Invitation** in the Subject box.

4   Press Enter, and in the message area, type **Hope to see you at the picnic on June 6th at 1:00 P.M. For directions to Cherry Creek Park, please see the attached map. See you there!**

Insert File

5 On the Standard toolbar in the message window, click the Insert File button.

The Insert File dialog box appears.

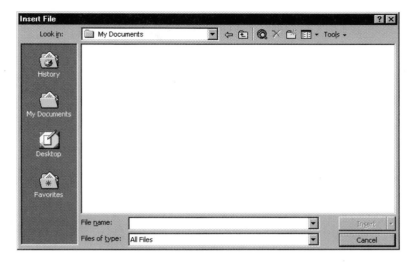

6 Click the Look In down arrow, and navigate to the Outlook Core Practice folder on your hard disk.

7 Double-click the Map file to attach it to your e-mail message.

Outlook attaches the Map file to the e-mail message, and the Insert File dialog box closes. Your screen should look similar to the following.

If you are sending an e-mail attachment to someone who connects to the Internet using a slow modem (33.6 KBps or slower), you should limit the attachment size to 300 KB or less. Messages with large attachments can take a long time for recipients' e-mail programs to receive.

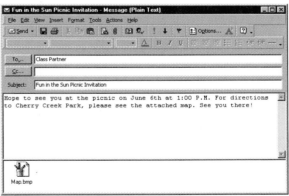

8 On the Standard toolbar in the message window, click the Send button.

The message is sent to your class partner.

Checking for E-Mail Messages

Just as Outlook sends e-mail every 10 minutes, Outlook automatically checks for new mail every 10 minutes. Later in this course, you will learn how to change this setting to a longer or shorter interval. Also, just as with sending e-mail, you can manually check for messages by clicking the Send/Receive button on the Standard toolbar. Any messages that are on the mail server appear in your **Inbox**.

important

Interoffice mail—e-mail sent over a local area network (LAN) or to a **Microsoft Exchange Server** post office—is usually sent almost instantaneously. However, when you send e-mail to someone outside of your LAN or Exchange Server, you send the message over the Internet. Your Internet service provider's mail server places incoming messages in a **mail queue**. The mail queue is a list of messages received by a mail server organized in the order in which the messages are received. In turn, messages are sent to recipients in the order in which the server received them. Sometimes this means you will have to wait a few minutes to receive an Internet mail message that was sent to you.

In this exercise, you check for incoming e-mail messages.

1   If necessary, on the Outlook Bar, click the Outlook Shortcuts group bar, and click the Inbox shortcut.

The contents of the Inbox folder appear, and message headers appear in the top pane of the message window for messages that you've already received.

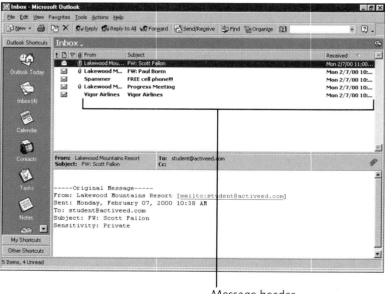

Message header

If you are using Exchange Server to send and receive e-mail messages, or if you have multiple e-mail accounts, point to Send/Receive on the Tools menu and click the account that you want to send to and receive from.

2   On the Standard toolbar, click the Send/Receive button.

A progress bar indicating that Outlook is sending and receiving messages appears briefly, and then new message headers appear in the top pane of the message window. The messages are from your class partner.

OL2000.1.1
OL2000.1.9

Reading Messages

The Inbox appears with the Preview Pane, the area at the bottom right of the Outlook window, open by default. You can read the body of a message in the Preview Pane by clicking the message header in the Inbox. Messages that you have read are shown with an open envelope icon to the left of the message header; unread messages appear with a closed envelope icon. If the Preview Pane is not visible, you can double-click the message header to open the message in a separate window.

Open envelope

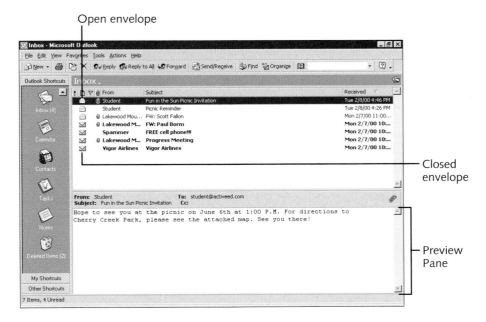

Closed envelope

Preview Pane

In this exercise, you read the e-mail messages that your class partner sent to you.

1   Click the *Picnic Reminder* message header.

The *Picnic Reminder* message header appears in the Preview Pane.

2   Double-click the *Fun in the Sun Picnic Invitation* message header.

The message appears in its own window. Notice the attachment icon in the message.

Be sure to single-click the *Picnic Reminder* message in step 1. Double-clicking the message has a different result.

3   Double-click the Map attachment icon.

A dialog box appears, asking if you would like to open the file or save it to disk.

You can also open an attachment in the Preview Pane. In the top-right corner of the Preview Pane, click the paper clip icon, and click the attachment.

4   Click the Open It option, and click OK.

The Map file opens in the program that has been set up to read picture files. By default, this program is Microsoft Internet Explorer, but it could be a different program if your computer has a program installed for viewing and editing graphics.

Close

5   In the top-right corner of the window that contains the map, click the Close button.

The application closes.

6   In the top-right corner of the message window, click the Close button.

The message closes, and the Inbox appears.

Using AutoPreview and the Preview Pane

The **AutoPreview** feature provides an extended view of each e-mail message that you receive. When you turn on AutoPreview, Outlook displays the first three lines of every e-mail message directly below the message header.

AutoPreview is useful if you receive dozens of e-mail messages each day and want to scan through them quickly to determine which messages to read first. You can also use AutoPreview to skim the contents of messages so that you can quickly spot junk e-mail messages that have deceptive headers.

Outlook automatically displays the content of the currently selected message in the Preview Pane. You can close the Preview Pane if you want to view more e-mail message headers at a time. Because both the Preview Pane and AutoPreview allow you to view portions of messages, you might find that it's not necessary to use both at the same time.

To turn AutoPreview on or off:

●   On the View menu, click AutoPreview.

To turn the Preview Pane on or off:

●   On the View menu, click Preview Pane.

> The AutoPreview and Preview Pane menu commands are on/off toggles. That is, if you click one of these commands while the feature is turned on, the feature is turned off. If you click one of these commands while the feature is turned off, the feature is turned on.

OL2000.1.6

Replying to and Forwarding Messages

If you receive an advertisement via postal mail, you might simply read it and discard the advertisement. If you receive a letter from a friend sent via postal mail, you might want to respond after you've read the letter, by writing and sending a reply to your friend.

E-mail is similar. Sometimes, you'll read the information in an e-mail message without replying to the message. At other times, you'll **reply** to e-mail messages sent to you by friends or coworkers. A reply sends a copy of the original message and additional text that you type, if any. The recipient will see the text *RE:* and the original subject in the message header. When you reply to a message, you can choose to reply to only the sender, or if other recipients received the same message, you can choose to reply to both the sender and all the other recipients.

After you receive an e-mail message, you might decide that the information contained in the message will be useful to others. If so, you can **forward** the message to other recipients. Forwarding a message lets you send a message to those not originally on the recipient list. All you do is click the Forward button on the Standard toolbar, type the e-mail addresses of the additional recipients in the To box, and then click the Send button. You can also type additional information at the start of the forwarded message prior to sending the message.

In this exercise, you reply to the message that was sent to you and forward that message to another member of your class.

1   In the Inbox, verify that the *Fun in the Sun Picnic Invitation* message header is selected.

2   On the Standard toolbar, click the Reply button.

A reply window opens with the original message displayed, and the insertion point is already in the message area.

3   In the message area, type **Yes, I will be attending the picnic**.

4   On the Standard toolbar in the message window, click the Send button.

The reply is sent to your class partner.

5   On the Standard toolbar, click the Send/Receive button.

A reply from your class partner appears in the Inbox.

6   In the Inbox, click the *Fun in the Sun Picnic Invitation* message header again.

7   Click the Forward button on the toolbar.

A forward window opens with the original message displayed.

8   In the To box, type an e-mail address for a class member other than your class partner.

9   On the Standard toolbar in the message window, click the Send button.

The message is forwarded to a class member.

10   On the Standard toolbar, click the Send/Receive button.

A forwarded message from a class member appears in the Inbox.

tip

You can also reply to or forward a message by clicking Reply or Forward on the Actions menu.

OL2000.1.4
OL2000.1.11

Printing Messages

It's often convenient to print a copy of a message so that you can read the message when you're not at your computer or to pass the message to somebody who does not have access to e-mail. For example, Lakewood Mountains Resort employees found it useful to print a copy of a message that provided directions to the company picnic. They then followed the directions to get to the park.

You can also print message attachments if the application used to create the attachment is installed on your computer. You can print an attachment by opening the attachment and using the Print command of the program that the attachment opens in, or by right-clicking the attachment icon in the message window and clicking Print on the shortcut menu. When printing an attachment, Outlook might display an alert box warning you of the possible danger of viruses hidden within attached messages. Click the Print button in the message box to continue the printing process.

Outlook includes several options for printing e-mail messages. Messages can be printed in Table style or Memo style. If you print using the Table style, you will see a list of messages in a table format that resembles the Inbox; the message headers that are currently in your Inbox will be listed under column headings, such as From, Subject, and Received. If you print using the Memo style, the printout will include your name at the top of the page, information about the message (who the message was from, when the message was sent, who the message was sent to, and the subject of the message); the actual message appears last.

Clicking the Page Setup button opens the Page Setup dialog box. In the Page Setup dialog box you can preview the page style, the size of the columns and rows (if you selected the Table style), and the fonts in which the message will be printed. If you click the Paper tab on the Print Setup dialog box, you can change the paper type, such as letter, legal, and A4, and page styles, including the Day-Timer and Franklin Day Planner styles.

In this exercise, you print an e-mail message in the Memo style, and you set up Outlook to print an e-mail message and its attachment.

1   In the Inbox, click the *Picnic Reminder* header message header.

The *Picnic Reminder* message header is selected

Print

2   On the Standard toolbar, click the Print button.

One copy of the e-mail message is printed.

3   Click the original *Fun in the Sun Picnic Invitation* message header.

4   On the File menu, click Print.

The Print dialog box appears.

You can also use the Print dialog box to print multiple copies of a message or attachment. Type the number of copies that you want to print in the Number Of Copies box, and click OK.

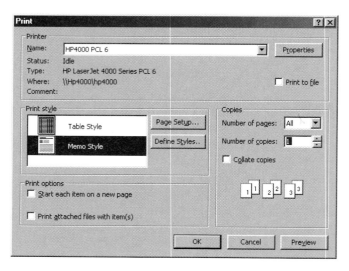

5   In the Print Options section, select the Print Attached Files With Item(s) check box, and click OK.

Outlook prints the e-mail message in the Memo style, and prints the attachment.

important

An alert box might appear, asking whether you want to open the attached file. To print the attachment, click the Open It option, and click OK.

OL2000.1.10

Finding Messages

If you send and receive a lot of messages on a regular basis, your Inbox and **Sent Items** folder might contain dozens or even hundreds of messages. At some point, you might need to track down a specific message sent to a recipient or a message received from a particular e-mail address. For example, one of the new employees at Lakewood Mountains Resort said he didn't receive directions to the picnic. The sender opened the Sent Items folder and then searched for a key word or phrase (such as *picnic directions*) that she knew was contained in the message. She then forwarded the message to the employee who had not received the directions.

In this exercise, you will find the messages that contain the word *directions*.

1   On the Standard toolbar, click the Find button.

The Find Items In Inbox pane appears.

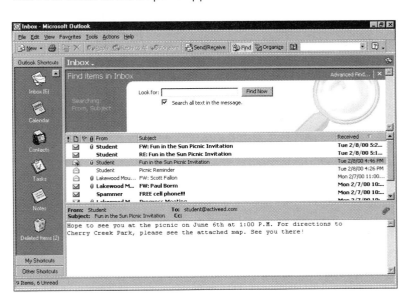

2   In the Look For box, type **directions**.

3   Click the Find Now button.

The results appear in the lower half of the screen. The directions messages should be the only messages listed.

> **tip**
> Depending on the folder that's currently open (Inbox, Sent Items, Outbox, Drafts, or Deleted Items), the search will look at particular fields, such as the To, Cc, or subject line. The fields are displayed to the left of the Look For box. The Search All Text In The Message check box is selected by default to expand the search to include the message text.

You can also click the Close button in the top-right corner of the pane to close the Find Items In Inbox pane.

4   On the Standard toolbar, click the Find button.

The Find Items In Inbox pane no longer appears.

OL2000.1.6

Recalling Messages

Outlook provides a way for recalling a message after it has been sent. You can **recall** a message and send an updated message when it's important to reissue information that might have been sent incorrectly the first time, or if you sent the message to the wrong recipient. For example, the recreation director at Lakewood Mountains Resort sent a message to the planning team announcing an upcoming event and accidentally typed the wrong date for the event. He recalled the message, made the correction to the date, and then resent it.

> **important**
> This procedure works only if you are using Outlook in the Corporate or Workgroup setting. If you use the Internet Only setting, the procedure will not work.

This procedure works only for recipients who are using Outlook and who have not read the message or moved it out of their Inboxes. (You will learn how to move messages later in this lesson.) The recipient will receive an e-mail message stating that the sender would like to recall the message. The recipient will still be able to read the message, but he or she has the option to delete the message per the sender's request.

On a Microsoft Exchange Server network, the message is deleted from the recipient's Inbox. Microsoft Exchange Server is a collaboration program that can be installed on a Microsoft Windows NT or Microsoft Windows 2000 server. It allows people in an organization to communicate via the network without going through the Internet and provides many additional benefits for collaborating with others on the organization's network.

> **important**
> To recall messages, you must set your e-mail service options to Corporate or Workgroup. To do so, on the Tools menu, click Options, click the Mail Delivery tab, and click the Reconfigure Mail Support button. In the E-Mail Service Options dialog box, click the Corporate Or Workgroup option, click the Next button, and then follow the instructions on your screen.

When you recall a message, you have a few options. These options appear in the Recall This Message dialog box, as shown on the following page. You can choose to delete the unread copies of the message, or delete the unread copies of the message and replace it with a new message. You can also have Outlook send you a message telling you whether the recall succeeds or fails for each recipient.

You can choose to delete the message even if you and the recipient are not using Outlook with Microsoft Exchange Server. However, the recalled message will be deleted from the recipient's mailbox only if he or she uses Outlook with Microsoft Exchange Server.

In this exercise, you create a message, send it to your class partner, and then recall the message. You also view a recall message from your class partner.

New Mail Message

1 On the Standard toolbar, click the New Mail Message button.

A mail message window appears.

2 In the To box, type the e-mail address for your class partner.

3 Press Tab twice, type **Picnic Activity Survey** in the Subject box, and press Enter.

The insertion point moves to the message area.

4 Type **Take a look at the list of activities below. Place an X next to the activities that interest you.**, and press Enter twice.

5 Type **Baseball** and press Enter.

6 Type **Soccer** and press Enter.

7 Type **Croquet** and press Enter.

8 On the Standard toolbar in the message window, click the Send button.

The message is sent to your class partner.

9 On the Standard toolbar, click the Send/Receive button.

A message from your class partner appears in your Inbox.

10 On the Folder Banner, click the folder name *Inbox*.

The Folder List appears.

Push Pin

11 In the top-right corner of the Folder List, click the Push Pin button.

The Folder List will now stay open.

12 Click Sent Items.

The contents of the Sent Items folder appears.

13 Double-click the *Picnic Activity Survey* message header.

The *Picnic Activity Survey* message opens in its own window.

You can click the Delete Unread Copies And Replace With A New Message option to open the recalled message, and type and send a new message.

14 On the Actions menu, click Recall This Message.

The Recall This Message dialog box appears, and the Delete Unread Copies Of This Message option is already selected.

15   Click OK.

Outlook recalls the message.

Close

16   In the top-right corner of the message window, click the Close button.

The message window closes.

17   In the Folder list, click Inbox.

The contents of the Inbox appear.

18   On the Standard toolbar, click the Send/Receive button.

A recall message from your class partner appears.

19   Click the *Recall: Picnic Activity Survey* message.

A message stating that your class partner would like to recall the *Picnic Activity Survey* message appears in the Preview Pane.

Deleting Messages

After reading new messages, you can leave them in the Inbox for as long as you want. However, you will find that over time your Inbox can become cluttered if you don't organize or remove messages regularly. You can choose to delete any outdated e-mail messages by clicking their message headers and clicking the Delete button on the Standard toolbar or pressing the Delete key.

When you delete messages, they are not permanently removed from Outlook. Instead, they are placed in the **Deleted Items** folder until you decide to empty it. This safeguard makes it possible to recall your messages if you accidentally delete them or realize that you still need certain deleted messages.

In this exercise, you delete a message from the Inbox, delete a message from the Sent Items folder, and empty the Deleted Items folder.

> To select multiple message headers that appear together, click the first message header, hold down the Shift key, and then click the last message header. To select multiple message headers that do not appear together, click the first message header, hold down the Ctrl key, and then click each additional message header.

1   In the Inbox, click the *Picnic Reminder* message header.

Delete

2   On the Standard toolbar, click the Delete button.

The message moves to the Deleted Items folder.

3   In the Folder List, click Sent Items.

The contents of the Sent Items folder appear, showing the messages that you've already sent.

> You can restore a deleted message by dragging the messsage from the Deleted Items folder to the Inbox shortcut on the Outlook Bar.

4   Double-click the *Picnic Activity Survey* message header.

5   On the Standard toolbar in the message window, click the Delete button.

The message moves to the Deleted Items folder.

6   In the Folder List, click Deleted Items.

The Deleted Items folder opens, showing the messages that you deleted.

7   Press the Shift key, and click the bottom message.

The messages are selected.

> You can also delete all messages in the Deleted Items folder by clicking Empty "Deleted Items" Folder on the Tools menu.

8   Press Delete.

An alert box appears, asking you to confirm the deletion.

9 Click Yes.

The items are removed from the Deleted Items folder and permanently deleted.

Saving Drafts

If you compose a message and are unable to complete it at that time, you can save it in your Drafts folder so that you can complete and send the message later. You can create a draft of a message in two ways:

Close

● In the top-right corner of the message window, click the Close button, and Outlook will ask if you want to save the message. Click Yes to save the message without sending it.

Or

Save

On the Standard toolbar in the message window, click the Save button, and click the Close button in the top-right corner of the message window.

You do not have to close the message to save it as a draft.

To retrieve a draft so that you can complete the message and send it:

1 Display the Folder List, and click the Drafts folder.

2 Double-click the desired message to open it.

3 Complete or edit the message, and send it just as you normally would.

Lesson Wrap-Up

This lesson introduced you to some of the capabilities of Outlook e-mail, including composing, saving, and sending e-mail. You learned how to read a message and how to reply to and forward messages. You also learned how to include an attachment in an e-mail message, find a message, recall a message, delete messages, and navigate between various folders.

If you are continuing to the next lesson:

Close

● In the top-right corner of the the Folder List, click the Close button.
The Folder list closes.

If you are not continuing to other lessons:

● In the top-right corner of the the Folder List, click the Close button.
The Folder list closes.

Lesson Glossary

attachment An external document included as part of a message.

AutoPreview An Inbox view that displays each message header and the first three lines of each message.

Deleted Items The folder where deleted messages (and other deleted Outlook items) are stored until the folder is emptied.

Drafts The folder that stores incomplete messages so that you can complete and send them at a later time.

e-mail Any communication that is sent or received via computers, either over the Internet or through a messaging program used with an organization's internal network.

file Any document stored on a disk, such as Word documents, Excel spreadsheets, Microsoft Access databases, and pictures.

flag A reminder attached to messsages to remind yourself or notify the recipient of the importance of a message being sent. Flags also can set the due date for the follow up to the message and carry a comment about the message, or why it is flagged.

forward An action that sends a message that you received to one or more other users who might be interested in the message content.

icon A graphic representation of an attached file or document.

Inbox The folder that contains received e-mail messages and those not yet deleted or moved.

interoffice mail Messages sent and received via computers that are connected within a local area network (LAN).

item Any Outlook reference, such as a contact, task, or note.

mail queue A list of messages received by a mail server, organized in the order in which messages are received.

message An item sent electronically by or to a user on an e-mail system.

message header The top of an e-mail message that includes the name of the sender, the subject of the message, and the date and time when the message was sent.

Microsoft Exchange Server A messaging system that enables members of an organization to exchange and share information with users on a local area network and the Internet.

Outbox The folder that contains messages waiting to be sent from your computer to the server.

recall To send a message regarding a previous message requesting that the recipient disregard it. If the sender and the recipient are on Microsoft Exchange Server, the message is automatically deleted.

reply To send a copy of an original message, and a response that you type, to the sender of the message.

Sent Items The folder that contains messages already sent.

Quick Quiz

1   How do you manually check for messages in Outlook without waiting for messages to be sent or received at the preset interval?

2   What are the steps you take to create an e-mail message?

3   What happens to a message when you delete it from your Inbox?

4   What is contained in the header information of a message?

5   How do you read an e-mail message?

6   How do you save a message without sending it so that you can complete or edit the message later?

7   What is the Inbox?

8   What can you insert into an Outlook e-mail message?

9   What is the value of AutoPreview?

Putting It All Together

Exercise 1: The training director at Lakewood Mountains Resort must send an Outlook 2000 class announcement to those who signed up for the class. The date, time, and location of the class should be included in the message. Use the date, time, and location for your Outlook class to provide this information. A syllabus for the class must be sent as an attachment. You can find the syllabus in the Outlook Core Skills folder on your hard disk.

Send the class announcement with the syllabus—and include a flag—to your partner, to another member of your class, and to yourself. When you receive the message, print the syllabus.

Exercise 2: After you sent the class announcement, you found out that the location of the class has changed. Recall the message and notify the recipients that the location of the class has changed. After you've completed this task, delete the message.

Customizing E-Mail

After completing this lesson, you will be able to:

✔ *Specify e-mail options.*

✔ *Customize the appearance of e-mail messages.*

✔ *Use stationery.*

✔ *Add a signature to an e-mail message.*

✔ *Set viewing options.*

✔ *Sort messages.*

✔ *Filter a view.*

✔ *Create folders.*

✔ *Move messages between folders.*

✔ *Organize the Inbox by using colors.*

✔ *Filter junk e-mail messages.*

✔ *Archive messages.*

As the popularity of the Internet increases, it's easy to become overwhelmed with e-mail messages from friends, family, and coworkers. You can make your e-mail more manageable by identifying, prioritizing, and storing the messages that you receive. If you use e-mail regularly and you receive a dozen messages or more per day, over time it can become difficult to find a particular message when it's in a list of perhaps hundreds of received messages. However, if you customize and organize the e-mail messages you send and receive, locating the right information is a simple process.

You can easily customize e-mail messages in Microsoft Outlook by selecting specific message options to apply to your message. Available options include attaching a level of importance or sensitivity to a message, automatically sending replies to others, and saving sent messages to a specified folder. You can also set options that will delay the delivery of a message (you compose a birthday greeting to a friend but don't want to send it until the recipient's birthday) or will render a message invalid after a specified date. Other options include receiving notification when an e-mail message is read, linking a message to a contact, and assigning a message to a category.

You can also customize e-mail messages by changing their appearance. In older e-mail programs, you were restricted to sending messages using only plain text, with no text-formatting, color, or graphics capabilities. Most of today's programs include some if not all of these capabilities. Using Microsoft Outlook, you can customize your e-mail messages with graphical backgrounds, borders, different fonts and colors, and text formatting, similar to what you can do in a full-featured word processing program. You can further customize your e-mail messages by adding a personalized **signature**, which is a text message inserted at the end of an e-mail message. In a signature, you might include information about yourself, such as your title, phone number, or e-mail address, and you can even include graphics, such as your organization's logo.

Another way to manage your e-mail is by organizing messages in your Inbox. Organizing messages makes finding them easier and keeps the clutter in your Inbox to a minimum. You can arrange e-mail messages in a specific order, by moving them to different folders, deleting messages you no longer use, and even color-coding your messages. For example, you can color-code or move unwanted e-mail messages from advertisers to the Deleted Items folder. Or you can remove old messages from the Inbox by placing them in a storage folder or by deleting them.

In this lesson, you will learn how to customize outgoing messages by adding options, backgrounds, images, borders, and a personal signature. You will learn how to view your messages by sender, subject, time, and other criteria. You will also learn how to use a **filter** to temporarily exclude from view items that don't meet conditions that you set, such as unread messages, messages flagged for attention, or messages with attachments. You will learn how to organize your Inbox by adding color to message headers so that you can identify at a glance particular senders, **junk e-mail** messages, or adult content. You will also learn how to create folders to organize and store messages by specific topics or projects. In addition, you will learn how to **sort** and how to store messages that are important to you.

No practice files are required to complete the exercises in this lesson.

> Your Outlook folders should already contain the Outlook items (e-mail messages and contact records) that are necessary to complete the exercises in this lesson. If you need to add these items to your Outlook folders, see the "Using the CD-ROM" section at the beginning of this book.

Practice files for the lesson

important

To complete some of the exercises in this lesson, you will need to exchange e-mail messages with a class partner. If you don't have a class partner or are performing the exercises alone, you can enter your own e-mail address instead of your class partner's and send the message to yourself.

Specifying E-Mail Options

You can customize e-mail messages so that they are sent according to the options you've specified. For example, you can alert recipients that your e-mail message is more or less important than normal or that the message contains sensitive information. You can set Outlook to forward a reply to other people or to save your sent message in a particular folder. You can even select what day and time you want a message to be sent and alert the recipient when the message is no longer relevant.

To add options to an e-mail message, you click the Options button on the Standard toolbar in the message window. The Message Options dialog box will appear.

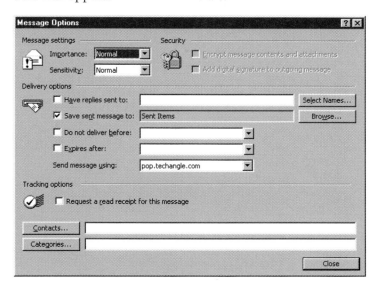

The e-mail options in the Message Options dialog box are explained in the following table.

Option	Description
Importance	Marks an e-mail message to be of high or low importance. When an e-mail message marked with high importance is received in Outlook, the message header displays a red exclamation point in the Importance column of the message header. A message of low importance displays a blue down arrow in the Importance column of the message header. All other e-mail messages are considered to be of normal importance, and no icon will appear in the Importance column when they are received.
Sensitivity	Recommends how the recipient should regard the e-mail message. You can mark messages as Normal, Personal, Private, or Confidential. A warning appears at the top of Personal, Private, and Confidential messages, stating the sensitivity of the e-mail message. Sensitivity doesn't restrict access to the message and shouldn't be considered a form of security.
Have Replies Sent To	Message replies are automatically sent to other e-mail addresses that you specify. For example, if you send a message that asks for more information about a particular topic, you could specify that you also want the reply sent to others who would benefit from the information.
Save Sent Message To	When you send an e-mail message, a copy of the message is automatically saved in the Sent Items folder. With this option, you can save a copy of a sent message in a folder that you specify.

(continued)

continued

Option	Description
Do Not Deliver Before	You can delay delivery of an e-mail message until a later date or time. For example, on Monday, the marketing director at Lakewood Mountains Resort remembered that she needed to send a birthday e-mail to her husband on Friday. Worried that she might forget to send the e-mail message on Friday, she created the message on Monday, and specified to have the message delivered on Friday.
Expires After	Some messages expire—that is, become invalid—after a certain date. You can include expiration dates for time-sensitive messages, such as invitations and deadlines. Messages that have expiration dates will appear dimmed or crossed out in the recipient's Inbox when the message has expired. An expired message that has not been read appears dimmed, although the message can still be opened. Expired messages that have been read appear with a line through them to indicate that the messages have expired. The messages will expire at the preset time of 5:00 P.M. (the end of the business day); however, you can change the preset time by deleting it and typing in a new time.
Send Message Using	Some large networks have more than one server that can send and receive e-mail messages. You can select which server you want to use to send the message by clicking the down arrow and selecting the server from the list. You might want to do this if one particular server seems busier than another server, in which case your messages will be sent faster if you select the server that has less traffic.
Request A Read Receipt For This Message	By selecting this check box, you can track whether the message has been read by the recipient. When the recipient opens the message, an alert box will appear asking whether Outlook can send a notification to the sender that you read the message. If the recipient agrees, Outlook will send an e-mail message to the sender, stating when the message was sent and read.
Contacts	You can click the Contacts button to link contacts to e-mail messages. For example, you could link a contact, such as the customer service manager, to an e-mail message sent from a satisfied customer.
Categories	You can click the Categories button to assign messages to categories. Categorizing messages can make it easier to find and group related messages.

Contacts and Categories are covered in Lesson 4, "Using Contacts."

In this exercise, you create a new message, mark the message as high priority, and then send it to your class partner. You also create another message, mark it as Confidential, and then send it to your class partner.

1   If necessary, on the Outlook Bar, click the Inbox shortcut.

The contents of the Inbox folder appear.

New Mail Message

2   On the Standard toolbar, click the New Mail Message button.

A message window appears.

3   On the Standard toolbar in the message window, click the Options button.

The Message Options dialog box appears.

> If you send the e-mail message to a recipient who also uses Outlook, any flags or other settings that you specified will appear in the recipient's message. Flags and other settings might not appear in a recipient's message if he or she is using an e-mail program other than Outlook (such as Netscape or Eudora).

4   In the Message Settings section, click the Importance down arrow, and click High.

5   Click the Close button.

The Message Options dialog box closes.

6   In the To box, type your class partner's e-mail address, and press the Tab key twice.

The insertion point moves to the Subject box.

7   In the Subject box, type **Health Insurance Files**, and press Enter.

The insertion point moves to the message area.

> You can mark a message as high importance by clicking the Importance: High button on the Standard toolbar in the message window.

8   Type **Review all health insurance files for inaccuracies.**

9   On the Standard toolbar in the message window, click the Send button.

The message is sent to your class partner.

10   On the Standard toolbar, click the New Mail Message button.

A message window appears.

New Mail Message

11   On the Standard toolbar in the message window, click the Options button.

The Message Options dialog box appears.

12   In the Message Settings section, click the Sensitivity down arrow, click Confidential, and click the Close button.

The Message Options dialog box closes.

13   In the To box, type your class partner's e-mail address, and press Tab twice.

The insertion point moves to the Subject box.

14   In the Subject box, type **Paycheck**, and press Enter.

The insertion point moves to the message area.

15   Type **Look for a $500 bonus in your next paycheck.**

16   On the Standard toolbar in the message window, click the Send button.

The message is sent to your class partner.

17   On the Standard toolbar, click the Send/Receive button.

Two messages from your class partner appear in the Inbox. Notice that a red exclamation point appears to the left of the *Health Insurance Files* message header.

18   Double-click the message *Paycheck*.

The message window opens. Notice that a comment appears in the top of the message window, stating that the message is confidential.

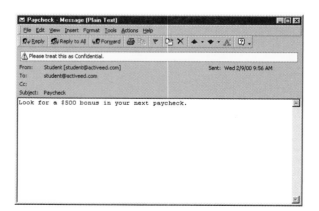

19   In the top-right corner of the message window, click the Close button.

The message window closes.

Close

OL2000.1.14

Customizing the Appearance of E-Mail Messages

In older e-mail programs, you were limited to sending e-mail messages in plain text in only a few fonts. With Outlook, you can send e-mail messages with graphical backgrounds and **formatted text**. Formatted text appears in different sizes, colors, styles, and alignments. You can use these formatting options to customize a message for a particular event or recipient. For example, you might send an e-mail invitation to a corporate shareholders meeting using a neutral background with a formal font, but you would probably send an e-mail invitation to a birthday party using a colorful background with text in a large, ornate font.

Outlook includes three message formats in which you can send and receive messages: HTML, Microsoft Outlook Rich Text, and Plain Text.

■   HTML is an acronym for Hypertext Markup Language, which is the formatting language used by Web browsers to format and display Web pages. Use HTML if you want to use text formatting, numbering, bullets, alignment, horizontal lines, backgrounds, animated graphics, pictures, and entire Web pages. Not all e-mail programs can display HTML formatting.

■   Microsoft Outlook Rich Text is a standard method of formatting text with tags and can be understood by most word processors and newer e-mail programs. Use Microsoft Outlook Rich Text if you want to use text formatting, bullets, and alignment. Microsoft Outlook Rich Text can't support the extensive Web capabilities of the HTML format such as animated graphics and Web pages. Not all e-mail programs can display Microsoft Outlook Rich Text formatting.

■ Plain Text is generic text that can be read by any e-mail program. Use Plain Text when you do not want to include any formatting in your messages. Plain Text is the safest option to choose because all e-mail programs can read text in this format.

2000
New!

You can choose whether to send e-mail messages in HTML, Rich Text, or Plain Text format—and you can change formats while composing the message.

You can specify one of the three message formats as a default format that will be used for your messages, but you can always switch to another message format for an individual message. Outlook uses the format of a received message as the format for your reply message. For example, if you reply to a message sent to you in plain text, Outlook creates a reply in plain text format.

You can also change how your replies and forwarded messages are formatted and how the original text is included in the message, if at all. You use the On Replies Or Forwards section of the E-Mail Options dialog box to change the appearance of replies and forwards.

The following table lists the reply and forward options.

When you click a reply or forward option in the E-Mail Options dialog box, a preview of the reply or forward appears to the right of the selected option.

Option	Description
Do Not Include Original Message	The message consists of your response only; the original message does not appear with the reply. This option is useful if you want to send short replies to a recipient who will have no difficulty understanding what you are replying to. This option is not available when forwarding a message, because when you forward a message, you want the original message text to be displayed.
Attach Original Message	The original message is included as an attachment in the reply or forward.
Include Original Message Text	The original message text is included in the message and appears below your comments.
Include And Indent Original Message Text	The original message text is included in the message and appears indented under your comments. This option helps you to easily distinguish original text from your message text.
Prefix Each Line Of The Original Text	The original message text is included in the message, and each line of original text has a prefix character, such as a ">". You can choose the prefix character in the E-Mail Options dialog box.

tip
You can also use the Format menu in the message window to change the text format of a message before or while you compose it. If you display the Format menu, and you see only the Plain Text formatting commands, click Plain Text, click Yes, and then redisplay the Format menu; HTML will appear as a third formatting command. If you display the Format menu, and you see only the Plain Text and HTML formatting commands, click Plain Text, click Yes, and then redisplay the Format menu. Rich Text will appear as a third formatting command.

In this exercise, you change the format of your replies so that original text is sent as an attachment, and change the format of your outgoing e-mail messages to Microsoft Outlook Rich Text. You also create an e-mail message, send it to your class partner, reply to a message from your class partner, and view a reply to your message.

1   On the Tools menu, click Options.

The Options dialog box appears.

2   Click the E-Mail Options button.

The E-Mail Options dialog box appears.

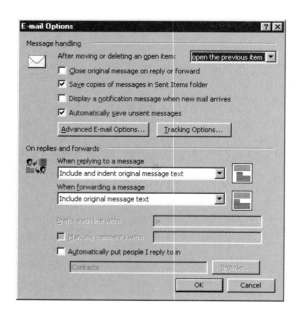

3   In the On Replies And Forwards section, click the When Replying To A Message down arrow, click Attach Original Message, and then click OK.

The E-Mail Options dialog box closes.

4   In the Options dialog box, click the Mail Format tab.

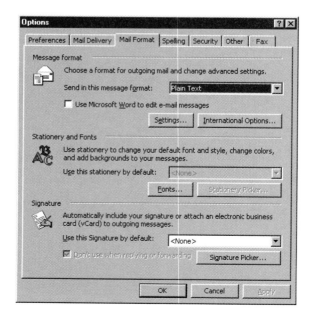

5   In the Message Format section, click the Send In This Message Format down arrow, click Microsoft Outlook Rich Text, and click OK.

The Options dialog box closes.

New Mail Message

6   On the Standard toolbar, click the New Mail Message button.

A message window appears.

7   In the To box, type your class partner's e-mail address, and press Tab twice.

The insertion point moves to the Subject box.

8   Type **Going Away Party,** and press Enter.

The insertion point moves to the message area.

> If you don't see the Monotype Corsiva font in the list, choose another font that appeals to you.

9   On the Standard toolbar in the message window, click the Font down arrow, scroll down, and click Monotype Corsiva.

The font Monotype Corsiva appears in the Font box.

10   On the Standard toolbar in the message window, click the Font Size down arrow, and click 20.

The font size is set to 20 points.

Font Color

11   On the Standard toolbar in the message window, click the Font Color button, and click the Maroon square (first row under the Automatic button, third square from the left).

The font will now appear in maroon.

12   In the message area, type **Please come to the LMR pavilion for Frank's going away party. RSVP.**

The text appears in Monotype Corsiva, 20 points, and is maroon.

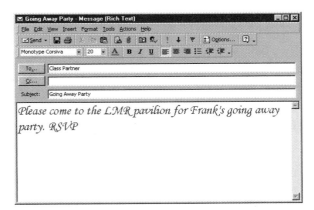

13   On the Standard toolbar in the message window, click the Send button.

The message is sent to your class partner.

14   On the Standard toolbar, click the Send/Receive button.

A message from your class partner appears in the Inbox.

15 In the Inbox, double-click the message *Going Away Party*.

The message window appears.

16 On the Standard toolbar in the message window, click the Reply button.

A reply window appears. Notice that the original *Going Away Party* message is now an attachment.

Close

17 In the message area, type **I will be there.**, click the Send button on the Standard toolbar in the reply window, and in the top-right corner of the message window, click the Close button.

The reply is sent to your class partner, and the reply window closes.

18 On the Standard toolbar, click the Send/Receive button.

A message from your class partner appears in the Inbox.

19 Double-click the reply from your class partner, and double-click the Going Away Party attachment icon.

The original message appears in its own window.

Close

20 In the top-right corners of each open window, click the Close button.

The windows close.

Using Stationery

When recipients receive a message that you've sent, they normally see the message text on a white background. However, with Outlook, you can send e-mail messages using more colorful and graphically interesting **stationery**. Outlook stationery is like an electronic version of paper stationery. Stationery has predefined images, backgrounds, and borders that you can add to special e-mail messages like party invitations or birthday wishes. Outlook has a variety of stationery designs you can choose from. To send a decorative e-mail message, you could use the Ivy design, which has an ivy border on the left side of a message and room for your text. If you want to announce that you are selling something, you could use the For Sale design. The Chicken Soup design is almost an e-mail message in itself, with *Get Well Soon* in large, bold letters. You can edit the text of these designs, or you can create your own text.

The marketing department at Lakewood Mountains Resort sends out birthday greetings to former guests via e-mail. To make the e-mail messages appear festive, they type Happy Birthday in large, colorful letters and add a cheerful stationery design in the body of the message.

You might choose a stationery design that Outlook informs you is unavailable because some stationery designs are not installed by default when you install Outlook. You can use the Microsoft Outlook or Microsoft Office 2000 CD-ROM to install additional stationery.

In this exercise, you send a birthday party invitation e-mail message, customized with stationery, to your class partner. You also view an invitation that you receive from your class partner.

1   On the Actions menu, point to New Mail Message Using, and click More Stationery.

The Select A Stationery dialog box appears.

2   Scroll down the Stationery list, and click Party Invitation.

The stationery appears in the Preview box.

3   Click OK.

A message window appears and displays the Party Invitation stationery in the message area, as shown on the following page.

4   In the To box, type your partner's e-mail address, and press Tab twice.

The insertion point moves to the Subject box.

5   In the Subject box, type **Mike's Birthday**, and press Enter.

The insertion point moves to the message area.

6   In the message area, if necessary, scroll down to the bottom of the stationery, click to the right of the word *Day* (after the colon), press the Spacebar, and type **Saturday, June 6th**.

7   Click to the right of the word *Time* (after the colon), press the Spacebar, and type **1:00 P.M**.

8   Click to the right of the word *Place* (after the colon), press the Space-bar, and type **Cherry Creek Park**.

9   On the Standard toolbar in the message window, click the Send button.

The message is sent to your class partner.

10   On the Standard toolbar, click the Send/Receive button.

A message from your class partner appears in the Inbox.

11   Double-click the *Mike's Birthday* message header.

The message window opens. Notice the stationery background.

Close

12   In the top-right corner of the message window, click the Close button.

The message closes.

OL2000.1.13

Adding a Signature to an E-Mail Message

Rather than typing your name, address, phone number, and other identifier information at the end of every message that you compose, you can create a signature that Outlook will add to the end of all messages that you send. Signatures usually include a name and can also include personal information such as a phone or fax number, a title, and even a graphic like a company logo. You can use a wide range of colors and fonts to create a unique and expressive signature. For example, one of the managers at Lakewood Mountains Resort ends her e-mail messages with a business signature, which includes her name, title, business name, phone number, and the LMR logo.

Clair Hector
Manager
Lakewood Mountains Resort
555-555-0155

You can create as many signatures as you need. In addition to a business signature, you could also have a personal signature that might include a nickname or a favorite quote. You can create a simple signature for messages sent in Plain Text format, and a more complex signature with a logo for messages sent in HTML or Microsoft Outlook Rich Text format. You can set up Outlook to automatically insert a signature in the message area, or you can select which signature you want to appear in the message area by pointing to Signature on the Insert menu and selecting the signature that you want.

If your signature contains colors or fonts, and you change the format of your message to Plain Text, the appearance of your signature will change.

In this exercise, you create a signature and send a message with the signature to your class partner.

1   On the Tools menu, click Options.

The Options dialog box appears.

2   Click the Mail Format tab.

3   Click the Signature Picker button.

The Signature Picker dialog box appears.

4   Click the New button.

The Create New Signature dialog box appears.

5   In the first box, type **class signature**.

6   Verify that the Start With A Blank Signature option is selected.

7   Click the Next button.

The Edit Signature dialog box appears.

In the Edit Signature dialog box, you can change the font and paragraph format of your signature by selecting your signature, clicking either the Font or Paragraph button, and then selecting the desired formatting options.

8   Type your name, press Enter, and type Outlook 2000 Class.

9   Click Finish, and click OK to close the Signature Picker dialog box.

The Options dialog box reappears.

10   Click OK to close the Options dialog box.

When you create a new e-mail message, your signature will appear in the message area.

Notice that the class signature now appears in the Use This Signature By Default box in the Signature section. This means that every time you create a message, your signature will automatically appear. If you no longer want your signature to automatically appear in the message window, click the Use This Signature By Default down arrow and click None.

11   On the Standard toolbar, click the New Mail Message button.

A message window appears. Notice that the signature you created appears in the message area.

12   In the To box, type your class partner's e-mail address, and press Tab twice.

The insertion point moves to the Subject box.

13   In the Subject box, type **Outlook Expert**, and press Enter.

The insertion point moves to the message area.

14   Type **Are you going to take the Outlook Expert course?**.

15   On the Standard toolbar in the message window, click the Send button.

The message is sent to your class partner.

16   On the Standard toolbar, click the Send/Receive button.

A message from your class partner appears in the Inbox.

17   Double-click the *Outlook Expert* message header.

The message window opens. Notice the signature below the text.

18   In the top-right corner of the message window, click the Close button.

The message closes.

Not all e-mail programs can display all the fonts that are available in Outlook or in your installation of Microsoft Windows. Similarly, if you receive a message that contains a font that you do not have installed, Outlook will substitute the font for one that you do have installed.

OL2000.2.3

Setting Viewing Options

The Inbox can appear in several different **views**, or groups, to help you locate messages. For example, you could group your messages by sender so that all messages from your supervisor would be grouped together to help you easily identify them. Or suppose your Inbox shows dozens or hundreds of messages—most of which you have read but some of which you have not read; you could temporarily change your Inbox view so that only the messages you have not read are displayed.

By using different views, you can find particular messages faster and easier. You can also see the relationships among different messages, the rate of e-mail correspondence, and even the date and time at which you sent and received an e-mail message.

In most views, messages appear in a table format with the following columns at the top of the Inbox window: Importance, Icon, Flag Status, Attachment, From, Subject, and Received. When you view messages in the By Conversation Topic, By Sender, or By Follow-Up Flag view, the messages are divided into groups. The groups are divided by expandable gray bars that summarize what each group contains. For example, if you display your messages in the By Sender view, instead of seeing the messages, you will see several gray bars that display the text *From: (name of sender) ([number] Items, [number] Unread)*. So if you had four messages from your mother (and you read two of them) and two messages from your supervisor, Marvin (and you read one of them), you would see two gray bars that displayed the text From: Mom (4 Items, 2 Unread) and From: Marvin (2 Items, 1 Unread). The messages will be hidden until you click the plus sign (+) located at the left end of the gray bar. To hide messages, click the minus sign (-) located at the left end of the bar. The ability to hide and show messages is just another way to help you locate the messages that you want to see.

For more information on flagging messages, see the Composing, Addressing, and Sending Messages section in Lesson 2, "Using E-Mail in Outlook."

The following table details each view.

View	Description
Messages	This is the default view for the Inbox. Message headers are arranged in a table with seven columns: (from left to right) Importance, Icon, Flag Status, Attachment, From, Subject, and Received.
Messages With	Message headers are arranged in a table and AutoPreview by category. From one to three lines of the body of the message appear under the message header.
By Follow-Up Flag	Messages appear sorted by Follow-Up Flag. Also, a new column, Due By, has been added.
Last Seven Days	Messages received in the last seven days appear. The Last Seven Days view is useful if you want to see only your most recent messages.
Flagged For The Next Seven Days	Messages that have a Due Date within the next seven days appear. The Flagged For The Next Seven Days view is useful if you want to see those messages requiring the most urgent attention.
By Conversation Topic	E-mail messages and replies are grouped according to their message threads (a sequence of replies regarding a single topic). A conversation topic is the subject of the original message in a message thread. The By Conversation Topic view is useful if you have many replies to messages. For example, if you and a co-worker have been sending e-mail messages back and forth regarding an upcoming picnic, the replies concerning the original message will appear indented under the original message in the order that they were received.
By Sender	E-mail messages appear sorted by the sender's e-mail address. The By Sender view is useful if you want to see all e-mail correspondence with a particular person or address.
Unread Messages	Only those e-mail messages that have not been opened and read appear in this view. This view is useful if your Inbox contains a combination of read and unread messages.
Sent To	Messages appear sorted by the address they were sent to. This view is useful if you want to see whether you sent a message or reply to a particular person or e-mail address.
Message Timeline	Instead of a table, messages appear on a timeline organized by when they were sent and received. Double-clicking a message header opens the e-mail message. The timeline increments can be viewed by Day, Week (the default timeline view), or Month. The timeline increments can be changed on the Standard toolbar by clicking the Day, Week, and Month buttons. This view is useful if you want to review your e-mail correspondence over time.

In this exercise, you change the Inbox view from the default Message view to the By Sender view, the Unread Messages view, and the Message Timeline view.

1   On the Standard toolbar, click the Organize button.

The Using Folders section of the Organize pane appears.

2   Click the Using Views link.

The Change Your View list appears. You can use this list to change the appearance and organization of messages.

Change Your View list

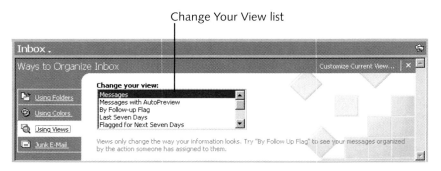

3   In the Change Your Views list, scroll down to the bottom, and click By Sender.

The message headers are grouped in a table by sender. All of the messages from your class partner are grouped in a gray bar with your class partner's name displayed on it. Notice that the number of messages on the gray bar appears in parentheses to the right of your class partner's name.

4   At the left end of your class partner's gray bar, click the plus sign (+).

The e-mail messages from your class partner appear. Notice that the plus sign (+) is now a minus sign (-).

5   At the left end of your class partner's gray bar, click the minus sign (-).

The e-mail messages from your class partner no longer appear. Notice that the minus sign (-) is now a plus sign (+).

6   Click the plus sign at the left end of a different gray bar to see the messages.

7   In the Change Your View list, click Unread Messages.

All unread messages appear.

8   In the Change Your View list, click Message Timeline.

The view changes to display message headers in a timeline.

9   In the Change Your View list, scroll to the top, and click Messages.

The view changes back to Messages—the default view.

OL2000.2.2

Sorting does not remove messages from view. To temporarily remove messages from view, you must apply a filter, which is covered in the next section.

You can sort by as many as four fields.

Sorting Messages

You can quickly manage many messages by sorting them. Sorting arranges the messages in your Inbox by the criteria you specify. You can sort according to age (how long the message has been in your Inbox), size, importance, and more. You can sort messages in any view, in either ascending order (A to Z) or descending order (Z to A), by a specific field or column header that appears at the top of a view's table, such as subject, sender, or flag status. When you sort in a view, the messages remain in the same view; however, they appear in a different order.

For example, the human resources manager at Lakewood Mountains Resort returned from vacation to find that her Inbox contained hundreds of unread messages. She wanted to reply to those messages that were most important, so in Messages view, she sorted the contents of her Inbox by order of importance. The messages marked with high importance appeared at the top of the list in ascending order. After she replied to the high-priority e-mail messages, she then wanted to reply to the remaining e-mail messages in the order she had received them. So she sorted her Inbox again—this time choosing the Received sort option.

You can also sort by more than one field, thus performing a sort within a sort. When you perform a second sort on messages that have already been sorted, the second sort further organizes the list of sorted messages. For example, if you sort your Inbox by Subject in ascending order and then sort by Attachment in descending order, the Inbox will appear sorted by Subject, and within the subjects, messages with an attachment will appear first.

In this exercise, you sort the list of messages in your Inbox by Attachment and by Subject. You then clear the sort.

1   In the top of the Organize pane, click the Customize Current View button.

The View Summary dialog box appears.

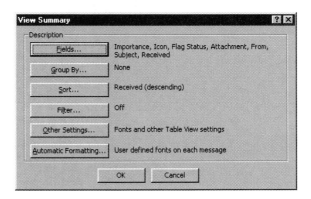

2   Click the Sort button.

The Sort dialog box appears.

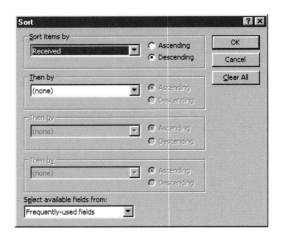

3   In the Sort Items By section, click the down arrow, scroll to the top, click Attachment, and then verify that the Descending option is selected.

4   Click OK twice.

The messages with attachments appear at the top of the message list. The attachments themselves are not sorted in any particular order.

> If necessary, scroll up through the Inbox so that you can see the messages at the top.

5   In the top of the Organize pane, click the Customize Current View button.

The View Summary dialog box appears.

6   Click the Sort button.

The Sort dialog box appears. Notice that Attachment still appears in the Sort Items By box.

7   In the Then By section, click the down arrow, scroll down to the bottom, click Subject, and if necessary, click the Descending option.

8   Click OK twice.

> If necessary, scroll up through the Inbox so that you can see the messages at the top.

The messages with attachments still appear at the top of the message list and are sorted by subject in descending order (Z to A). (Outlook ignores the text *FW:* and *RE:* in the subject and uses the first letter that appears after the text *FW:* and *RE:* to sort by the subject.)

9   In the top of the Organize pane, click the Customize Current View button.

The View Summary dialog box appears.

> When messages are sorted in the Inbox, a small arrow appears in the associated column heading to indicate whether the messages are being sorted in ascending or descending order. The arrow points upward if messages are sorted in ascending order, and the arrow points downward if messages are sorted in descending order. You can also sort messages by clicking the column heading.

10   Click the Sort button.

The Sort dialog box appears.

11   Click the Clear All button.

The sort criteria are removed.

12   Click OK twice.

The message headers no longer appear in the sort criteria you specified.

OL2000.2.5

Filtering a View

You apply a filter if you want to display only items or files that meet certain conditions. For example, you could create a filter that displays only messages sent by a particular person or only messages that have a certain subject. Filtering makes finding a particular message much easier because messages that don't meet the conditions are removed from view. The more conditions, the more specific your list of messages will be.

A customer service representative at Lakewood Mountains Resort had dozens of messages in his Inbox and wanted to quickly find messages sent from his manager about a company picnic. So he filtered his Inbox for messages that had the word *picnic* in the subject line and were sent from his manager. This action saved him the time and the effort it would have taken to scroll through all his messages.

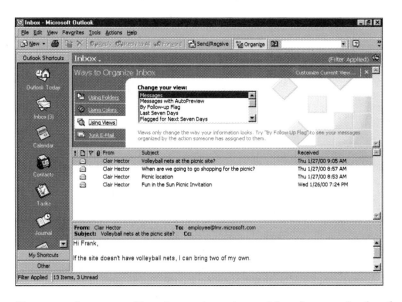

You can also use a filter in conjunction with other methods of organizing messages. For example, after you sort the Inbox, you can filter the remaining e-mail messages. You can also filter messages as they appear in a view. For example, the training director at Lakewood Mountains Resort received numerous e-mail messages over the weekend regarding the results of a current training program. Some messages had instructor evaluations attached, and others did not. The training director wanted to reply to all the messages without evaluations first and then reply to those with evaluations. To speed up the process, he applied the Unread Messages view, filtered messages containing the word *training*, and then sorted those messages by Attachment in ascending order. (Messages with attachments appeared at the bottom of the list.)

> A filter is different from a sort because a filter removes messages in a folder from view that do not meet the conditions, while a sort simply rearranges all the messages in a folder.

You use the Filter dialog box to apply a filter to a folder. (To display the Filter dialog box, you click the Customize Current View button in the Using Views section of the Organize pane, and then click Filter.) The Filter dialog box is divided into conditions that can be applied to filter a folder. The conditions are listed in the following table.

Condition	Description
Search For The Word(s)	You can filter a folder by a specific word or words. By default, Outlook will filter messages based on words in the subject field only, but you can also filter according to words in the subject and message body as well as by frequently used text fields. This approach is useful if you know a particular key word will be unique to the messages you want to view. For example, if you want to view a message regarding a daily report, you could filter by the words *daily report* in the subject field.
From	This option filters messages by sender. Clicking the From button in the Filter dialog box opens the Select Names dialog box. Select the name or e-mail address of the person or persons you want to filter for.
Sent To	This option filters messages by the recipient. Like the From button, clicking the Sent To button in the Filter dialog box opens the Select Names dialog box. Select the name or e-mail address of the person or persons you want to filter for.
Where I Am	This option filters out messages according to where your name or e-mail address appears in the message header. You can filter out messages in which you are the only person on the To line, messages in which you are on the To line with other people, or messages you have received as a courtesy copy.
Time	This option filters messages by time. You use two boxes to select options: The first box contains options that establish an action to filter for, such as messages received or sent, and the second box contains options for setting the time criterion, such as yesterday or today. For example, you could filter a folder to search for messages sent this week or for messages received that have a due date of tomorrow.

You must remove a filter to show all the messages in the Inbox. You remove filters by clicking the Clear All button in the Filter dialog box.

In this exercise, you apply a filter to display only those messages that contain the word *party* in the subject or message body.

1   Click the Customize Current View button.

The View Summary dialog box appears.

2 Click the Filter button.

The Filter dialog box appears.

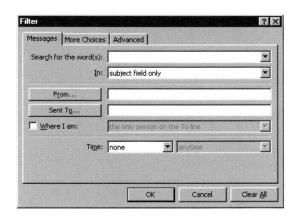

3 In the Search For The Word(s) box, type **party**.

4 Click the In down arrow, and click Subject Field And Message Body.

5 Click OK twice.

The Inbox appears with the filter applied. Only those messages containing the word *party* in the subject or message body appear.

6 Click the Customize Current View button.

The View Summary dialog box appears.

7 Click the Filter button.

The Filter dialog box appears.

8 Click the Clear All button.

The Filter dialog box is cleared.

9 Click OK twice.

The Inbox no longer appears with a filter.

Notice that, although the message header *Mike's Birthday* does not contain the word *party* in the subject, the message still appears in the Inbox because the stationery used for the message contains the word *party* in the message body.

OL2000.2.1

Creating Folders

A folder organizes stored messages or other files and Outlook items. When you first start Outlook, several folders already exist, including the Inbox (where new e-mail messages appear), Sent Items (which contains copies of messages that you've already sent), Drafts (where unfinished messages are stored), and Deleted Items (which contains items that you deleted in other Outlook folders). You can create your own folders—such as folders for coworkers, managers, or projects—to organize messages more effectively.

When you create a folder, you must first consider where the folder is to be placed. Most Outlook folders are located within one or more other folders. For example, the Inbox folder is located in the Outlook Today folder. You can see which folders are inside of other folders by displaying the Folder List.

important

A folder created in Outlook must contain only a specific type of Outlook item—such as mail items only or contact items only. You identify which type of item that can appear in the folder when you create the folder. Any item moved to this folder will be converted to that type of item, regardless of what the item was originally created as. For example, if you create a folder to hold mail items, and then move a task to the folder, a message window will appear with task information displayed in the subject and message area. The To box is empty, ready for you to address the message that contains information about the task, and then send it.

When creating a folder, you can also create a shortcut to the folder on the Outlook Bar. Creating a shortcut is especially useful if you plan to open and use the folder often.

In this exercise, you create a new folder called Parties, which will be used to store all messages that you receive about the upcoming Lakewood Mountains Resort parties.

1   In the Organize pane, click the Using Folders link.

The Using Folders section of the Organize pane appears.

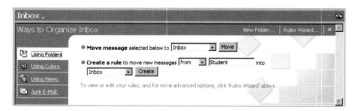

2   In the top of the Organize pane, click the New Folder button.

The Create New Folder dialog box appears.

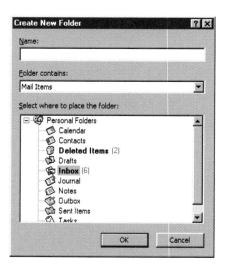

3 In the Name box, type **Parties**.

Notice that Mail Items appear in the Folder Contains box.

4 Verify that Inbox is selected In the Select Where To Place The Folder list, and click OK.

The Add Shortcut To Outlook Bar dialog box appears, asking if you want to place a shortcut on the Outlook Bar.

You can also create a new folder by pointing to Folder on the File menu and clicking New Folder.

5 Click Yes.

The Parties folder is created. The My Shortcuts group bar on the Outlook Bar flashes for a few seconds as the Parties shortcut is moved to the My Shortcuts group.

6 On the Outlook Bar, click the My Shortcuts group bar.

The Parties shortcut appears on the Outlook Bar.

Parties —

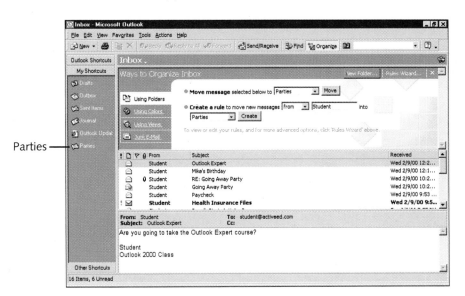

7 On the Folder Banner, click the folder name *Inbox*.

The Folder List appears.

8 If necessary, in the Folder List, click the plus sign (+) to the left of Inbox.

Notice that, although the folder has been added to the My Shortcuts group, the folder is located within the Inbox folder.

You will add messages to this folder in the next exercise.

9 Click outside the Folder List.

The Folder List closes.

OL2000.4.2

Moving Messages Between Folders

When you want to organize many Outlook items with similar subjects or content, you can group the items together in a folder. Folders not only store the items, but other folders can be created within the folder to further subdivide items more specifically. This system of organization can be helpful when you have a large project that requires many items dealing with many subjects. For example, the training director at Lakewood Mountains Resort has a folder for messages regarding training. This folder is further subdivided into folders for messages regarding each training class. You can use four different methods to move a file from its current location to another folder: drag the message from its current location to a folder, click the Move To Folder button on the Standard toolbar, use the Move Message option in the Using Folder section of the Organize pane, and create a rule to automatically move messages from one folder to another.

Move To Folder

You manually move a selected message into a folder by dragging the message from the Inbox (or its current location) to the desired folder. Dragging is convenient if you want to move a message to a folder that is visible in the Outlook window. Messages can be dragged to folders (represented by icons) on the Outlook Bar and in the Folder List. For example, if you receive a message in your Inbox and want to move it to the Notes folder, you drag the message header onto the Notes shortcut on the Outlook Bar.

The Notes folder is covered in Lesson 7, "Using Notes."

Move To Folder

Clicking a message header and then clicking the Move To Folder button on the Standard toolbar opens a menu of folders into which the message can be moved. The list of folders on the menu changes to reflect folders based on the frequency with which you've used them. For example, if you frequently move messages to a folder called Picnic but never move them to the Tasks folder, the Picnic folder will appear on the menu, but the Tasks folder will not.

The Using Folders section of the Organize pane contains a Move Message option that moves selected messages to a desired folder. Like the Move To Folder option, the message or messages must be selected and then the desired folder must be selected from the Move Message list. This method is convenient if you have just used the New Folder button in the Using Folders section of the Organize pane to create a folder and want to move messages into that folder.

In the Using Folders section of the Organize pane, you can also create a **rule** (a set of conditions, actions, and exceptions that perform a particular process) so that a message from a particular address is moved to a particular folder. Creating this rule is a helpful way to organize messages if messages sent from a particular address will always be moved to a particular folder. For example, the head chef of the Lakewood Mountains Resort has a friend who sends him recipes via e-mail. To help him stay organized, the chef created a rule so that any e-mail messages he receives from his friend are moved to his Recipes folder. With this rule, the chef doesn't have to sort through his Inbox for new recipes; he can simply access any recipe messages in the Recipes folder.

When you no longer want to use a rule, you click the Rules Wizard button in the Using Folders section of the Organize pane, and delete the rule.

tip

After you send a message, Outlook saves a copy of the message in the Sent Items folder. However, you can create a rule that will copy sent messages to a folder other than the Sent Items folder. For example, if you want all the messages that you've sent to your supervisor copied to another place, you could create a folder named Supervisor, and create a rule so that any messages sent to the supervisor's e-mail address will be copied to the Supervisor folder. In the Using Folders section of the Organize pane, click the Create A Rule To Move New Messages down arrow, click Sent To, and then type the e-mail address or name of the person in the box to the right. Then click the second down arrow below the text *Create a rule*, click a folder, and click the Create button.

In this exercise, you move messages into the Parties folder, create a folder called Class, and then create a rule for moving incoming e-mail messages from your class partner to the Class folder. You then send a message to your class partner to test the rule. You also use the Rules Wizard to delete the rule.

1   In the Inbox, click the *Mike's Birthday* message header to select it, press Ctrl, and then click the two *Going Away Party* message headers.

The messages are selected.

2   In the Using Folders section of the Organize pane, verify that *Parties* appears in the Move Messages Selected Below To box.

3   Click the Move button.

The messages are moved to the Parties folder. The messages no longer appear in the Inbox.

If you move a message into the wrong folder, immediately after you've moved it, you can click Undo Move on the Edit menu to move the message back to its previous location.

4   In the My Shortcuts group on the Outlook Bar, click the Parties shortcut.

The Party messages appear in the Parties folder.

5   On the Standard toolbar, click the Organize button.

The Organize pane appears.

6   In the top of the Organize pane, click the New Folder button.

The Create New Folder dialog box appears.

7   In the Name box, type **Class**.

8   In the Select Where To Place The Folder list, click Inbox, and click OK.

The Add Shortcut To Outlook Bar dialog box appears, asking if you want to place a shortcut on the Outlook Bar.

9   Click Yes.

The Class folder is created and the Class shortcut is added to the My Shortcuts group on the Outlook Bar.

10 In the Organize pane in the first Create A Rule To Move New Messages box, verify that the word *from* appears.

11 If necessary, in the next box, type your class partner's e-mail address.

12 In the box under the text *Create a rule*, verify that the word *Class* appears.

13 Click the Create button.

An alert box appears, notifying you that the new rule will be applied to incoming messages. The alert box also asks if you would like the rule to be applied to the current contents of this folder.

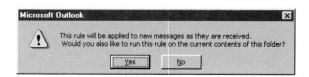

14 Click No so that the rule is not applied to the current contents of the folder.

The rule is created. Messages sent from your class partner will be sent to the Class folder.

New Mail Message

15 On the Standard toolbar, click the New Mail Message button.

A message window appears.

16 In the To box, type your class partner's e-mail address, in the Subject box, type **Testing**, and in the message area, type **Is this message in the Class folder?**

17 On the Standard toolbar in the message window, click the Send button, and on the Standard toolbar, click the Send/Receive button.

A message from your class partner is automatically moved to the Class folder.

18 In the My Shortcuts group on the Outlook Bar, click the Class shortcut.

The *Testing* message header appears in the Class folder.

19 On the Standard toolbar, click the Organize button, and click the Rules Wizard button at the top of the Organize pane.

The Rules Wizard appears. The rule that you created is selected in the Apply Rules In The Following Order box, as shown below.

20 Click the Delete button, click Yes in the alert box to confirm the deletion, and click OK.

The rule is no longer applied to the messages sent by your class partner.

Color-Coding Message Headers

You can create rules to color-code message headers that meet specific criteria. Organizing your Inbox by color helps you find specific messages when you have many e-mail messages in your Inbox. For example, the training director at Lakewood Mountains Resort created a rule to color-code in purple all message headers from the senior manager. When a purple message header appears, the training director knows to give it special attention.

To create a rule to color-code message headers, in the Using Colors section of the Organize pane (as shown below), you click the first down arrow, and click From or Sent To.

Clicking From will color message headers in the Inbox; clicking Sent To will color message headers in the Sent Items folder. The next box is for the e-mail address of the sender's message you want to color-code. You can type the e-mail address in the box or, if you have an e-mail message from the sender in your Inbox, click the message header, and the e-mail address will appear in the box. The third box indicates what color you want the message headers to be coded. (To change the color, click the box's down arrow.) Click the Apply Color button. This will color all messages from or to the selected e-mail address in the chosen color.

When you no longer want to color-code messages, you click the Automatic Formatting button in the Using Colors section of the Organize pane, and delete the rule to color-code.

In this exercise, you color-code in blue all message headers from your class partner. You then send a message to your class partner to test the rule. You also delete the rule.

1   On the Outlook Bar, click the Outlook Shortcuts group bar, and click the Inbox shortcut.

2   On the Standard toolbar, click the Organize button.

   The Organize pane appears.

3   In the Organize pane, click the Using Colors link.

   The Using Colors section of the Organize pane appears.

4   In the Organize pane, verify that the word *from* appears in the first Color Messages box.

5   In the Inbox, click one of the e-mail messages from your class partner.

Your class partner's name appears in the second Color Messages box in the Organize pane.

6   In the Organize pane, click the down arrow of the third Color Messages box.

A list of colors appears.

7   Click Blue.

The word *Blue* appears in the third box.

8   Click the Apply Color button.

Messages sent from your class partner appear in blue. Any future messages that your class partner sends to you will also appear in blue.

New Mail Message

9   On the Standard toolbar, click the New Mail Message button.

A message window appears.

10   In the To box, type your class partner's e-mail address, and in the Subject box, type **Feeling blue**.

11   On the Standard toolbar in the message window, click the Send button, and on the Standard toolbar, click the Send/Receive button.

A blue message header from your class partner appears in the Inbox.

12   In the top of the Organize pane, click the Automatic Formatting button.

The Automatic Formatting dialog box appears, as shown below.

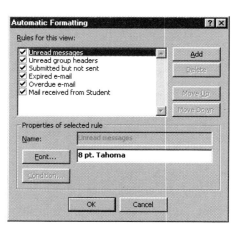

If you don't want to delete the rule, you can clear the check box to the left of the text *Mail received from [class partner]*. The rule will still exist but will no longer be applied. You can reapply the rule at any time by selecting the check box.

13   In the Rules For This View list, click the text *Mail received from [class partner]* to select it, click the Delete button, and click OK.

The rule to color-code is no longer applied to the messages sent by your class partner.

Filtering Junk E-Mail Messages

Junk e-mail (unsolicited and unwanted e-mail, also known as *spam*) is an annoying problem for many Internet users. Junk e-mail can fill an Inbox with dozens, even hundreds, of advertisements, chain e-mails, and other nuisances. Unfortunately, many individuals and companies use junk e-mail as a major marketing tool because it is so inexpensive. Another form of junk e-mail is unsolicited messages with adult content that might be offensive or inappropriate for some people.

Outlook includes built-in junk e-mail filters that can identify e-mail messages containing text and message headers identified by Microsoft as common to junk e-mail. Messages with terms common to junk e-mail—such as *SPECIAL PROMOTION*, *$$$*, and *Money back guarantee*—can be color-coded, moved to a different folder, or deleted. This system of identifying junk e-mail prevents your Inbox from becoming cluttered with junk e-mail and allows you to either review the filtered messages at your convenience or just have them automatically deleted.

Outlook also includes a separate category of filters to identify messages suspected of having adult content. As with the junk e-mail filters, messages with terms common to adult content messages, such as *over 21* and *adults only*, will be color-coded or moved to a different folder.

The junk e-mail and adult e-mail filters might not catch all such messages, however. Those who send junk e-mail can easily revise their message text and message headers to include text not identified as junk or adult content and thus bypass the filters. If you find that you are receiving many junk e-mail messages and the filters are not effective, you can add new junk e-mail addresses to the filter by right-clicking the messages and clicking Junk E-mail on the shortcut menu.

You can also add new junk e-mail addresses to the junk e-mail filter by using the Organize pane. You can specify that junk e-mail message headers and message headers with adult content be displayed in the Inbox in a color of your choice. When these message headers appear in your Inbox, you will recognize the color and can delete the messages before reading them.

> **A list of the terms Outlook uses to filter suspected junk e-mail messages is provided in a folder called Filter in Windows Explorer. The location of this folder depends on the operating system you are using.**

tip

You can connect to the Outlook Web site, *officeupdate.microsoft.com/ articles/junkmail.htm*, directly from the Junk E-mail section to download new junk e-mail filters. Click the Click Here link in the Junk E-Mail section, and click the Outlook Web Site link.

In this exercise, you turn on the Junk E-Mail message filter to color junk e-mail message headers teal, and add an address to the Junk E-Mail Senders list.

1   In the Organize pane, click the Junk E-Mail link.

The Junk E-Mail section of the Organize pane appears.

2   If necessary, in the Organize pane, click the first Automatically down arrow, and click Color.

3   Click the Junk Messages down arrow, and click Teal.

4   Click the Turn On button.

The Junk E-Mail filter is activated. The pane changes to say *New Junk messages will appear Teal*. The Turn On button is now the Turn Off button. The *Free Cell Phone* messages header appears teal.

5   Double-click the *Vigor Airlines* message header.

This is junk e-mail; however, Outlook did not recognize it as junk e-mail.

6   In the top-right corner of the message window, click the Close button.

The message closes.

7   Right-click the *Vigor Airlines* message header.

A shortcut menu appears.

8   Point to Junk E-Mail, and click Add To Junk Senders List.

An alert box appears, notifying you that the selected message has been added to the junk e-mailers list and that if you want to see the list, go to the Junk E-Mail section of the Organize pane.

9   Click OK.

Any message that you receive from this company will automatically be colored teal.

10 In the bottom of the Organize pane, click the Click Here link.

More junk e-mail options appear.

You might have to scroll down through the Inbox to see the *Free Cell Phone* message.

You can automatically move junk e-mail to the Deleted Items folder. In the Junk E-Mail section of the Organize pane, click the first Automatically down arrow, and click Move, click the Junk Messages To down arrow, click Deleted Items, and click the Turn On button.

11   On the second line, click the Edit Junk Senders link.

The Edit Junk Senders dialog box appears. The e-mail address of Vigor Airlines has been added to the junk e-mailers list.

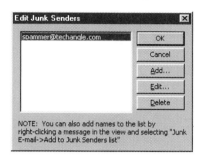

There are several organizations that fight junk e-mailers by alerting government authorities to illegal spamming and promoting further legislation to restrict junk e-mail. Search for them with your Web browser using the keywords *spam* or *junk e-mail*.

12   Click OK.

13   On the last line of the Junk E-Mail window, click the Back To Junk E-Mail link.

The original junk e-mail options are redisplayed.

OL2000. 2.4

Archiving Messages

When you first install and run Outlook, all your folders are empty (except for one welcome message from Microsoft in your Inbox). But after a few months, that pristine condition will probably change drastically. E-mail messages in your Inbox and Sent Items boxes can number in the hundreds unless you're in the habit of moving or deleting your e-mail periodically. If you tend to keep all your messages in their original folders, and you don't like to permanently delete e-mail messages (in the event that you might need to return to them later), you might want to take advantage of Outlook's **archive** feature.

Using the Outlook Archive feature, you can store old (*you* determine what length of time is considered "old") Inbox and Sent Items content within a single, compressed file stored in a folder on your hard disk, leaving you with only the most current information. When you archive outdated messages in a folder, they are removed from your Outlook folder and are copied to a .pst file on your hard drive. Archiving merely helps to remove the clutter from your Outlook folders.

You can instruct Outlook to AutoArchive your Outlook folders for you, in which case Outlook periodically archives your folders so that you don't have to be concerned with the process. Or you can archive the folders manually, in which case Outlook archives items that are older than the period of time that you specify for determining what should be archived.

In this exercise, you manually archive the Inbox.

1   On the File menu, click Archive.

The Archive dialog box appears. Notice that the Archive This Folder And All Subfolders option is selected, and the Inbox is selected.

2   Click the Archive Items Older Than down arrow.

A mini-calendar appears.

3   If necessary, click the left or right arrow at the top of the mini-calendar to display the current month, and click yesterday's date.

4   Click the Browse button, click the Save In down arrow to navigate to the Outlook Core Practice folder on your hard disk, and then click OK twice.

All e-mail messages older than yesterday's date are archived. The archived messages are removed from the Inbox.

It might take a few seconds for the messages to be removed from the Inbox.

5   Display Windows Explorer and navigate to the Outlook Core Practice folder on your hard disk.

A file called Archive appears.

You might have to scroll down in the Inbox to see that the older messages (such as the *Free Cell Phone* message or the *Vigor Airlines* message) no longer appear.

6   In the top-right corner of the Windows Explorer window, click the Close button.

Windows Explorer closes and Outlook reappears.

tip

To import an archive file, click Import And Export on the File menu to display the Import And Export Wizard. Verify that the Import From Another Program Or File option is selected, and click Next. In the next wizard dialog box, scroll down, click Personal Folder File (.pst), and click Next. In the next wizard dialog box, click the Browse button, navigate to the folder the archive is stored in, and double-click the archive file. Click Next to display the final wizard dialog box, and click Finish. The files will be restored to the Inbox.

Lesson Wrap-Up

This lesson covered how to customize your e-mail messages and organize your Outlook Inbox. In this lesson, you learned about e-mail options such as importance, sensitivity, and delivery options. You also learned how to customize the appearance of your e-mail messages by creating them in the Plain Text, Microsoft Outlook Rich Text, and HTML formats. You learned about creating messages with stationery and creating a signature. You learned how to set viewing options and how to sort and filter the Inbox. You learned how to create a folder and move messages between folders. In addition, you learned how to organize your Inbox by color-coding messages and filtering junk e-mail. Finally, you learned how to archive old messages.

If you are continuing to the next lesson:

● On the Standard toolbar, click the Organize button.
   The Organize pane closes.

If you are not continuing to other lessons:

Close

● In the top-right corner of the Outlook window, click the Close button.
   The Outlook window closes.

Lesson Glossary

archive A process in which older Inbox and Sent Items messages and attachments are combined into a single file, compressed, and stored in a folder on your hard disk.

filter The process of specifying criteria and then using Outlook to display only those items that match your criteria.

formatted text Text that appears in different sizes, colors, styles, and alignments.

junk e-mail Unsolicited and unwanted e-mail that is used for advertising purposes and is more commonly known as spam.

rule A set of conditions, actions, and exceptions that define and control the process for managing incoming e-mail messages.

signature Personal information, such as your title, phone number, or address, that is automatically added to the end of each e-mail message that you compose and send.

sort To arrange messages in ascending or descending order by the criteria you specify, such as by sender, subject, or flag status.

stationery Ready-made designs, including images, backgrounds, and borders, that can be applied to an e-mail message.

views Ways to group and view related items in an Outlook folder.

Quick Quiz

1   How do you assign high-importance status to a message?

2   What is a view?

3   What does a filter do?

4   What is one way to distinguish messages from a specific person?

5   What is a signature in an e-mail message?

6   How can you store outdated messages?

7   What can you use to format a message with a predefined design?

8   What levels of Importance does Outlook let you set for a message?

9   Where in Outlook do you filter junk e-mail?

Putting It All Together

Exercise 1: The new marketing director at Lakewood Mountains Resort needs to set up his e-mail workspace. First, create two folders for the new projects—Pool and Tennis Courts—starting next week. Place these folders in the Inbox folder.

Next, set up a business signature to include his name (David Perry), title (marketing director), and phone number (555-555-0154). Set this signature as the default signature. Finally, the director has little time for junk e-mail, so set up the filters to identify and delete junk e-mail.

Exercise 2: The general manager of Lakewood Mountains Resort wants to invite a new member of the staff to a manager's meeting. Send an e-mail message to someone@microsoft.com using the Formal Announcement stationery announcing the managers meeting on Tuesday, at 3:00 P.M., in the dining room. Indicate that the message is important.

LESSON 4

Using Contacts

After completing this lesson, you will be able to:

✔ *Open the Contacts folder.*

✔ *Create and edit contacts.*

✔ *Create multiple contact records for people at the same company.*

✔ *Use the Office Clipboard to paste from multiple copied items.*

✔ *Delete and restore contacts.*

✔ *Use folders, views, and categories.*

✔ *Assign items to a category.*

✔ *Modify the Master Category List.*

✔ *Sort contacts.*

✔ *Send e-mail from the Address Book and the Contacts folder.*

✔ *Send and receive contact information by e-mail.*

✔ *Create a letter for a contact by using the Letter Wizard.*

To communicate efficiently with personal and business associates, many people keep track of important phone and fax numbers, addresses, and other relevant information in an address book or a business card holder. Using the tools in Microsoft Outlook, you can also create and organize your contact information at your computer. In Outlook, a **contact** is a collection of information about a person or a company. Contact information is stored in the **Contacts folder,** which is essentially an electronic organizer that you can use to create, view, sort, and edit contact information. Contacts are integrated with other components of Outlook and other Microsoft Office programs so that name, address, and phone information is available for use with other Outlook folders and Office programs.

One of the chief values of the Contacts folder is that each time you create a new contact, the name, e-mail address, and phone numbers are added to your **Address Book.** When you compose an e-mail message, you can then use the Address Book to insert the appropriate e-mail address in the To or Cc box—you don't have to manually type the addresses.

In this lesson, you will learn how to create, edit, and delete contacts. You will also learn how to sort contacts and organize them by using folders and views. In addition, you will learn how to use the Address Book and Contacts to send e-mail messages as well as learn how to send contact information as a **vCard,** or a virtual business card. At the end of this lesson, you will learn how to compose and send letters in Microsoft Word by using contact information from Outlook.

**Practice files
for the lesson**

No practice files are required to complete the exercises in this lesson.

Your Outlook folders should already contain the Outlook items (e-mail messages and contact records) that are necessary to complete the exercises in this lesson. If you need to add these items to your Outlook folders, see the "Using the CD-ROM" section at the beginning of this book.

important

To complete some of the exercises in this lesson, you will need to exchange e-mail messages with a class partner. If you don't have a class partner or are performing the exercises alone, you can enter your own e-mail address instead of your class partner's and send the message to yourself.

Viewing Contacts

When you click the Contacts shortcut on the Outlook Bar, the contents of the Contacts folder appear. Outlook provides several different formats for viewing contact information. Contacts appear in the **Address Cards** view by default. From the Address Cards view, you can see a contact's title bar, a follow-up flag (if one is present to remind you that you need to make a follow-up phone call or send additional information to the contact), a mailing address, and the company with which the contact is associated. You can also see four fields for storing telephone and fax information, and up to three of the contact's e-mail addresses.

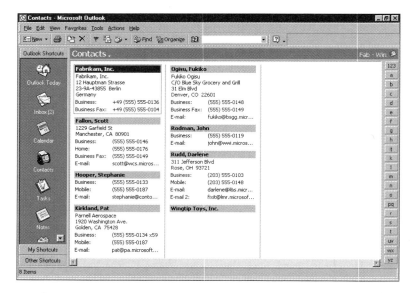

You can get more detailed information about a contact by double-clicking the contact. The contact window that appears contains a menu bar, a Standard toolbar, and five tabs—General, Details, Activities, Certificates, and All Fields. You'll use the General tab most frequently when you create or look up contact information; you might also want to use the Details tab to add more information about contacts.

Standard toolbar

Tabs

Contact
name

Address

Notes
box

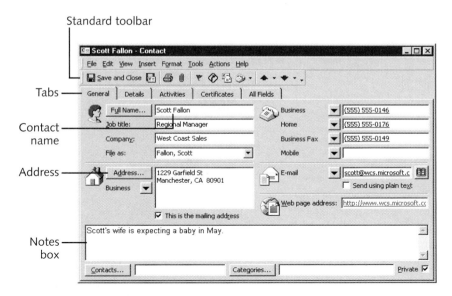

When you open a contact window, the General tab appears by default. The General tab contains all the information that appears on the contact in the Address Cards view, as well as a box for a Web page address, an area for notes, links to other contacts, and Outlook categories the contact is assigned to. When you create a new contact, you must enter at least a full name, a company name, or an e-mail address. (Only one of these is required so that the contact can be sorted properly.) All other entries are optional. If you enter an e-mail address but don't include a full name or company name, Outlook will suggest that you provide one of these names before you save the contact.

The Details tab contains more specific information about the contact—the contact's office, department, profession, manager's name, assistant's name, the contact's nickname, spouse's name, and the contact's birthday and anniversary, as well as e-mail address information. All entries on the Details tab are optional.

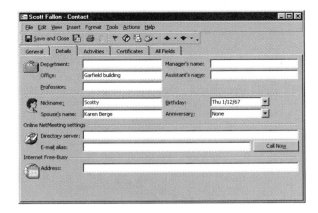

If you open a contact window for a particular contact, and then close Outlook, the contact window will remain open so that you can continue to view or modify the information for this contact.

You can be in any Outlook folder and view contact information. On the Tools menu, click Advanced Find. Click the Look For down arrow, and click Contacts. In the Search For The Words box, type the first few letters of the contact's name, and click the Find Now button. The contact will appear in the bottom pane of the Advanced Find window. Double-click the contact to view information in the contact window.

To close a contact window, click the Save And Close button or, in the top-right corner of the contact window, click the Close button.

In this exercise, you view contact information.

1   On the Outlook Bar, click the Contacts shortcut.

The contents of the Contacts folder appear.

2   Double-click the title bar of the Fabrikam, Inc., contact.

The Fabrikam, Inc., contact window appears with the information on the General tab visible.

3   Click the Details tab.

The Details tab appears; there is no information in the Details section of the contact.

4   Click the General tab.

The General tab appears.

Close

5   In the top-right corner of the contact window, click the Close button.

The contact window closes.

Display Map Of Address

tip

When you want directions to a contact's home or business, you can get that information in Outlook by using its mapping feature. Double-click the contact record, and under the Address button, click the down arrow to select the type of address (business, home, or other) that you want to find on a map. Then, on the Standard toolbar in the contact window, click the Display Map Of Address button. Your Web browser opens so that you can use the service on the Microsoft Expedia Web site to display a street map for the contact's location.

OL2000.5.1

New Contact

Creating and Editing a New Contact

Creating a contact is simply a matter of typing information in boxes in the contact window (as shown below). Each box represents a field, or a single item of contact information, such as an individual's name, a company name, or a phone number. All the fields that you enter for a contact form a **contact record**. On the Standard toolbar, you click the New Contact button to display a blank contact window. To enter information in a box (field), you click the box and type the information. To move to the next box, you press Tab or you can click in the box.

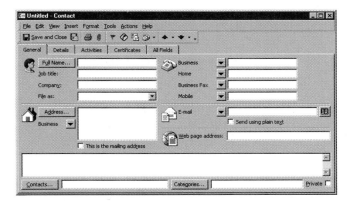

When you create a contact for a company and do not have a specific person as a contact at the company, enter the company name in the Company box and leave the Full Name box blank. Outlook interprets any information in the Full Name box as an individual's name, and it will attempt to store the contact by the name, last name first. For example, if you were to create a contact for Lakewood Mountains Resort, you would enter Lakewood Mountains Resort in the Company box. If you typed Lakewood Mountains Resort in the Full Name box, the contact would be stored as Resort, Lakewood Mountains.

Because some people have multiple phone numbers, addresses, and e-mail addresses, the Address, Phone, and E-Mail boxes can have multiple field entries. To enter more than one number, address, or e-mail address, you click the down arrow next to the box to display a list of entry descriptions (as shown in the following illustration).

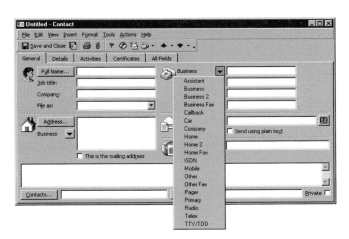

You click the most appropriate entry description and enter the information in the box. For example, a customer service representative at Lakewood Mountains Resort is entering information for a contact who has both a pager and a mobile phone. In the first box, the representative clicks the down arrow, clicks Pager, and types the pager number. In the next box, the representative clicks the down arrow, clicks Mobile, and types the mobile phone number.

You can also store a contact's Web page address in the contact window, if applicable. Unlike e-mail addresses, you can store only one Web page address at a time.

When you finish entering information for a contact, click the Save And Close button on the Standard toolbar in the contact window to save the information as a contact record, and close the contact window.

In this exercise, you create three contact records.

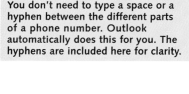

New Contact

1   On the Standard toolbar, click the New Contact button.

A contact window appears with the insertion point already in the Full Name box.

> When you type a name in the Full Name box and then move to a different box, the title bar removes the word *Untitled* and replaces it with the name you have entered.

2   In the Full Name box, type **Erik Gavriluk**, and press Tab.

The insertion point moves to the Job Title box. Outlook automatically inserts Gavriluk, Erik in the File As box.

3   Type **Director**, and press Tab.

The insertion point moves to the Company box.

4   Type **ProElectron, Inc**.

5   Click in the Address box.

6   Type **4567 Coolidge St.**, and press Enter.

7   Type **Cherry Hills, NY 09472**.

> You don't need to type a space or a hyphen between the different parts of a phone number. Outlook automatically does this for you. The hyphens are included here for clarity.

8   Click in the Business box, and type **555-555-0142**.

9   Click the Mobile down arrow.

A list of entry descriptions appears. Notice that Business has a check mark to the left of it. This is because you already typed the Business phone number in the Business box.

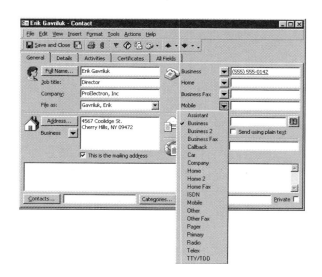

10   Click Pager.

The word Pager appears in place of the word Mobile.

11   In the Pager box, type **555-555-0143**.

12   Click in the E-Mail box, type **erik@proelectron-inc.microsoft.com**, and then press Enter.

A line appears under the e-mail address.

You can open your Web browser and access a site directly from the contact window by clicking on the Web address.

13   Click in the Web Page Address box, type **www.ProElectron.microsoft.com**, and then press Enter.

A Web page link is created, and the insertion point moves to the notes box.

14   Type **Erik is a mountain bike enthusiast.**

Save And New

15   On the Standard toolbar in the contact window, click the Save And New button.

The contact record is saved, and a blank contact window appears.

OL2000.5.5

tip

To help you remember which contacts are related to certain activities, you can use the contacts window to link the current contact record to activities— such as tasks or e-mail messages. To link a contact, display the contact window, and then on the Actions menu, point to Link, and click Items. In the Look In list, click a folder that contains the activity that you want to link the contact to, in the Items list, click an item, such as an appointment, and click OK. After you link activities to a contact, you can see these activities on the Activities tab of the contacts window.

You will use your contact information and your class partner's contact information for many exercises in this lesson. If you are working on these exercises at home or at your office, you can send and receive e-mail messages to yourself; however, you might need to adjust some of the steps in the exercise to accommodate the existing contact information on your computer. If possible, you can work through these exercises independently by asking a coworker or friend to participate as your exercise partner.

16   Add yourself as a new contact. At this point, do not include personal information such as home phone or address (you will add this information later), but you must type your name in the Full Name box and the e-mail address assigned to you at the beginning of class in the E-Mail box.

17   On the Standard toolbar in the contact window, click the Save And New button.

A contact record containing your information is saved.

18   Type your class partner's information for the new contact record. Again, do not include any address or phone number information, but you must type your class partner's name in the Full Name box, and the e-mail address assigned at the beginning of class in the E-Mail box.

19   On the Standard toolbar in the contact window, click the Save And Close button.

The contact is saved. The three contacts that you've added appear in the Contacts folder.

Entering Multiple Contacts for the Same Company

When entering multiple contacts for different people at the same company, you don't have to type company information for each new contact. You can click an existing contact for the company, and on the Actions menu, click New Contact From Same Company. A new contact window appears with the company name, address, business phone, and business fax automatically inserted. You can then enter new information about the individual (such as the person's name, home phone, and personal Web site address).

In this exercise, you create a new contact record by using an existing contact who works at the same company as the new contact.

1   In the Contacts folder, click the Erik Gavriluk contact that you created in the previous exercise.

The contact is selected.

> Outlook will not automatically add the same Web and e-mail addresses for employees at the same company because many people have their own Web pages and different e-mail addresses. When you want to specify a Web or e-mail address, you must type it in the appropriate box.

2   On the Actions menu, click New Contact From Same Company.

A new contact window appears. The contact window contains the same company name, address, and business phone number as the contact Erik Gavriluk.

3   Type the following contact information in the appropriate boxes:

Full Name   **Wendy Vasse**

Job Title   **Sales Representative**

Mobile   **555-555-0110**

E-Mail   **wendy@proelectron-inc.microsoft.com**

> You can click the Pager down arrow, and click Mobile to add a mobile phone number.

4   Click the Details tab.

The Details tab appears.

5   Click in the Department box, and type **Sales**.

6   On the Standard toolbar in the contact window, click the Save And Close button.

The information about Wendy Vasse is saved as a new contact and appears in the Contacts folder.

OL2000.4.7

Using the Office Clipboard

Copying and pasting—duplicating information from one location to one or more other locations—can be a useful method to use in Outlook. For example, suppose that one of your contacts has made his or her mobile phone the primary business phone as well; to update your contact record for this individual, you could copy the phone number in the Mobile box and paste it in the Business box. Normally, you would use the Microsoft Windows Clipboard to do this. You simply copy the desired information from a contact record or other Office document (Windows places the copy on the clipboard), and then paste it in the desired record, folder, or document.

If you want to copy multiple selections and then paste them to different locations in a contact record or in different folders or different locations in a document, Outlook (and other Microsoft Office applications) provides a feature that you can use to do this easily. For example, suppose you've created a letter in Microsoft Word, including the name, company, and address of the recipient at the top of the letter. You then want to use this information to create a new contact record. So you need to copy the recipient's name from the letter into the Full Name box in the contact window, you need to copy the company name into the Company box, and you need to copy the recipient's address into the Address box.

By using the **Office Clipboard,** you can store multiple copied items so that the different copied items can be pasted into other Outlook locations or to and from other Microsoft Office documents. The difference between the Office Clipboard and the general Windows Clipboard is this ability to collect and paste several items at the same time. With the Windows Clipboard, if you copy or cut text, graphics, or some other object to the Windows Clipboard, the item replaces the existing content (if any) of the Windows Clipboard. With the Office Clipboard, however, you can copy and store up to 12 items at the same time. You can then select which stored item you want to paste.

You access the Office Clipboard by displaying the **Clipboard toolbar,** which appears as a floating toolbar. (To display the Clipboard toolbar in Contacts, open the contact record, and on the View menu, point to Toolbars, and click Clipboard.) To copy and paste, you select the desired text from an Outlook item, and click the Copy button on the Clipboard toolbar. The text is copied to the Clipboard and appears as a page icon with the Outlook icon on the Clipboard toolbar. Clicking this icon pastes the selected text, starting at the location of the insertion point. You can continue to copy up to 11 more selected items to the Office Clipboard and then selectively paste the items into Outlook or other Microsoft Office documents as desired. You can paste each selection individually, or you can paste all copied selections at one time by clicking the Paste All button on the Clipboard toolbar.

Copy

The Office Clipboard and the corresponding Clipboard toolbar are available only in Microsoft Word 2000, Microsoft Excel 2000, Microsoft Access 2000, Microsoft PowerPoint 2000, and Microsoft Outlook 2000. They are not available in other Microsoft Office programs or in non-Microsoft programs.

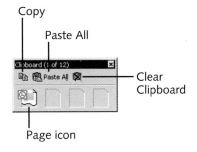

To help you identify different items in the Office Clipboard, up to the first 50 characters of the copied or cut text for each item appears as a ScreenTip when you position the mouse pointer over the item in the Clipboard toolbar. If you copy a graphic or other object to the Office Clipboard, the ScreenTip for the item will appear as a numbered object.

important

You cannot access the Clipboard toolbar from the View menu in the Outlook window. You can access the Clipboard toolbar on the View menus of the message window, the appointment window, the contact window, the task window, and the journal entry window.

When you have finished using items that you have copied to the Office Clipboard, you can delete all the copied selections by clicking the Clear Clipboard button on the Clipboard toolbar. You should clear the Office Clipboard periodically if you no longer need to paste from any of the current items in the Office Clipboard. This removes clutter from the Clipboard toolbar and makes room for new items that you want to copy and paste.

In this exercise, you use the Office Clipboard to copy address and phone information from one contact to another, and then you delete the contents of the Office Clipboard.

1   Double-click the Scott Fallon contact record.

The contact window appears.

2   On the View menu, point to Toolbars, and click Clipboard.

The Clipboard toolbar appears.

> The Clipboard toolbar might contain an icon for a previously copied selection (even from a different Microsoft Office program). If the Clipboard already displays an icon from Outlook or another Office application, the next copied text will appear in the next blank box. You can remove this item by clicking the Clear Clipboard button on the Clipboard toolbar.

3   Click the Address down arrow, and click Home.

The home address for Scott Fallon appears in the Address box.

4   Select the address.

Copy

5   On the Clipboard toolbar, click the Copy button.

An Outlook icon representing the copied address appears in the first box of the Clipboard toolbar.

> Notice that you do not need to keep a contact window open to retain its contents in the Office Clipboard. The selected and copied contents remain open even after you close the contact window.

6   Select the home phone number, and click the Copy button on the Clipboard toolbar.

Both the home address and home phone number appear as separate items in the Clipboard toolbar.

Close

7   In the top-right corner of the contact window, click the Close button.

The contact window and the Clipboard toolbar close.

New Contact

8   On the Standard toolbar, click the New Contact button.

A blank contact window and the Clipboard toolbar appear.

9   In the Full Name box, type **Karen Berge**.

10   Click in the Address box, and click the first Outlook icon on the Clipboard toolbar.

The address is pasted in the Address box.

11 Click in the Home phone number box, and click the second Outlook icon on the Clipboard toolbar.

The phone number is pasted in the Home phone number box.

Clear Clipboard

12 On the Clipboard toolbar, click the Clear Clipboard button.

The contents of the Office Clipboard are deleted.

Close

13 In the top-right corner of the Clipboard toolbar, click the Close button.

The Clipboard closes.

14 On the Standard toolbar in the contact window, click the Save And Close button.

The new contact record is saved, and the contact window closes.

Deleting and Restoring Contacts

OL20005.1

Just as it is important to clean up your e-mail folders by deleting old messages occasionally, it's important to remove outdated contacts occasionally. If you no longer do business with a particular company, for instance, or if particular employees no longer work at your company, you will probably want to delete their corresponding contact records in Outlook. Deleting old or unwanted contact records helps you find and organize the contacts that you do use more easily.

When you delete a contact, Outlook doesn't ask whether you are sure you want to delete the record; Outlook simply moves the contact to the Deleted Items folder. The contact is not permanently deleted when you do this, so you could still access the deleted contact by opening the Deleted Items folder and double-clicking the contact. However, if you delete a contact in the Deleted Items folder, or if you empty the contents of the Deleted Items folder, the contact is permanently deleted.

The Deleted Items folder can be set to empty—permanently delete—all items in the folder whenever you exit Outlook. To set the Deleted Items folder to be emptied when you exit Outlook, on the Tools menu, click Options, and click the Other tab. Select the Empty The Deleted Items Folder Upon Exiting check box, and click OK.

If the last step you performed was to delete a contact record, you can quickly restore the record by clicking Undo Delete on the Edit menu.

If you delete a contact accidentally or change your mind and want to keep the contact, you can do so provided you haven't yet emptied your Deleted Items folder. To return a deleted contact to the Contacts folder, drag the contact from the Deleted Items folder onto the Contacts shortcut on the Outlook Bar.

In this exercise, you delete and restore a contact.

1 Click the Fukiko Ogisu contact record.

The contact record is selected.

Delete

2 On the Standard toolbar, click the Delete button.

The record is moved to the Deleted Items folder.

Deleted Items

3 On the Outlook Bar, scroll down if necessary, and click the Deleted Items shortcut.

The contents of the Deleted Items folder appear.

4   Drag the Fukiko Ogisu contact to the Contacts shortcut on the Outlook Bar.

The Fukiko Ogisu contact no longer appears in the Deleted Items folder.

Contacts

5   On the Outlook Bar, click the Contacts shortcut.

The contents of the Contacts folder appear. Notice that the Fukiko Ogisu contact record appears in the Contacts folder.

Using Folders to Organize Contacts

You can use folders to organize your contacts just as you did your e-mail messages in Lesson 3, "Customizing E-Mail." In addition to the folders that are installed with Outlook, you can create your own folders to organize your contacts more efficiently. For example, Lakewood Mountains Resort uses many different contractors to perform maintenance at the resort. The office manager decided to move all the contact information for these contractors into a folder called Maintenance so that she can easily locate a particular contractor without having to look through her long list of contacts.

In this exercise, you create a folder and move a contact into it.

1   On the Standard toolbar, click the Organize button.

The Organize pane appears.

2   In the Organize pane, click the Using Folders link.

The Using Folders section of the Organize pane appears.

3   In the top-right corner of the Organize pane, click the New Folder button.

The Create New Folder dialog box appears.

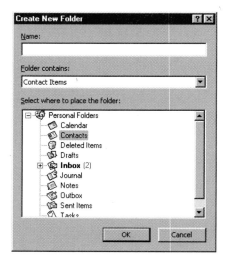

4   In the Name box, type **Personal**.

5   In the Folder Contains box, verify that Contact Items appears, and click OK.

The Add Shortcut To Outlook Bar dialog box appears, asking if you want to make this folder a shortcut.

6   Click the No button.

The Folder List appears. Notice that the Personal folder is located below the Contacts folder.

7   In Contacts, drag the horizontal scroll bar to the right to display the Wingtip Toys contact record.

8   Click the Wingtip Toys contact record.

The contact record is selected.

9   In the Organize pane, click the Move button.

The Wingtip Toys contact moves to the Personal folder.

10   In the Folder List, click Personal.

The contact Wingtip Toys appears in the Personal folder.

11   In the Folder List, click Contacts.

The contents of the Contacts folder appear.

12   In the Folder List, click the Close button.

The Folder List closes.

Using Views to Organize Contacts

Like e-mail messages, contact records can appear in several different views, or groups, which can help you find contacts faster and easier. For example, if you are looking for a particular contact and you know the contact's company, you could group your contact records by Company to locate contacts more easily.

In the Address Cards (the default view) and Detailed Address Cards views, contacts appear as cards, similar to business cards in a card file. In all other views, contacts appear in a table format with columns and rows. Each contact appears in a row, separated by columns that correspond to fields in the contact, such as Company and Business Phone. The contents of the columns change to reflect the contents of the selected view. In the views in which contacts appear in tables, the contacts are divided into groups with expandable gray bars that summarize the contents of each group. For example, when you display your contacts in the By Location view, you will see several gray bars that display the text Country/Region: (location)([number] items). If you had four contacts located in the United States and two in the United Kingdom, you would see two gray bars that displayed the text Country/Region: United States of America (4 items) and Country/Region: United Kingdom (2 items). To see the contacts, click the plus sign (+) located at the left end of the bar. To hide the contacts, click the minus sign (-) located at the left end of the bar.

The following table details each view.

View	Description
Address Cards	Contacts are arranged as cards in a row, displaying both blank fields and fields with information.
Detailed Address Cards	Contacts are arranged as cards displaying only those fields with information. This view is useful when you want to see only the known information about a contact.
Phone List	Contacts appear in rows and columns, with each telephone field displayed. As the name suggests, this view makes it easy to find a contact's telephone number.
By Category	Contacts appear grouped by categories. Categorizing contacts facilitates finding contacts. Categories are covered in the next section in this lesson.
By Company	Contacts appear grouped by Company. This view is useful for finding contacts based on the contents of the Company box. If you have several contacts that are in the same company, you can use this view to identify the job title and the department for each contact.
By Location	Contacts are grouped by Country/Region based on the contents in the Address box. This view is useful when you have international contacts.
By Follow-Up Flag	Contacts are grouped by Follow-Up Flag. This view is useful when you have marked a contact for follow-up—for example, you might add a follow-up flag for a contact who you need to call back or send additional information.

To use views to organize contacts, on the Standard toolbar, you click the Organize button. When the Organize pane appears, you click the Using Views link and click a view in the Change Your View box.

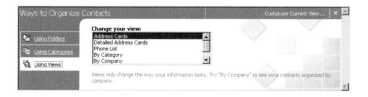

In this exercise, you display contact records in different views.

1   On the Standard toolbar, click the Organize button.

The Organize pane appears.

2   In the Organize pane, click the Using Views link.

The Using Views section of the Organize pane appears.

3   In the Change Your View list, click Detailed Address Cards.

The Contacts view changes to list your contacts in Detailed Address Cards view.

Some contacts will not have any of the entries used to sort contacts for a particular view. These contacts are grouped together with the text *(none) ([number] items)* appearing on the gray bar.

4   In the Change Your View list, click Phone List.

The Contacts view changes to list your contacts by name, e-mail address, and phone numbers.

5   In the Change Your View list, click By Category.

The Contacts view changes to list your contacts by category.

6   In the Change Your View list, click By Company.

The Contacts view changes to list your contacts by company.

7   Scroll down the Change Your View list, and click By Location.

The Contacts view changes to list your contacts by geographic location.

8   Scroll down the Change Your View list, and click By Follow-Up Flag.

The Contacts view changes to list your contacts by follow-up flag.

You can also change views by pointing to Current View on the View menu and clicking a view.

9   Scroll to the top of the Change Your View list and click Address Cards.

The Contacts view changes to list contacts by Address Cards.

OL2000.4.6
OL2000.5.3

Using Categories to Organize Contacts

Outlook provides other approaches that you can use to organize and group contacts—including the use of categories. A **category** is a keyword or phrase associated with an Outlook item, such as a contact. (You can assign categories to other contacts, such as tasks, which you will learn about later in this course.) A category is typically a brief description of the way in which a contact should be grouped with other contacts—for example, Business, Personal, Key Customer, and so on.

Outlook provides dozens of ready-made category descriptions, but you can also create your own. For example, the operations manager at Lakewood Mountains Resort could assign the ready-made Outlook category *Suppliers* to all companies from whom the resort purchases products and services on a regular basis. Whenever she needs a list of the resort's suppliers, she can view her Contacts folder by category. All contacts that have been assigned to the Suppliers category appear grouped together. She could narrow the categorization further by creating her own custom categories for each resort department, such as *Restaurant Suppliers, Business Office Suppliers, Housekeeping Suppliers,* and so on.

To assign a contact to a category, you select the contact, and click the Using Categories link in the Organize pane. In the first line, click the Add Contacts Selected Below To down arrow to view a list of categories you can select from, such as Holiday, Business, or International, and then click the Add button. The contact will be added to the selected category.

To create your own category, click the Using Categories link in the Organize pane, and in the second box, enter the category name. Click the Create button to create the category. Then you can assign the contacts you want to the new category.

In this exercise, you create a new category, assign two contacts to the category, and view your contacts by category.

1   In the Organize pane, click the Using Categories link.

The Using Categories section of the Organize pane appears.

2   Click in the Create A New Category Called box, and type **Finance**.

3   Click the Create button.

The Finance category is created.

4   In the Contacts folder, scroll to the right, and click the John Rodman contact record.

The contact record is selected.

5   In the Organize pane, click the Add button.

The contact record is assigned to the new Finance category.

6   In the Contacts folder, click the Scott Fallon contact record.

The contact record is selected.

7   In the Organize pane, click the Add button.

The contact record is assigned to the Finance category.

8   In the Organize pane, click the Using Views link.

9   If necessary, scroll down the Change Your View list, and click By Category.

The Contacts view changes to list your contacts by category.

10   On the left side of the Finance gray bar, click the plus sign (+).

Scott Fallon and John Rodman appear as the contacts in the Finance category.

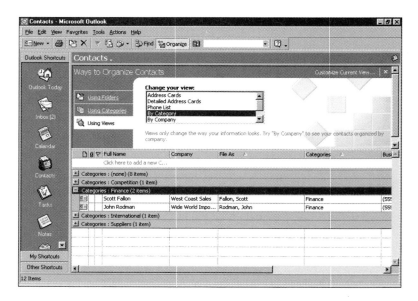

11   In the Organize pane, in the Change Your View list, click Address Cards.

The Contacts folder returns to the Address Cards view.

OL2000.4.5

Assigning Items to Multiple Categories

Relationships with contacts can be complex, so it's not unusual when a contact doesn't fit neatly into a single category. For example, Lakewood Mountains Resort hosts an international convention organized by a company in Mexico. The contact of the convention organizer can be assigned to the International, Key Customer, or Business category—or to all three.

Fortunately, you can assign contacts to more than one category. By assigning multiple categories to a contact, you make the contact record more accurately reflect your relationship to the contact and you enhance your ability to sort that contact by a particular category.

To assign a contact to an additional category or to change an existing category, double-click the contact, click the Categories button, and select the appropriate check box. Selecting a check box that already has a check mark in it removes the contact from that category.

In this exercise, you assign the contact Scott Fallon to two additional categories—Business and Supplier.

> You can open a contact record from within any view in the Contacts folder.

1   In the Contacts folder, double-click the contact record for Scott Fallon.

The contact window appears.

2   In the contact window, click the Categories button.

The Categories dialog box appears and shows that Scott Fallon is already assigned to the Finance category.

Categories	? ✕
Item(s) belong to these categories:	
Finance	Add to List
Available categories:	
☐ Business	
☐ Competition	
☐ Favorites	
✔ Finance	
☐ Gifts	
☐ Goals/Objectives	
☐ Holiday	
☐ Holiday Cards	
☐ Hot Contacts	
☐ Ideas	
☐ International	
☐ Key Customer	
☐ Miscellaneous	
☐ Personal	
OK Cancel Master Category List...	

3   In the Categories dialog box, select the Business check box, scroll down, select the Suppliers check box, and then click OK.

The categories are now added to the contact record. The categories you selected appear in the Categories box.

4   On the Standard toolbar in the contact window, click the Save And Close button.

The contact record is saved and closed.

5   In the Organize pane, in the Change Your View list, click By Category.

The contacts are organized by category.

6   On the left side of the Business and the Suppliers gray boxes, click the plus signs (+).

The contact record for Scott Fallon appears under each category. Notice that Fabrikan, Inc., is also listed under the Suppliers category.

7   In the Change Your View list, click Address Cards.

The contacts appear in Address Cards view.

Modifying the Outlook Master Category List

OL2000.4.4

Outlook's ready-made list of categories is called the **Master Category List** (as shown in the following illustration). The Master Category List contains many useful categories, such as Hot Contacts, Holiday, and VIP, but you can add your own categories. In a previous exercise, you used the Organizer pane to create a custom category called Finance. Outlook automatically added that category to the Master Category List. You can also open the Master Category List directly and add other custom categories to the list. In fact, you can customize the Master Category List in just about any way you want. You can delete categories that you don't use, and you can reset the Master Category List to restore the default categories if you decide you want to start fresh.

In this exercise, you add a category to the Master Category List, delete a category from the Master Category List, and reset the Master Category List to its original content.

1   On the Edit menu, Click Categories.

The Categories dialog box appears.

2   Click the Master Category List button.

The Master Category List dialog box appears.

3   In the New Category box, type **Charities**, and click the Add button.

Charities is added to the Master Category List.

> Notice that the Finance category that you created in the previous exercise appears in the Master Category List.

4   In the Master Category List, click Ideas.

5   Click the Delete button.

Ideas is deleted from the Master Category List.

6   Click the Reset button.

An alert box appears, stating that the Master Category List will be reset to contain only those categories that were installed with Outlook. It also states that items assigned to categories that are deleted will keep their assignments. In this case, the Finance category will be deleted along with the Charities category, because neither category is part of the original Master Category List. However, the two contacts that have been assigned to the Finance category will retain their category assignments.

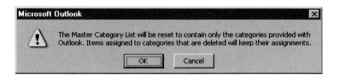

7   Click OK.

The Master Category List is reset. The custom Finance and Charities categories are deleted and the Ideas category is restored.

8   Click OK twice.

The Master Category List dialog box closes and the Categories dialog box closes.

OL2000.5.6

Sorting Contacts

Sorting contacts can help you find a contact faster and easier. You can sort contacts in any view, in either ascending order (A to Z) or descending order (Z to A) by a specific field, or by a particular column header that appears at the top of the view's table, such as Company, Job Title, or Personal Home Page. When you sort in a view, the contacts remain in the same view; however, they appear in a different order.

For example, the human resources manager at Lakewood Mountains Resort needed to find a contact but could only remember that the contact's first name was Kim. She sorted her Contacts folder by First Name, and the contacts were displayed in alphabetical order by the first name. She could have also used the Find button on the Standard toolbar to search for *Kim*. However, because the Find feature looks for a match in the name, company, address, and categories fields, it might find matches that she did not intend (for example, Kimball Museum of Science would have produced a match). Sorting by a particular column heading can often be faster.

> Unlike a filter, the Sort command displays all contacts.

You can also add an additional field, thus performing a sort within a sort. When you include a second field in the sort, the second sort narrows the first sort criterion even further. For example, you can sort Contacts by Country/Region in ascending order and then sort by Business Address in ascending order. The folder appears sorted by Country/Region, and within the Country/Region groups, contacts are sorted by Business Address.

In this exercise, you sort the list of contacts in Phone List view by Business Phone number.

1 In the Organize pane, in the Change Your View list, click Phone List.

Contacts are displayed in Phone List view.

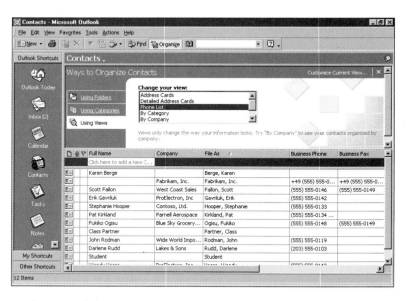

2 At the top of the Organize pane, click the Customize Current View button.

The View Summary dialog box appears.

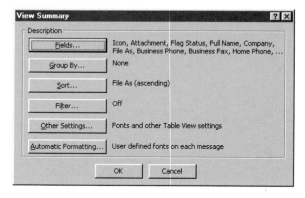

3 Click the Sort button.

The Sort dialog box appears.

4 In the Sort Items By section, click the down arrow.

5 Scroll up if necessary, click Business Phone, and, if necessary, click the Ascending option.

6   Click OK twice.

The contents of the Contacts folder appear sorted by Business Phone within each category.

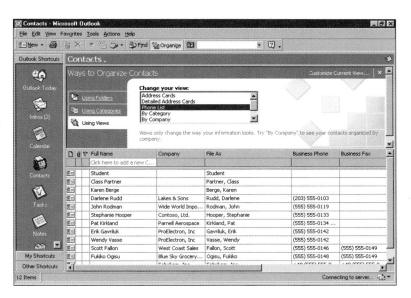

7   In the Organize pane, click the Customize Current View button.

The View Summary dialog box appears.

8   Click the Sort button.

The Sort dialog box appears.

9   Click the Clear All button, and then click OK twice.

The contents of the Contacts folder are no longer sorted by Business Phone.

10   In the Organize pane, in the Change Your View list, click Address Cards.

The Contacts view is changed to Address Cards.

When you click the Clear All button and close the Sort dialog box, Outlook no longer sorts the contents of the Contacts folder by the criterion you specified. Instead, contacts are sorted by the default.

OL2000.1.7
OL2000.1.16

Using the Address Book to Send E-Mail

As mentioned at the outset of this lesson, when you create a new contact record, some of the information automatically is copied to the Address Book, which can store names, e-mail addresses, and phone numbers. You can open the Address Book from any folder in Outlook by clicking the Address Book button on the Standard toolbar.

important

If your computer is set up for the Corporate or Workgroup e-mail service, your Address Book will look slightly different (and have different options) than the one discussed in this lesson.

Within the Address Book window is a toolbar and a listing of contact information for each record listed in the Contacts folder. The toolbar contains six buttons—New, Properties, Delete, Find People, Print, and Action. The buttons are described in the table below.

> You can also add names, e-mail addresses, and phone numbers directly in the Address Book without having to create contact records first. On the Standard toolbar, click the Address Book button. On the Address Book toolbar, click New, and click New Contact. Enter information just as you would do in a contact window.

Button	Description
New	You can use the New button to add a new contact or group of contacts to the Address Book.
Properties	Displays a summary of information about a contact. You can add or edit contact information in the Properties dialog box.
Delete	Permanently deletes a contact. The selected contact does not go to the Deleted Items folder.
Find People	Opens the Find People dialog box, where you can conduct searches in selected folders based on criteria you select.
Print	You can use this button to print individual contact records or to print the entire contents of the Address Book.
Action	You can use this button to perform actions, such as send an e-mail message in the Address Book or use the Windows Dialer to dial a phone number.

> You can also press Ctrl+Shift+B to open the Address Book.

If a contact has an e-mail address, you can send messages to the contact directly from the Address Book, so you don't have to copy or manually type the e-mail address into the To box of a new message window.

Address Book buttons

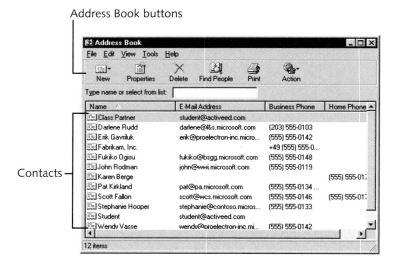

Contacts

In this exercise, you open the Address Book, select an e-mail address, and send an e-mail message.

Address Book

1 On the Standard toolbar, click the Address Book button.

The Address Book appears.

2 If necessary, click your class partner's name.

3   On the toolbar, click the Action button, and click Send Mail.

A message window appears. Your class partner's address is in the To box.

Because this message will not be used in another part of the lesson, it is not necessary that the message be sent and received immediately. Therefore, there is no need to click the Send/ Receive button (see Lesson 2, "Using E-Mail in Outlook").

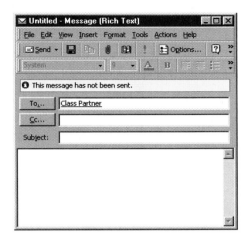

4   In the Subject box, type **Address Book**.

5   Click in the message area, and type **You are in my address book**.

6   On the Standard toolbar in the message window, click the Send button.

The message is sent to your class partner.

Close

7   In the top-right corner of the Address Book, click the Close button.

Using Contacts to Send E-Mail

OL2000.1.16

*New Message
To Contact*

You can send e-mail directly from the Contacts folder without having to open the Inbox folder first. To send an e-mail message to a contact from the Contacts folder, you first click the contact record in the Contacts folder. Then on the Standard toolbar, click the New Message To Contact button. A message window appears, with the e-mail address of the contact you selected in the To box. You can type any further information for the e-mail message, and, on the Standard toolbar in the message window, click the Send button.

You can send e-mail messages from Contacts even when the recipient is not a contact. On the Standard toolbar, click the down arrow to the right of the New button, and click Mail Message. A blank message window will appear so that you can create and send a message.

In this exercise, you send a message to your class partner from a contact window. You also send an e-mail message to your class partner from the Contacts folder.

If a recipient is in the Address Book, you can click the To button in the message window to display the Select Names dialog box. Click the name of the recipient, click the To button, and click OK.

1   In the Contacts folder, double-click your class partner's contact record.

Your class partner's contact window appears.

*New Message
To Contact*

2   On the Standard toolbar in the message window, click the New Message To Contact button.

A message window appears with your class partner's e-mail address in the To box. The insertion point appears in the Subject box.

3   Type **A question**, and press Enter.

The insertion point moves to the message area.

4   Type **How is the Outlook class going?**, and click the Send button.

The message is sent, and the contact window reappears.

Close

5   In the top-right corner of the contact window, click the Close button.

The contact window closes, and your class partner's contact record is still selected.

New Message To Contact

6   On the Standard toolbar, click the New Message To Contact button.

A message window appears with your class partner's e-mail address in the To box. The insertion point appears in the Subject box.

7   Type **FYI**, and press Enter.

The insertion point moves to the message area.

Because these messages will not be used in another part of the lesson, it is not necessary that the message be sent and received immediately. Therefore, there is no need to click the Send/Receive button (see Lesson 2, "Using E-Mail in Outlook").

8   Type **You can send a message directly from the Contacts folder.**

9   On the Standard toolbar in the message window, click the Send button.

The message is sent to your class partner. The Contacts folder reappears.

OL2000.5.2
OL2000.1.16

Sending Contact Information via E-Mail

important

To use vCards in Outlook, you must have the VcViewer program installed and Outlook must be set up using the Internet Only configuration. If an alert box appears, stating you do not have the VcViewer program installed, you can install it from the Outlook or Microsoft Office 2000 CD-ROM.

You can use the vCard format to send and receive contact information as an e-mail attachment so that it can be added easily to your or a recipient's Contacts folder. You can create a vCard for yourself, forward a vCard (sent to you from another person), send a contact as a vCard to other recipients so that they can add it to their Contacts folder or Address Book, and you can include a vCard as part of a signature.

Exchanging contact information using vCards is fast and convenient. Rather than sending a text message containing the contact information, and then typing it in as a new contact, you can send a vCard and the recipient can add it directly to his or her Contacts folder. For example, the head chef of Lakewood Mountains Resort attaches a vCard with his address and phone information to his signature. When he sends e-mail to other people, they receive the vCard and can easily add it to their Contacts folder. To send a vCard from Contacts, right-click the contact you want to send information about, and click Forward As vCard. A new message window opens with the contact information appearing as a vCard attached to the message. In the To box, type the e-mail address of whomever you want to receive the vCard, and click the Send button.

In this exercise, you forward your contact information as a vCard to a member of your class, make the vCard part of your signature, and send a message to a class member with a vCard as part of your signature.

1   In the Contacts folder, double-click your contact record.

Your contact window appears.

2   In the Address box, type the address for your company, your home address, or a fictitious address.

3   In the Business or Home box, type your business phone number, your home phone number, or a fictitious phone number.

4   On the Standard toolbar in the contact window, click the Save And Close button.

The contact window closes and the Contacts folder reappears, with your contact record still selected.

5   Right-click your contact record.

A shortcut menu appears.

6   Click Forward.

A new message window appears with *FW: [Your Name]* in the Subject box. The vCard appears in the bottom of the message window as an attachment.

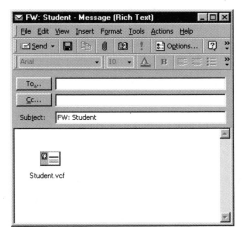

7   Click the To button.

The Select Names dialog box appears.

8   In the Select Names dialog box, click your class partner's name, click the To button, and click OK.

The Select Names dialog box closes, and your class partner's name appears in the To box.

9 On the Standard toolbar in the message window, click the Send button.

Your contact information is sent as a vCard.

10 On the Tools menu, click Options.

The Options dialog box appears.

11 Click the Mail Format tab, and click the Signature Picker button.

The Signature Picker dialog box appears.

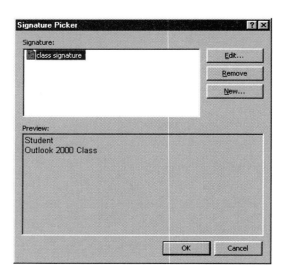

12 Verify that the signature you created in Lesson 3, "Customizing E-Mail," is selected, and click the Edit button.

The Edit Signature dialog box appears.

13 At the bottom of the dialog box, click the New vCard From Contact button.

The Select Contacts To Export As vCards dialog box appears.

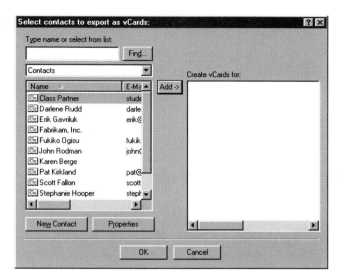

14 Click your name, click the Add button, and then click OK.

In the Edit Signature dialog box, notice that your name appears in the Attach This Business Card (vCard) To This Signature box.

15 Click OK three times to close the open dialog boxes.

16 Click your class partner's contact record.

*New Message
To Contact*

17 On the Standard toolbar, click the New Message To Contact button.

A new message window appears. Your class partner's e-mail address appears in the To box, your signature appears in the message area, and a vCard is attached to the message.

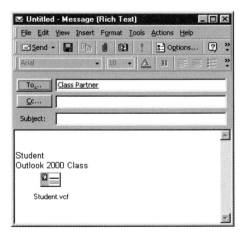

18 In the Subject box, type **My new signature**, in the message area, type **Look at my new signature**, and then click the Send button on the Standard toolbar in the message window.

The message is sent to your class partner.

You will view your class partner's e-mail messages sent to you in the next exercise.

19 On the Outlook Bar, scroll up if necessary, and click the Inbox shortcut.

The contents of the Inbox folder appear.

20 Click the Send/Receive button.

The messages from your class partner appear in the Inbox.

Receiving Contact Information via E-Mail

When you receive a vCard, it appears as an attachment to an e-mail message. You can open it by double-clicking the vCard icon just like any other attachment. The vCard opens as a contact window. You can add any additional information you want, such as who sent you the card, or edit existing information. You click the Save And Close button to add the vCard to your Contacts folder.

If the vCard is a duplicate of an existing contact, an alert box appears. You can choose to add the contact as a second record, or you can elect to add updated information from the new contact to the existing contact.

In this exercise, you receive two vCards and save them as a single contact record.

Because both messages contain a vCard, it does not matter which message you select first.

1 Double-click one of the messages that you received from your class partner in the previous exercise.

A message window appears. The vCard appears as an attachment to the message.

If an alert box appears, asking whether you want to open or save the file, click the Open It option, and click OK.

2 Double-click the vCard.

The vCard appears as a contact window.

important

If you're using Microsoft Windows 2000, a properties dialog box appears. In the dialog box, click the Add To Address Book button, and click OK. An alert box appears telling you that the record is a duplicate. Click Yes to update the existing contact.

3 Click the Save And Close button.

Because you should already have a contact record for your class partner, an alert box will probably appear indicating that this is a duplicate record.

4 When the alert box appears, verify that the Update New Information From This Contact To The Existing One option is selected, and click OK.

The vCard is saved as a contact record (or updates your class partner's contact information) in the Contacts folder.

5 In the top-right corner of the message window, click the Close button.

Close

6 Double-click the remaining message from your class partner.

A message window appears.

7 Double-click the vCard.

The vCard appears as a contact record.

8   Click the Save And Close button.

An alert box appears indicating that this is a duplicate record.

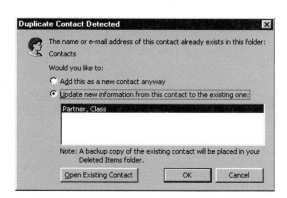

9   Verify that the Update New Information From This Contact To The Existing One option is selected, and click OK.

Outlook saves the vCard as a contact record in the Contacts folder.

Close

10   In the top-right corner of the message window, click the Close button.

11   On the Outlook Bar, click the Contacts shortcut.

The Contacts folder appears.

Contacts

12   In the Contacts folder, find your class partner's contact record and verify that the address and phone information in the vCard you received is now a part of your class partner's contact record.

OL2000.7.1

Creating a Letter for a Contact Using the Letter Wizard

Outlook e-mail capabilities are integrated with all other Microsoft Office applications. This means you can initiate some activities directly in an Office application that you would otherwise have to do from within Outlook. For example, you can use your Address Book (which Outlook updates each time you create a new contact) to create and send documents in Microsoft Word. After you create a document in word, on the File menu, you can point to Send To and then click E-Mail Recipient or E-Mail Recipient (As Attachment) to send the document as the body of an e-mail message or as an attachment to an e-mail message. You can also click the E-Mail button on the Standard toolbar in Word to quickly send the document as an e-mail message.

Conversely, you can also initiate an e-mail message in letter format from within Outlook, which can then launch Word so that you can compose the body of the letter. You don't need to type the recipient's address in the letter if it already exists in a contact record.

For example, an administrative assistant at Lakewood Mountains Resort needs to write a letter to a client regarding his account. Instead of opening Word and typing the client's information in the top-left corner of the letter, the assistant creates the letter from the contact record in Outlook, and the contact information is automatically added to the letter.

Although Outlook starts the letter-creation process, you actually create and compose the letter in Microsoft Word. Outlook starts Word and then starts the Letter Wizard. The Letter Wizard dialog box appears in Word and contains four tabs, each relating to a step in the letter-creation process. In the first step, on the Letter Format tab, you choose a letter format, including letterhead, page design, and letter style. In the second step, on the Recipient Info tab, you select the recipient's name, mailing address, and a salutation. In the third step, on the Other Elements tab, you can select options concerning reference lines, mailing instructions, attentions, subjects, and courtesy copies. In the fourth and final step, on the Sender Info tab, you select information about the person sending the letter (either yourself or someone else), and letter closing options. After the fourth step is finished, the Letter Wizard closes and you can begin to type the body of the letter. You need only type the body of the letter.

important

To complete the next exercise, you must have Microsoft Word installed on your computer.

In this exercise, you use the Letter Wizard to format and compose a letter to contact Erik Gavriluk.

1   In the Contacts folder, click the Erik Gavriluk contact.

2   On the Actions menu, click New Letter To Contact.

Word is opened, and the first dialog box of the Letter Wizard appears.

If the Office Assistant appears, right-click the Assistant and click Hide on the shortcut menu that appears.

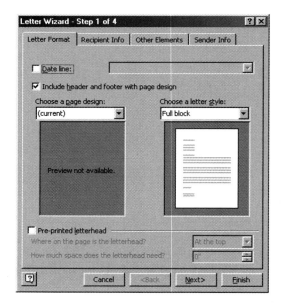

3 Select the Date Line check box to add the date to the letter.

Today's date appears in the box. Notice that the Include Header And Footer With Page Design check box is already selected.

4 Click the Choose A Page Design down arrow to view the letter design options, and click Professional Letter.

The Professional Letter design template appears. Notice that the Full Block letter style option appears in the Choose A Letter Style box. This letter style prints the letter with the date, return address, and closing aligned left. The margins of the letter text are justified on both the left and right margins.

5 Verify that the text *At the top* appears in the Where On The Page Is The Letterhead box.

The wizard will provide room at the top of the page for your (or your company's) pre-printed letterhead information.

6 Select the Pre-Printed Letterhead check box, and in the How Much Space Does The Letterhead Need box, select the original text, and type **1.5**.

7 Click the Next button.

The Recipient Info tab of the Letter Wizard appears. Erik Gavriluk's name and address already appear in the dialog box.

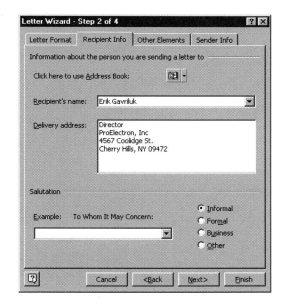

8 In the Salutation section, click the Formal option to change the salutation to Dear Erik Gavriluk.

9   Click the Next button.

The Other Elements tab of the Letter Wizard appears.

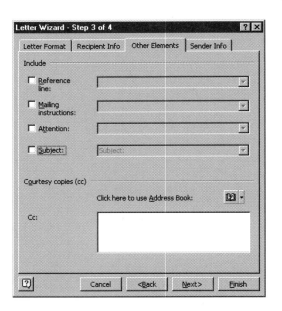

You can see a list of frequently used text for this field by clicking the down arrow next to each item.

10   Select the Subject check box, click after the word *Subject*, press the Spacebar, and type **Bids for signs**.

11   Click the Next button.

The Sender Info tab appears.

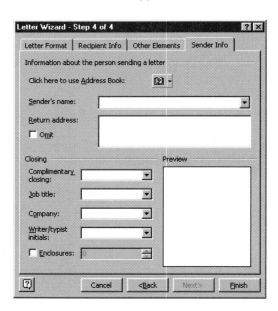

You can also choose a name from the Address Book to be inserted here. Click the Address Book button and select the name. The name can be yours or, when you are writing the letter for someone else, his or her name.

12   If your name does not appear in the Sender's Name box, click the Sender's Name down arrow, and click your name in the list. If your name does not appear in the list, type your name in the Sender's Name box.

13 Select the Omit check box.

The return address will not be printed in the letter.

14 In the Closing section, click the Complimentary Closing down arrow, scroll down, and click Sincerely,.

15 Click in the Job Title box, and type **Marketing Director**.

16 Click the Finish button.

The Letter Wizard closes and the letter is displayed in Word. You can now add the body text to the letter. The text *Type Your Text Here* is selected, ready for you to type over it.

> If the Office Assistant appears, asking if you want to do more with the letter, click Cancel.

17 Complete the letter by typing **We at Lakewood Mountains Resort are now taking bids for new signs. If you would like to obtain more information and place a bid, contact us at 555-555-0129.**

18 On the Standard toolbar, click the Save button.

The Save As dialog box appears.

19 Click the Save In down arrow, and navigate to the Outlook Core Practice folder on your hard disk.

20 In the File Name box, select the text, type **Letter to Erik Gavriluk**, and then click the Save button.

The letter is saved in the Outlook Core Practice folder.

Lesson Wrap-Up

This lesson covered how to create and use contacts, a central feature of Microsoft Outlook. In this lesson, you learned how to view contacts and how to create and edit contacts; how to sort and organize contacts using folders, views, and categories; how to use the Address Book and contacts to send e-mail messages; how to send contact information as a virtual business card, or vCard; and finally, you learned how to create a letter to a contact using the Letter Wizard and Microsoft Word.

If you are continuing to the next lesson:

Close

● In the top-right corner of the Microsoft Word window, click the Close button.

Microsoft Word closes.

If you are not continuing to other lessons:

Close

1 In the top-right corner of the Microsoft Word window, click the Close button.

Microsoft Word closes.

Close

2 In the top-right corner of the Outlook window, click the Close button. Outlook closes.

Lesson Glossary

Address Book A repository for storing names, e-mail addresses, and phone and fax numbers. You can use the Address Book to quickly insert e-mail addresses in the To and Cc boxes when you compose a message.

Address Cards The default view of Contacts in which the contact's basic information appears.

category A keyword or phrase associated with a contact that helps to organize and group Outlook items according to a common usage (such as Business or Personal). You can group contacts into categories, but you can also group other Outlook items, especially tasks, into categories.

Clipboard toolbar A toolbar available in some Microsoft Office programs, including Outlook, that can be used to copy multiple selections and store them simultaneously, and then can be used to selectively paste items stored in the Office Clipboard into folders or other Microsoft Office documents.

contact A record of a person's or company's addresses, phone and pager numbers, and e-mail addresses. The record can include personal information, such as birthdays and anniversaries, and company information.

contact record All the fields entered for a contact, such as name, company, and phone number.

Contacts folder An address book and information record where you store, sort, and arrange contacts. The Contacts folder is often referred to as Contacts.

Master Category List A list of available categories you can use to group items or find items. Outlook provides 20 ready-made categories, but you can add your own custom categories.

Office Clipboard A storage area available in some Microsoft Office applications in which multiple selections can be copied and stored in the Office Clipboard simultaneously. The Clipboard toolbar can then be used to selectively paste items from the Office Clipboard into folders or documents.

vCard A virtual business card containing contact information that can be sent to others via e-mail so that the recipients can view the contact information or add it to their Contacts folder or Address Book.

Quick Quiz

1 How can the Address Book save you time in addressing a new message?

2 Can you add categories to the Master Category List? If so, how?

3 What is a category?

4 How do you enter multiple contacts for the same company?

5 What is a vCard?

6 What happens when you click the Save And New button after entering contact data?

7 For a contact record to be complete, what box(es) in the contact window are you required to fill in?

8 In general, what is the Contacts folder used for?

9 Where does a contact go when you delete it, and how do you permanently delete a contact?

Putting It All Together

Exercise 1: The new marketing director at Lakewood Mountains Resort needs to add two new contacts for the advertising agency of Ferguson & Bardell. The members of the agency are Kathryn Wilson, President, and Sue Jackson, Ad Consultant. The address for the company is 55 Pine Terrace, Suite 400, San Jose, CA 11111. Each contact is to be assigned to the Business and Strategies categories. The additional information the marketing director has for each person is the business phone, mobile phone, pager, and e-mail address.

Enter the following contact information for Kathryn Wilson:

Name	**Kathryn Wilson**
Job Title	**President**
Business Phone	**555-555-2636**
Pager	**555-555-7988**
Mobile Phone	**555-555-7981**
E-Mail Address	**kathryn@ferguson&bardell.microsoft.com**

Enter the following contact information for Sue Jackson:

Name	**Sue Jackson**
Job Title	**Ad Consultant**
Pager	**555-555-6536**
Mobile Phone	**555-555-5581**
E-Mail Address	**sue@ferguson&bardell.microsoft.com**

You must complete Exercise 1 before you can continue to Exercise 2.

Exercise 2: Compose a formal letter to the president of Ferguson & Bardell indicating what a pleasure it was to meet with her team and expressing confidence that the advertising campaign for Lakewood Mountains Resort is in good hands. Save or print the letter.

LESSON 5

Using the Calendar

After completing this lesson, you will be able to:

✔ *Navigate within the Calendar.*

✔ *Change Calendar views.*

✔ *Schedule appointments and events.*

✔ *Create recurring appointments.*

✔ *Set reminders.*

✔ *Edit appointments.*

✔ *Delete appointments.*

✔ *Organize appointments using categories and views.*

✔ *Plan meetings with others.*

✔ *Print a Calendar.*

✔ *Save a Calendar as a Web page.*

✔ *Integrate the Calendar with other Outlook components.*

For many busy businesspeople, there never seem to be enough hours in the day to get through all their tasks. To keep track of all your day-to-day duties, meetings, and appointments, it's important to stay organized. To do this, you can jot down your appointments and other scheduling information in a day planner or enter the information into a palm-size computer. But you can also use Microsoft Outlook to plan your day and your week. And because Outlook uses the full power of your computer, you can often take advantage of features not available with a day planner or a palm-size computer. For instance, in Outlook, you can set an alarm to notify you of an upcoming appointment. You certainly can't expect your day planner to sound an alarm, and many palm-size computers can't do this either.

The **Calendar** is a component of Outlook that can be used similarly to the way you might use a desk calendar or a day planner, although with Outlook you have many additional features at your fingertips. In the Calendar, you can create information about activities that are to take place at scheduled times, called **appointments**. You can also keep track of and plan **events**, which are activities that occupy long periods of time, such as vacations or conventions. You can also schedule **meetings**, which are appointments that you invite or request others to attend.

Using the Calendar, you can set reminders, create a list of daily tasks that you need to perform, change appointment times easily, and automatically mark meetings that occur on a regular basis (such as a weekly management meeting). You can print your daily, weekly, or monthly calendar and take it with you when you are away from your desk or your office, and you can make your schedule available to others over a network (via Microsoft Exchange Server) or over the Internet so that they can see when you are available for meetings.

In this lesson, you will learn how to navigate within the Calendar and schedule and edit appointments and events. You will also learn how to set reminders and plan meetings with others. You will learn how to print a copy of the Calendar and integrate the Calendar with other Outlook components. Finally, you will learn how to book office resources and save a schedule as a Web page.

Practice files for the lesson    No practice files are required to complete the exercises in this lesson.

important

To complete some of the exercises in this lesson, you will need to exchange e-mail messages with a class partner. If you don't have a class partner or are performing the exercises alone, you can enter your own e-mail address instead of your class partner's and send the message to yourself.

Understanding Appointments and Meetings

Many people use the terms appointment and meeting interchangeably. In the Outlook Calendar, however, there is a clear distinction between an appointment and a meeting. This distinction can sometimes seem confusing, so it's helpful if you understand the difference before you begin the exercises for this lesson.

In the Outlook Calendar, an appointment is anything that is scheduled—a doctor appointment, a business trip, a management meeting, a luncheon engagement, a racquetball game, and so on. A meeting, though, is a *kind of appointment*. Specifically, a meeting is an appointment in which you use the Outlook Calendar to request the attendance of other people. For example, if you plan a management meeting for two hours on Tuesday and then use the Calendar to e-mail the other managers a request to attend the meeting, Outlook does indeed consider this to be a meeting. If you plan the management meeting and then phone each manager to see if he or she can attend, and then schedule the meeting time in the Outlook Calendar, Outlook does not consider this to be a meeting, just an appointment.

(continued)

continued

So if you schedule an activity but don't use the Outlook Calendar to request the attendance of others, you are scheduling an appointment. If you use the Outlook Calendar to request the attendance of others to a scheduled activity, you are creating a *type of appointment* called a meeting. Even if *you* call something a meeting, Outlook might not.

OL2000.3.1

Calendar

Navigating Within the Calendar

When you click the Calendar shortcut on the Outlook Bar, the Calendar opens and the Day view of your schedule appears by default. This view shows the Calendar divided into three sections—the Appointment Area, the Date Navigator, and the TaskPad.

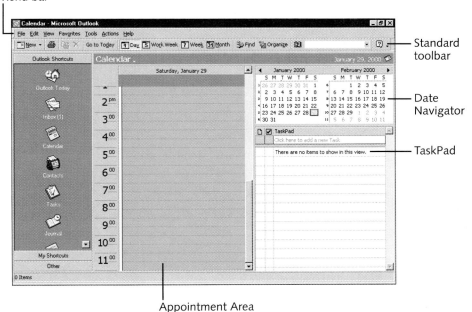

Menu bar

Standard toolbar

Date Navigator

TaskPad

Appointment Area

Section	Description
Appointment Area	The **Appointment Area** resembles a daily planner. Use the Appointment Area to schedule activities, which can be displayed by day, work week, week, or month. By default, the workday starts at 8:00 A.M. and ends at 5:00 P.M. The time slots outside this workday period appear shaded. You can use the scroll bars to show entry lines for any time of the day or night.
Date Navigator	The **Date Navigator** displays two full-month calendars. You can scroll backward and forward through different months and years to find dates by using two different options. First, you can use the left or right arrows at the top of the Date Navigator to scroll backward and forward through the months. Or, you can click and hold the month name to display a list of months, and then click a month in the list to display it in the Calendar. You can also use the Date Navigator to switch to different days in the Appointment Area.
Task Pad	You use the **TaskPad** to record tasks that you want to accomplish. This function works directly with the Tasks folder in Outlook.

In this exercise, you navigate through the Calendar in both the Appointment Area and the Date Navigator.

Calendar

1   On the Outlook Bar, click the Calendar shortcut.

   The contents of the Calendar appear.

2   In the Appointment Area, drag the scroll bar to the top.

   The Appointment Area is divided into 30-minute increments, starting with 12:00 A.M.

3   In the Appointment Area, drag the scroll bar to the bottom.

   The Appointment Area increments end with 11:30 P.M.

4   In the Date Navigator, click tomorrow's date.

   The Appointment Area switches to tomorrow's date.

5   At the top of the Date Navigator, click the left arrow.

   The previous month appears, but the date in the Appointment Area remains the same.

6   At the top of the Date Navigator, click and hold the right arrow on the month bar for a few seconds.

   Later months rapidly appear in the Date Navigator.

7   In the Date Navigator, click and hold the name of one of the currently displayed months.

   A menu of months appears.

8   Move the pointer to the month at the top of the list and release the mouse button.

   The Date Navigator displays the selected month.

9 On the Standard toolbar, click the Go To Today button.

The current day appears in the Appointment Area and in the Date Navigator.

tip

You can quickly display a different date by right-clicking any part of the Appointment Area, clicking Go To Date, clicking the Date down arrow, clicking a date, and clicking OK.

OL2000.3.7

Changing the Calendar View

Many personal planners show appointment and task information in a variety of ways. You can view the Calendar in a number of ways as well. Although the default display in the Calendar is the Day view, you can change the view to appear by **Work Week** (five business days), Week (seven days), Month, or you can view it with the Preview Pane, which allows you to view any notes you might have for a particular appointment. For example, you could use the Appointment Area to enter a brief description of the appointment. Then you could double-click the appointment to display an appointment window. You can then add notes (such as the purpose of the appointment, the agenda, or other preparatory notes) in the bottom section of the appointment area. After you save and close the appointment window, you can view your notes quickly by displaying the Preview Pane in the Calendar. You can close and reopen the Preview Pane at any time, depending on whether you need to view notes for one or more appointments.

In this exercise, you change the view of the Calendar.

The days of the work week are normally Monday through Friday, but you can change them to fit a different work schedule. On the Tools menu, click Options. On the Preferences tab, click the Calendar Options button. In the Calendar Work Week section, select the check boxes of the days of the week that you want to display, and click OK twice.

1 On the Standard toolbar, click the Work Week button.

The five days of a standard work week appear in five columns.

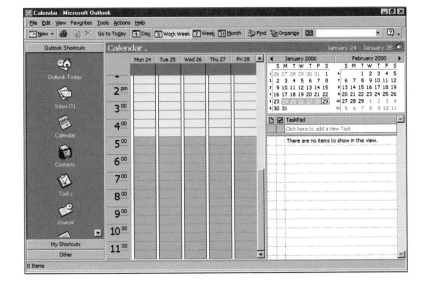

2   On the Standard toolbar, click the Week button.

The view changes to seven days.

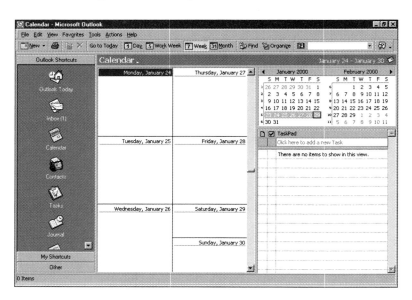

3   On the Standard toolbar, click the Month button.

The view changes to display a month.

Days not in the current month but included on the calendar are shaded. You can still view activities that you've entered for these days.

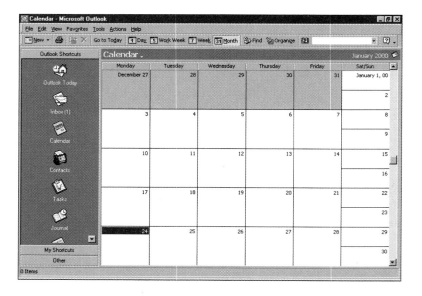

If you added any appointments, they would appear in the Calendar. If you added any notes in the memo area of the appointment window, the notes would appear in the Preview Pane.

4   On the View menu, click Preview Pane.

The window splits. In the top section, the Calendar view is displayed. In the bottom section, the Preview Pane is displayed.

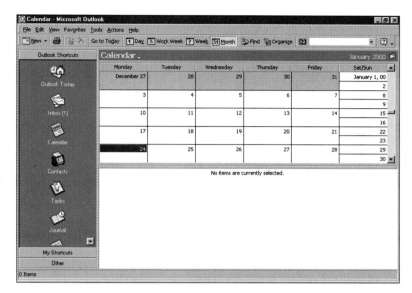

5   On the View menu, click Preview Pane.

The Preview Pane closes, and the month calendar is no longer split.

6   On the Standard toolbar, click the Day button.

The calendar appears in Day view.

OL2000.1.17
OL2000.3.9

Customizing Menus and Toolbars

You can easily change the way the menus and toolbars appear to fit the way you like to work. To customize the toolbars and menus in Outlook, click Customize on the Tools menu. Three tabs appear in the Customize dialog box. You can display additional toolbars as well as create new ones by using the Toolbars tab. Using the Commands tab, you can add buttons to the toolbar and commands to menus by dragging commands from the dialog box to the appropriate position on the toolbar or menu. You can control the way menu commands appear by using the Options tab. If you want to move a toolbar button to a different location or delete it from a toolbar, hold down the Alt key and drag the button to a different location on the toolbar or drag it off the toolbar to delete it. If you delete a toolbar button and later decide that you want to use it, you can display the Commands tab of the Customize dialog box and drag the command back to the appropriate toolbar.

OL2000.3.2

Scheduling Appointments and Events

An appointment is an activity that takes place at a scheduled time that does not require you to request the attendance of other people. Examples of appointments include lunch engagements, visits to the doctor, or any other activity that can be scheduled (such as *Suit is ready at Dry Cleaners*). When you enter an appointment into the Calendar, the appointment appears in one slot. Because the slots are in increments of 30 minutes, by default, an appointment is then 30 minutes in duration. However, you can increase the duration of an appointment by dragging the top or bottom border of the blue box (that surrounds the appointment entry) up or down. For example, the marketing director at Lakewood Mountains Resort has a doctor's appointment Monday morning at 9:00 A.M. Her doctor always seems to run at least an hour behind schedule, so to be safe, the marketing director wants to specify that the appointment goes until 11:30 A.M. She scheduled the appointment time by clicking the bottom border of the 9:00 A.M. time slot in the Appointment Area and dragging down to the top of the 11:30 A.M. time slot.

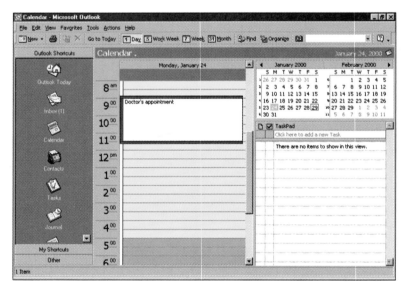

You can add details to an appointment by double-clicking a time slot. The detailed appointment window appears, and looks similar to the following illustration.

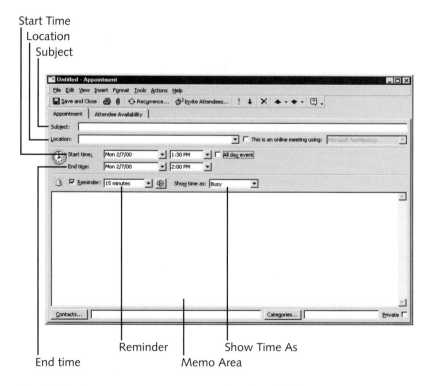

Start Time
Location
Subject

End time   Reminder   Show Time As
Memo Area

The following components appear in the window:

Component	Description
Subject	You can change the text of an appointment directly within the Appointment Area, or you can change it in the Subject box.
Location	You can use this box to type in the location of the appointment. Outlook maintains a list of previously entered locations. You can scroll through the Location box to select a previous appointment location.
Start Time	Outlook uses the starting time in the Appointment Area by default. You can change the starting time in the appointment window if you want.
End Time	Outlook automatically inserts the ending time based on the ending time that appears in the Appointment Area. You can also use the appointment window to change the ending time.
Reminder	Use this list to specify how soon before the appointment you want Outlook to remind you. If you do not want a reminder, clear the Reminder check box.
Show Time As	Use the Show Time As option to let others know that you are busy, free, or out of the office or that the appointment is tentative.
Memo Area	Use the text area at the bottom of the dialog box to type any notes or additional reminders that you want to include. If you add text to the memo area, you can view the text in the Calendar by viewing the Preview Pane.

You can also schedule a lengthy event in the Calendar. An event is a function that usually makes you unavailable for the entire day or for multiple days—such as a vacation, business trip, or off-site seminar. Events show up in the Calendar as a banner at the top of the Appointment Area. You can schedule appointments and meetings during an event. For example, suppose you mark the next two days as an event because you will be attending a convention. You can still make appointment entries for different lectures and presentations that you will be attending during the course of those two days. Double-clicking an event opens an event window, which is very similar to the appointment window.

In this exercise, you create two appointments and one multiday event.

1   In the Date Navigator, click tomorrow's date.

The Appointment Area displays tomorrow's date.

2   In the Appointment Area, if necessary, scroll up, and click the 12:00 P.M. time slot.

The 12:00 P.M. time slot is selected.

3   Type **Lunch with caterer,** and press Enter.

The half-hour appointment is entered.

4   Click in the 2:00 P.M. time slot, and drag the mouse pointer down to the top of the 3:30 P.M. time slot.

Three slots are selected, indicating an hour-and-a-half appointment.

5   Type **Meeting with Picnic Planning Committee**, and press Enter.

Two appointments for tomorrow are created.

> If you see a bell icon to the left of the appointment, this indicates that you will be reminded to attend the appointment before the appointment occurs. Setting reminders will be discussed later in this lesson.

> In step 4, you'll notice that the 3:30 time slot is not labeled. Only the start of each hour is labeled. The 3:30 time slot is directly under the 3:00 time slot.

6   In the Date Navigator, click Monday of the following week.

The Appointment Area displays the Monday of the following week.

New Appointment

7   On the Standard toolbar, click the New Appointment button.

An appointment window appears with the insertion point already in the Subject box.

8 In the Subject box, type **Vacation**, and press Tab.

The insertion point moves to the Location box.

9 In the Location box, type **Hawaii**.

10 Select the All Day Event check box.

Notice that the window is now called Vacation - Event.

11 Click the End Time down arrow.

A mini-calendar appears.

OL2000.3.5

12 In the mini-calendar, click a date two weeks from the shaded date.

When you close the appointment window and return to the Calendar, it will show a two-week vacation.

13 Click the Show Time As down arrow, and click Out Of Office.

Your Calendar will indicate to others that you are out of the office for this two-week period.

> You can also display the event window by clicking New All Day Event on the Actions menu.

14 On the Standard toolbar in the event window, click the Save And Close button.

The window closes. The event, Vacation (Hawaii), appears at the top of the Appointment Area, and in the Date Navigator, the vacation days appear in bold type.

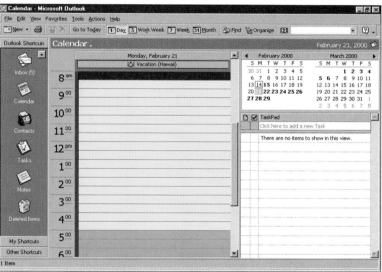

OL2000.3.8

Creating Recurring Appointments

Some meetings and appointments are held on a regular basis at the same time and on the same day each week. These appointments are referred to as **recurring** appointments. For example, the office manager at Lakewood Mountains Resort calls in a supply order every Friday morning at 10:00 A.M. To remind herself of this task, she created a recurring appointment in her Calendar.

For daily appointments, you can specify whether they occur every day (Monday, Tuesday, Wednesday, Thursday, Friday, Saturday, and Sunday) or every weekday (Monday, Tuesday, Wednesday, Thursday, and Friday). For weekly appointments, you can specify the number of weeks to pass before repeating the appointment (every two weeks, for example), and the day of the week (such as every other Monday). For monthly appointments, you can specify the day of the month, and for yearly appointments, you can specify the day of the year.

In this exercise, you create a recurring appointment.

1   In the Date Navigator, click four Tuesdays into the future.

The fourth Tuesday into the future is displayed in the Appointment Area.

2   In the Appointment Area, click the 8:30 A.M. time slot, and drag down to the top of the 10:00 A.M. time slot.

Three slots are selected, indicating an hour-and-a-half appointment.

3   Type **Weekly sales meeting**, and press Enter.

Weekly sales meeting is entered as an appointment.

4   Double-click the appointment.

The appointment window appears. The subject of the appointment is the same name that you just typed in the Appointment Area.

5   On the Standard toolbar in the appointment window, click the Recurrence button.

The Appointment Recurrence dialog box appears. Notice that the appointment time is the same time you specified in the Appointment Area.

> You can make an existing appointment a recurring appointment. Double-click the existing appointment, and on the Standard toolbar in the appointment window, click the Recurrence button. Enter the recurrence information, click OK, and click the Save And Close button.

> Recurring meetings, appointments, and events can be scheduled on multiple days in one week. Notice in the Appointment Recurrence dialog box that you can select any and as many days of the week as needed.

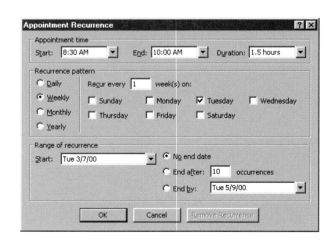

6   In the Recurrence Pattern section, click the Weekly option if necessary.

7   If necessary, select the Tuesday check box, and then clear any other day check boxes.

8   In the Range Of Recurrence section, click the End After option.

9   In the End After box, double-click 10, and type **8**.

The appointment will recur weekly on Tuesdays, eight times.

10   Click OK.

The dialog box closes, and the appointment window reappears.

11   Click in the Location box, and type **Lakewood Mountains Resort Pavilion**.

12   On the Standard toolbar in the appointment window, click the Save And Close button.

13   In the Date Navigator, click a few Tuesdays into the future.

The recurring meeting message continues to appear in the Appointment Area.

14   On the Standard toolbar, click the Go To Today button.

Today's date is displayed in the Calendar.

> If the recurring appointment conflicts with another appointment in the future, Outlook will show a warning. You can choose to reschedule or cancel the appointment.

tip

When creating a recurring appointment in the Appointment Area, the date does not have to be on the same day of the week as the appointment. You can change the day of the week in the Appointment Recurrence dialog box.

OL2000.3.3

Setting Reminders

When you are extremely busy or preoccupied with a particular task, you can easily forget about an upcoming appointment. With Outlook, you can let the Calendar do your reminding for you. When you set up an appointment, you can choose to be reminded, and if you choose this option, you can also select how far in advance of the appointment you want to be reminded. The appointment appears with a bell next to its description, indicating that you will be reminded of the appointment. You can also choose a sound that will play (if any) when the reminder appears on the screen. The following reminder dialog box appears before the appointment begins.

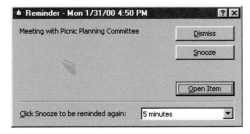

important

Outlook must be running for the Reminder dialog box to appear. If you are using a different program, and Outlook is running, the Reminder dialog box will appear on top of any open windows and documents.

In this exercise, you set a reminder for the appointment *Meeting with Picnic Planning Committee* that you entered in a previous exercise.

1   In the Date Navigator, click tomorrow's date.

The appointments for tomorrow appear.

2   Double-click the appointment *Meeting with Picnic Planning Committee.*

The appointment window appears.

3   If necessary, select the Reminder check box.

4   Click the Reminder down arrow, scroll up, and click 10 Minutes.

Outlook will remind you that you have an appointment 10 minutes before the start of the appointment.

Reminder

5   Click the Reminder button.

The Reminder Sound dialog box appears. The default setting is selected.

To hear the reminder sound, your computer must have a sound card and speakers that are turned on. Whether or not you have sound capabilities, Outlook will still display the Reminder dialog box, notifying you that the appointment is impending.

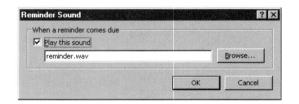

6   Click OK.

7   On the Standard toolbar in the appointment window, click the Save And Close button.

The reminder is set.

Editing Appointments

In addition to setting reminders for appointments, you can add information about the appointment—such as who is involved or whether the appointment is going to last the entire day—and you can attach files for reference or mark the appointment as private. You can also set the level of importance for an appointment. By default, the level of an appointment is set for Medium, but you can change this to either High or Low. And of course, you can use the appointment window or the Appointment Area to change appointment information—such as the start and end times or the location—at any time.

For example, when the marketing director at Lakewood Mountains Resort meets with clients, she jots down the attendees' names and the topics she wants to discuss in the memo area of her appointment window. If her appointment has to be rescheduled for later in the day, she changes the start and end times and sets a reminder.

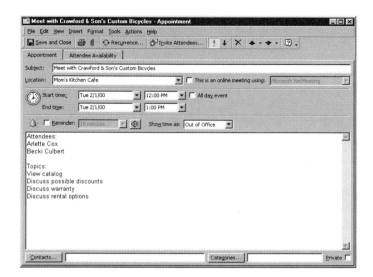

In this exercise, you edit the appointment *Lunch with caterer* created earlier in the lesson and change the date of the appointment.

1   Double-click the appointment *Lunch with caterer*.

    The appointment window appears.

2   Click in the Location box, and type **Mom's Kitchen Cafe**.

3   Click the first Start Time down arrow.

    A mini-calendar appears.

4   In the mini-calendar, click the day after tomorrow's date.

5   Click the Show Time As down arrow, and click Out Of Office.

Importance: High

6   On the Standard toolbar in the appointment window, click the Importance: High button.

7   In the bottom-right corner of the window, select the Private check box.

    The appointment will be considered private. Others with access to this schedule can see that there is an appointment and that you will be out of the office, but they cannot see any details.

8   On the Standard toolbar in the appointment window, click the Save And Close button.

9   On the Navigation Bar, click the day after tomorrow's date.

    The appointment is displayed for tomorrow, the location of the appointment appears next to the subject, and a key icon appears to the left of the subject, indicating that the appointment is private.

tip

You can change the time or duration of an appointment in the Appointment Area by dragging an appointment from one time entry to another. In Month view, which displays multiple days, you can also drag an appointment to a different day.

Deleting Appointments

If an appointment is cancelled or if its occurrence has already passed, you can remove the appointment from the Calendar. When you delete an appointment, it's moved to the Deleted Items folder, just as with e-mail messages and contacts. The deleted appointments remain there until you empty the Deleted Items folder. You can restore an appointment from the Deleted Items folder by dragging it back into the Calendar folder.

important

When you try to delete a recurring appointment, Outlook will ask you whether you want to delete the current selected appointment or all occurrences of the appointment.

In this exercise, you delete a normal appointment, a recurring appointment, and restore an appointment.

1   Click the appointment *Lunch with caterer*.

Delete

2   On the Standard toolbar, click the Delete button.

The appointment moves to the Deleted Items folder.

You can also right-click an appointment that is not currently selected, and then click Delete on the shortcut menu that appears.

3   In the Date Navigator, click one of the Tuesdays that appear in bold (after the vacation days).

The recurring appointment for the selected date appears in the Appointment Area.

You might need to scroll up the Appointment Area to see the appointment.

4   Click anywhere on the appointment *Weekly sales meeting*.

5   Click the Delete button.

An alert box appears, asking whether you want to delete the currently selected appointment or all occurrences. The Delete This One option is already selected.

If you had clicked the Delete All Occurrences option, Outlook would have deleted every occurrence of the appointment *Weekly sales meeting*.

6   Click OK.

The selected appointment is deleted, but all other occurrences remain.

7   On the Outlook Bar, if necessary scroll down, and click the Deleted Items shortcut.

The contents of the Deleted Items folder appear.

8   Drag the appointment *Lunch with caterer* onto the Calendar shortcut on the Outlook Bar.

9   On the Outlook Bar, click the Calendar shortcut.

The contents of the Calendar appear.

10 On the Date Navigator, click the day after tomorrow's date.

Notice that the appointment *Lunch with caterer* has returned to its original date and time.

Organizing Appointments by Using Categories

You can organize appointments by categories just as you can contacts to make it easier to view just the appointments you need. In the Using Categories section of the Organize pane, you can select one of the existing categories, such as Holiday, Business, or Gifts. Also, you can create your own category and assign appointments or events to that category.

In this exercise, you create a category and assign a category to the appointment *Meeting with Picnic Planning Committee* that you entered in a previous exercise.

1 On the Standard toolbar, click the Organize button.

The Organize pane appears with the Using Categories section displayed.

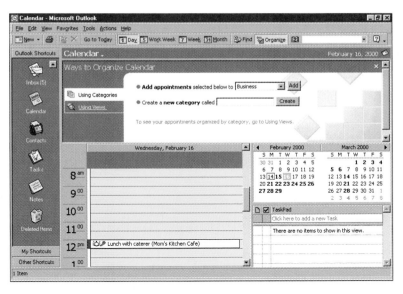

2 In the Organize pane, click in the Create A New Category Called box, and type **Planning.**

3 Click the Create button.

The category, Planning, is created and now appears in the Add Appointments Selected Below To box in the Organize pane.

4 In the Date Navigator, click tomorrow's date, and in the Appointment Area, scroll down and click the appointment *Meeting with Picnic Planning Committee.*

5 In the Organize pane, click the Add button.

The appointment *Meeting with Picnic Planning Committee* is assigned to the Planning category.

You will use the By Category view to locate this appointment in the next exercise.

Organizing Appointments by Using Views

You've already seen how to use the Day, Week, Work Week, and Month buttons to change the view of the Calendar. With Outlook, you can also determine which appointments appear in the Calendar so that you see only a specific type of appointment or only those appointments for a particular period. View categories include Active Appointments, Events, Annual Events, Recurring Appointments, and By Category. Changing the view in this manner allows you to quickly identify a particular type of appointment. For example, if you just want to see appointments that take up a full day or multiple days, you could display the Calendar in Events view. If you've assigned appointments to different categories, you can elect to view appointments by category so that you can identify related appointments.

To change views, you can use the Organize pane, just as you did to change views for your contacts, or you can point to Current View on the View menu and click the desired view.

In this exercise, you use the Organize pane to organize appointments according to different views.

1   In the Organize pane, click the Using Views link.

The Using Views section of the Organize pane appears.

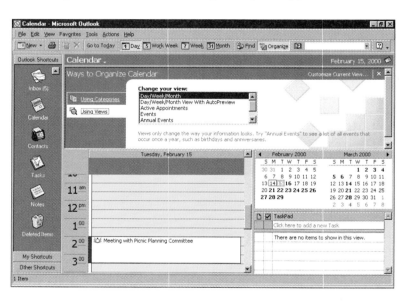

2   In the Change Your View list, scroll to the bottom, and click By Category.

The appointments are divided into categories.

3   If necessary, click the plus sign (+) on the left side of the Planning gray bar.

The appointment that you added to the Planning category in the previous exercise appears.

If you double-click the appointment, the appointment window will appear so that you can read the details of the appointment or edit it if necessary.

4 In the Organize pane, click Recurring Appointments in the Change Your View list.

Only recurring appointments appear.

5 In the Change Your View list, click Active Appointments.

All upcoming appointments appear in table format.

6 In the Change Your View list, scroll up to the top, and click Day/ Week/Month.

The view returns to the default Calendar view.

7 On the Standard toolbar, click the Organize button.

The Organize pane closes.

OL2000.3.11

New!

Outlook now provides this easier way to schedule a meeting.

Planning Meetings

Getting all the people you need to a meeting can be difficult because you have to coordinate multiple schedules. You can play phone tag all day with your prospective meeting attendees, attempting to schedule them for a commonly available meeting time, or you can use the Outlook Calendar. When you set up a meeting in Outlook, you send each prospective attendee a meeting request. For each prospective attendee, you can specify that his or her attendance is required or optional. (If you specified that a particular attendee's attendance is required and he or she declines to attend the meeting, you need to reschedule it.) The meeting request is an e-mail message that tells people what the meeting is about and where and when the meeting will take place.

When somebody sends you a meeting request via e-mail, a message appears that includes buttons that you can use to accept, decline, or tentatively accept the invitation to go to the meeting. If you accept, the meeting is added to your Calendar, and an e-mail response stating your acceptance is sent to the meeting organizer. If you decline, you can elect to decline with or without a response. For example, you might want to decline but let the person who sent the meeting request know when you are available.

important

In an Exchange Server environment, Outlook makes it easy to view coworkers busy times and have them view yours. You can't see the actual appointments for other people on your network, but you can observe which periods on which days have been blocked off as busy for a particular employee. This approach helps to ensure that you have scheduled a meeting for a time that is available to all your prospective attendees. Then when you send your meeting requests via e-mail, you are more likely to receive acceptances from most or all the prospective attendees.

In this exercise, you create a meeting and invite your class partner to the meeting. You also receive a meeting request from your class partner, and accept the invitation to attend the meeting.

1 On the Navigation Bar, click the last Monday of next month.

The last Monday of next month appears in the Appointment Area.

2 Click the 9:00 A.M. time slot.

3 On the Standard toolbar, click the down arrow to the right of the New Appointment button, and click Meeting Request.

The meeting window appears.

4 Click the To button.

The Select Attendees And Resources dialog box appears.

For attendees who are not required to attend a meeting, you can click the attendee, and then click the Optional button.

5 Scroll down if necessary, click your class partner's name, and click the Required button.

6 Click OK.

The meeting window reappears. Your class partner's name is now in the To box.

7 Click in the Subject box, type **Client Review meeting**, and press Tab.

The insertion point moves to the Location box.

8 In the Location box, type **Conference Room 3**.

The date, start time, and end time are already specified.

9 Click in the memo box, and type **Looking forward to discussing the project's requirements**.

10 On the Standard toolbar in the meeting window, click the Send button.

The meeting request is sent to your class partner. The meeting appears in the Calendar with a bell icon (indicating that a reminder has been set) and an icon that resembles two heads (indicating that other people are invited to the meeting).

OL2000.3.10

tip

If necessary, after a meeting has been set up in the Calendar, you can revise the list of meeting attendees by adding or removing attendees. Double-click the meeting, and on the Actions menu, click Add Or Remove Attendees to display the Select Attendees And Resources dialog box. To delete an attendee, click the attendee in the Message Recipients list, and press Delete. To add an attendee, click the attendee's name in the Name list and click the Required or Optional button. When you are finished, click OK, and click the Save And Close button on the Standard toolbar. In the alert box that appears, click the desired option concerning sending updates to attendees, and click OK.

11 In the Appointment Area, click the meeting.

Delete

12 On the Standard toolbar, click the Delete button.

An alert box appears, stating that attendees have not been notified that the meeting has been cancelled. You can either send a cancellation and delete the message, or delete the meeting in your calendar without sending a cancellation.

You deleted this message for classroom purposes. Normally you would not delete a meeting you just organized (unless you made a mistake), but because you are going to receive a meeting request to attend this same meeting from your class partner, you need to have this time open so that Outlook will not find a scheduling conflict.

13 Click the Delete Without Sending A Cancellation option, and click OK.

The meeting is deleted.

14 On the Outlook Bar, scroll up if necessary, and click the Inbox Shortcut.

The contents of the Inbox appear.

15 On the Standard toolbar, click the Send/Receive button.

A meeting request from your class partner appears in the Inbox.

16 Double-click the meeting request.

The meeting request opens.

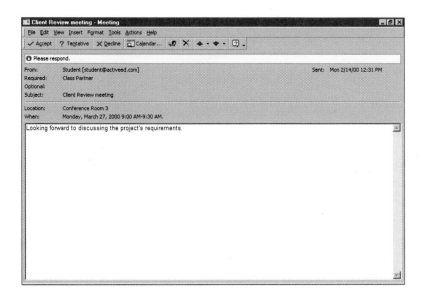

17 On the Standard toolbar in the meeting request window, click the Accept button.

An alert box appears, asking if you want to include comments with your response. The Send The Response Now option is already selected.

18 Click OK.

A response is sent to your class partner.

19 On the Standard toolbar, click the Send/Receive button.

A message header from your class partner appears with the subject *Accepted: Client Review meeting* in the Inbox.

20 On the Outlook Bar, click the Calendar shortcut, and in the Date Navigator, click the last Monday of next month.

The meeting *Client Review meeting* reappears in the Appointment Area because you accepted your class partner's meeting request to attend this meeting.

OL2000.3.13

Reserving Meeting Resources

In addition to inviting people to meetings, you can also schedule resources, such as conference rooms, flip charts, or computers. For example, when the office manager at Lakewood Mountains Resort scheduled the budget review meeting for the president, she booked a large conference room and an overhead projector through Outlook.

In order for you to schedule a resource, the resource must have its own mailbox on your server. One person, usually the office manager, sets up and administers the mailbox for the resource. The resource is self-sufficient because it automatically accepts and rejects invitations. For example, if you attempt to reserve a conference room for a particular period and somebody has already reserved the conference room, your meeting request will be rejected for the conference room resource.

To reserve a resource, you invite it to the meeting just as you would a person. In the Select Attendees And Resources dialog box, click the resource, and click the Resources button. The resource is added to your message list. If the resource you scheduled is free, the meeting is automatically entered in the resource's calendar so that no one else can reserve the same resource at the same time.

OL2000.3.4
OL2000.3.6

Printing Calendars

Many people who use Outlook as their scheduling tool like to have a printed copy of their schedule that they can take with them when they leave their desk or their office. As you might expect, Outlook provides several printing options for your Calendar. Specifically, you can print different views of the Calendar, such as a daily, weekly, or monthly view. You can then use the Print dialog box to specify the range of days that you want to print and the style that you want the days to be printed in. The Print dialog box includes five styles: Daily (the days that you specify will be printed one day per page), Weekly (the weeks that you specify will be printed one week per page), Monthly (the months that you specify will be printed one month per page), Tri-fold (it is divided into three columns: the first column will contain a day view, the second, the TaskPad, and the third, a week view), and Calendar Details (appointments, meetings, and events scheduled in the Calendar are described and listed under the day on which they occur).

The events coordinator at Lakewood Mountains Resort likes to attach a printout of a calendar in the Monthly Style to her newsletter so that readers can get an at-a-glance view of upcoming events at the resort.

In this exercise, you specify print options and print a two-month calendar in the Monthly Style.

Print

1   On the Standard toolbar, click the Print button.

The Print dialog box appears.

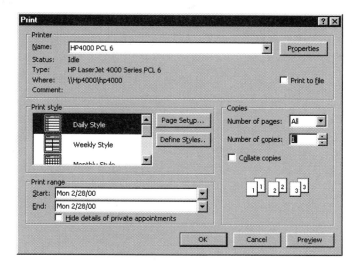

2   In the Print Style section, scroll down, and click Monthly Style.

3   In the Print Range section, click the Start down arrow.

A mini-calendar appears.

> You might need to display the current month first by clicking the left or right arrows at the top of the mini-calendar.

4   Click the first day of this month.

5   In the Print Range section, click the End down arrow.

A mini-calendar appears.

6   Click the last day of next month.

7   Click OK.

The Print dialog box closes and a two-month calendar prints in the Monthly Style.

tip

You can also print the Calendar in a Day-Timer or a Franklin Day Planner format. In the Print dialog box, click the Page Setup button, click the Paper tab, and then click the desired page size in the Size list.

OL2000.3.12

Saving a Calendar as a Web Page

If you want, you can save your Calendar as a Web page so that people can access your Calendar via the Internet. When you save a Calendar as a Web page, Outlook converts the Calendar to HTML (Hypertext Markup Language) format. HTML is the formatting language that all Web browsers (such as Microsoft Internet Explorer) use to display text and graphics properly when you access Web pages on the Internet. A Calendar can be placed on a Web site or can remain in a file that others can download for later access. When you save a Calendar as a Web page, you can specify the Calendar time frame that you want to share, include appointment details, or add a background.

For example, the events coordinator at Lakewood Mountains Resort used to attach a copy of the monthly events Calendar to the newsletter she sends out to employees each month. However, since the company's intranet was established, she now posts the Calendar information to the company's Web site instead.

In this exercise, you save your Calendar as a Web page.

A schedule saved as a Web page can also be sent as an attachment in a message.

1   On the File menu, click Save As Web Page.

The Save As Web Page dialog box appears.

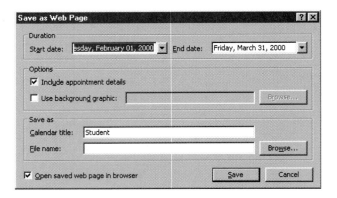

You might need to display the current month first by clicking the left or right arrows at the top of the mini-calendar.

2   In the Duration section, click the Start Date down arrow and click the first day of the current month.

3   In the Duration section, click the End Date down arrow and click the last day of the current month.

4   In the Calendar Title box, type your name (if necessary), press the Spacebar, and type **Class Calendar**.

5   Click the Browse button.

The Calendar File Name dialog box appears.

Do not include any spaces when you name a Web page file. If the name of the file is part of a Web address (such as *www.calendars.microsoft.com/ MyClassCalendar.htm*), the space will not be recognized and the file will not be available for viewing on the Web.

6   Click the Save In down arrow, and navigate to the Outlook Core Practice folder.

7   In the File Name box, type **MyClassCalendar**.

8   Click the Select button.

The Save As Web Page dialog box reappears.

9   Click the Save button.

If an alert box appears telling you that you need to install the feature that will publish the Calendar to the Web, click Yes, insert the Microsoft Office 2000 or Microsoft Outlook CD-ROM into the disk drive, and click OK.

The calendar is saved as a Web page and appears in Internet Explorer.

important

If Internet Explorer does not automatically display the Web calendar, you can manually open the calendar in Windows Explorer. Display the Windows Explorer (on the Windows taskbar, click the Start button, point to Programs, and click Windows Explorer). Navigate to the Outlook Core Practice folder, and double-click the My Class Calendar folder. You will see that many files were created as a result of creating the Web calendar. Double-click the file called MyClassCalendar.htm. Internet Explorer will then open and display the Web calendar.

Close

10 In the top-right corner of the Internet Explorer window, click the Close button.

Adding an Outlook Bar Shortcut to a Web Page

After a calendar has been saved as a Web page, it can be added as a shortcut to the My Shortcuts group on the Outlook Bar. You can create a **shortcut** on the Outlook Bar to any Web site and view that site in Outlook.

To add an Outlook Bar shortcut to a Web site, on the View menu, point to Toolbars and click Web. On the Web toolbar, click in the Address box, type the Web address for the Web site that you want to add as a shortcut, and then press Enter. The Web page will appear in the Outlook window.

On the File menu, point to New and click Outlook Bar Shortcut To Web Page. Click OK in the alert box that appears to add the shortcut to the bottom of the My Shortcuts group.

To access the Web site, click its shortcut on the Outlook Bar in the My Shortcuts group.

Integrating the Calendar with Other Outlook Components

OL2000.3.14
OL2000.6.5

At the beginning of this lesson, you looked at the three major components of the Calendar—the Appointment Area, Date Navigator, and TaskPad. You use both the Appointment Area and the Date Navigator to schedule appointments and meetings. You use the TaskPad to enter task descriptions, such as to create a weekly status report or to list phone calls that you need to make. Each row on the TaskPad indicates a separate task. The tasks in Calendar are also displayed in the Outlook Tasks folder, which you can access by clicking the Tasks shortcut on the Outlook Bar.

Tasks

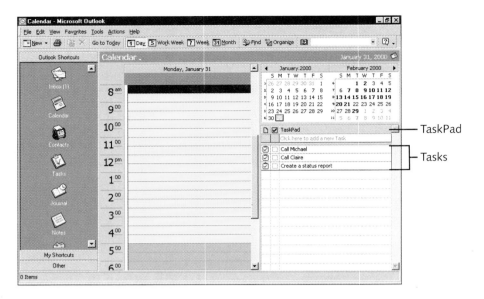

In this exercise, you create a task and mark it as completed.

1   In the TaskPad, click in the box that contains the text *Click Here to Add a New Task*.

The text is replaced with a blank line and an insertion point.

2   Type **Buy toothpaste**, and press Enter.

The task *Buy toothpaste* appears in the task list.

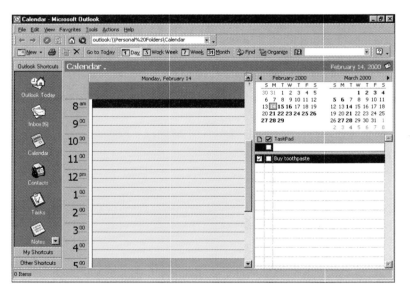

3   On the Outlook Bar, click the Tasks shortcut.

The contents of the Tasks folder appear. The task *Buy toothpaste* appears in the task list.

4   On the Outlook Bar, click the Calendar shortcut.

The contents of the Calendar folder appear.

5 In the TaskPad, select the check box to the left of the task.

A check appears in the check box, and the task appears with a strikeout line through it.

6 On the Outlook Bar, click the Tasks shortcut.

The contents of the Tasks folder appear. The task *Buy toothpaste* also appears with a line through it.

Lesson Wrap-Up

This lesson covered the parts of Outlook's Calendar—the Appointment Area, Date Navigator, and TaskPad. You learned how to navigate through the Calendar, change views, and create and edit appointments and events. You learned how to create recurring appointments and meetings and how to set reminders. You also learned how to organize appointments and meetings by category and views, and how to plan meetings with others and send meeting invitations by e-mail. You learned how to print a calendar as well as save a calendar as a Web page. Finally, you learned how to use the TaskPad to create a task and how to mark it as completed.

If you are continuing to the next lesson:

● On the Outlook Bar, click the Calendar shortcut.

The contents of the Calendar folder appear.

If you are not continuing to other lessons:

Close

● In the top-right corner of the Outlook window, click the Close button. Outlook closes.

Lesson Glossary

appointments Messages to yourself or other users about an activity to take place at a scheduled time but that does not involve inviting others or reserving office resources.

Appointment Area The place within the Calendar where you enter and schedule activities, which can be displayed by day, work week, week, or month.

Calendar A component of Outlook that you can use to create and schedule appointments, meetings, and tasks.

Date Navigator A wall-type calendar that appears in the Outlook Calendar and shows dates for up to six months. The Date Navigator can be used to switch to different days, months, and years in the Appointment Area.

events Activities that usually make you unavailable at the office for a full day or longer, such as a vacation, convention, or off-site meeting. Events appear as a banner in the Appointment Area.

meetings Types of appointments in which you request the attendance of others. Recipients of a meeting message have the option of accepting or declining the meeting invitation.

recurring An event, scheduled in the Calendar, that occurs at multiple times or regular intervals.

shortcut An icon on the Outlook Bar that displays a folder when you click it. You can create your own shortcuts to any file, folder, or Web page. When you click a shortcut to a Web page, the Web page appears in the right pane of the Outlook window.

TaskPad An area in the Calendar in which you record tasks that you need to perform. This area is integrated with the Tasks folder.

Work Week A new view for the Calendar in Outlook 2000 in which you can view the days of the week for those days on which you work.

Quick Quiz

1   How do you invite others to a meeting?

2   What is the Appointment Area?

3   Time slots in the Calendar are divided into what increment of time?

4   Can you change the Work Week view to be days other than Monday through Friday?

5   What is the Date Navigator?

6   In what styles can you print a Calendar?

7   What are three ways you can view the Calendar?

8   What is a recurring appointment?

9   How can you tell that you will be reminded of a meeting?

10 In addition to printing your Calendar, how can you make it accessible to others?

Putting It All Together

Exercise 1: The marketing director at Lakewood Mountains Resort wants to get her team on board for the new ad campaign. She wants to schedule a weekly team meeting on Fridays from 10:00 A.M. until noon in Conference Room 2 for the next four months. At the meeting, they will discuss the progress and status of the ad campaign project. Schedule this as a meeting, invite any member of your class to attend, and indicate that this class member's attendance is required.

Exercise 2: The marketing director will be taking a vacation to Tahiti after the ad campaign project is underway—five months from now. She wants anyone who looks at her schedule to know that she is out of the office for the two weeks she is in Tahiti. Schedule this event for a two-week period five months from now.

LESSON 6

Using Tasks

After completing this lesson, you will be able to:

✔ *Create tasks in Outlook.*

✔ *Add task details.*

✔ *Sort tasks.*

✔ *Organize tasks by using folders.*

✔ *Organize tasks by using categories.*

✔ *Assign tasks to others.*

✔ *Accept or decline tasks.*

✔ *Mark tasks as complete.*

✔ *Manually record a task in the Journal.*

✔ *Delete tasks.*

As your responsibilities at work and home increase, it can become difficult to keep track of everything you have to do each day. A great way to manage your daily activities is to create a to-do list. Seeing a list of the things you have to do might help you to organize and prioritize more efficiently. Also, checking off the entries one by one can create a sense of accomplishment. For example, the marketing director at Lakewood Mountains Resort creates a daily list of things to do based on her daily activities, special projects, and obligations to friends, family, and business associates.

The Microsoft Outlook **task list** provides a place for you to record to-do lists or to track tasks required to complete a project. If you've worked through Lesson 5, "Using the Calendar," you've seen the TaskPad that appears in the Calendar. When you make entries in the Calendar TaskPad, the entries are also recorded in the task list, which provides several options (for organizing and viewing tasks) that are not available in the Calendar TaskPad.

In this lesson, you will learn how to enter a **task**—a personal or work item to be completed. You will also learn how to add details to a task, mark tasks as complete, and delete a task. You will learn how to sort tasks and organize tasks by using folders and categories. Finally, you will learn how to assign tasks to others, accept or decline tasks assigned to you, mark tasks as complete, and manually record a task in the Journal.

Practice files for the lesson ➡ No practice files are required to complete the exercises in this lesson.

OL2000.6.6

Changing Task Views

As you have learned in previous lessons, when you change the view of a folder, items are displayed based on the criteria specified in the view. The same is true for the task list. Different views can help you to see your tasks in greater or more meaningful detail. For example, you might want to display only tasks that are due on a specific day. To apply a different view to the task list, on the View menu, point to Current View, and click the desired view.

When you change the task list view, different columns appear. You can change details about a task by clicking the appropriate column. If you click in the Importance, Due Date, Date Complete, or Status column, a down arrow appears. You click the down arrow to display a list of items from which you can choose.

OL2000.6.1

Adding Task Details

Often the Simple List view for the task list does not show all the columns you need for adding information about a more complicated task. For example, the marketing director at Lakewood Mountains Resort set up a task to create a project plan for the upcoming advertising campaign. This task is crucial to the project and therefore needed a high priority and a definite due date. The marketing director created the task, assigned the task a high priority flag, assigned a due date, and assigned the task to a category.

When you want to add several details to a task, it's often easiest to use the task window or to switch to the Detailed List view. The task window (shown below) has two tabs—Task and Details. Most of the details that appear in the task list are on the Task tab. The Details tab contains boxes for you to add information regarding the actual hours of work it took to complete a task, information about mileage and billing, and information regarding any companies involved with a task.

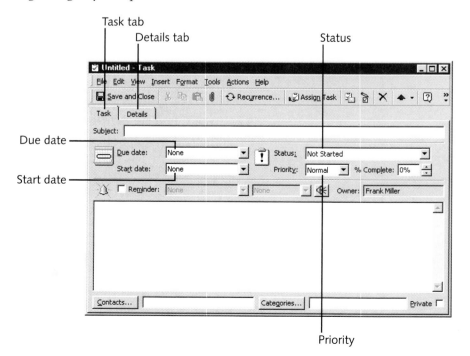

The task window appears when you double-click a task or click the New Task button. In the task window, the boxes on the Task tab correspond to the column headings that appear in the different task list views. The different options you select in these boxes or the information you enter can be used as criteria for organizing your tasks. Some of the options on the Task tab are described in the following table.

Box/Button	Description
Subject	The text of the task appears as the Subject. You can change the text of the task by editing it here.
Due Date	You can specify a date for when the task must be completed.
Start Date	You can set a date for when the task begins.
Status	You can mark a task's progress as Not Started, In Progress, Completed, Waiting On Someone Else, or Deferred.
Priority	You can specify the importance of the task. You can choose Low, Normal, or High importance.
% Complete	You can indicate the amount of work done on a task. You can enter any percentage from 0% to 100%, and the task status changes to reflect the percentage.
Reminder	You can specify how soon before the specified end date or time for the task you want to be reminded. If you don't want to be reminded, clear the Reminder check box. Click the appropriate down arrows to display a list of dates or times.
memo area	You can use the text area at the bottom of the window to jot down any notes or additional reminders.
Contacts	Click this button to display the Select Names dialog box, and select contacts that you can link to this task.
Categories	Click this button to display the Categories dialog box, and assign the task to a category.
Private	By selecting this check box, you can hide this task so that others who have access to your schedule cannot see it.

tip

Outlook understands natural language in most date boxes. For instance, in the Due Date or Start Date box, you can type **yesterday** to display yesterday's date, or type **next Monday** and Outlook will display next Monday's date, or type **one week from today** and Outlook will display the date seven days from the current date. Be specific, though. If you type in a vague expression like **soon** or **ASAP**, Outlook will display an error message. You can also enter a natural-language date in the Due Date column of the task list.

In this exercise, you change the task view, create a new task with details, and add information to an existing task.

1 On the View menu, point to Current View, and click Detailed List.

The tasks are displayed in Detailed List view, with new columns for Sort By: Priority, Attachment, Status, % Complete, and Categories.

New Task

2 Click the New Task button.

The task window appears, with the insertion point already in the Subject box.

> You can also display a new task window by pressing Ctrl+N.

3 In the Subject box, type **Call Joan to arrange a birthday dinner for Sarah.**

4 Click the Due Date down arrow.

A mini-calendar appears.

5 Click the date three days from today.

The selected date appears in the Due Date box.

6 Click the Status down arrow, and click In Progress.

In Progress appears in the Status box.

7 Click the Priority down arrow, and click Low.

Low appears in the Priority box.

8 On the Standard toolbar in the task window, click the Save And Close button.

The task window closes, and the task appears in the task list. Notice that a down arrow icon appears in the Priority column, indicating that the task is low priority.

9 Double-click the task *Call Cherry Creek Park to reserve sheltered picnic area.*

A task window appears. A note at the top of the task window indicates that the task is due in four days. The Subject box already contains the subject that you typed in the task list in the previous exercise.

10 Click the Start Date down arrow.

A mini-calendar appears.

11 Click tomorrow's date.

Tomorrow's date appears in the Start Date box.

12 On the Standard toolbar in the task window, click the Save And Close button.

The task is updated.

Sorting Tasks

The task list is automatically sorted alphabetically, based on the text in the Subject column. However, it might be more appropriate to sort tasks by a different field, such as Status, Priority, or Due Date. For example, the marketing director at Lakewood Mountains Resort sorted her task list for the ad campaign by Due Date so that she could more easily plan her upcoming deadlines.

To sort the task list, you click a column heading. The task list is sorted according to the contents of that column. Clicking the same column heading a second time reverses the sort order. For example, if you click the Subject column heading, Outlook sorts tasks alphabetically from Z to A. If you click the Subject column heading again, Outlook sorts tasks alphabetically from A to Z.

You can also sort tasks by right-clicking an empty area of the tasks list and clicking Sort. Select the desired sort criteria in the Sort dialog box, and click OK.

Subject

Tasks sorted from Z to A →

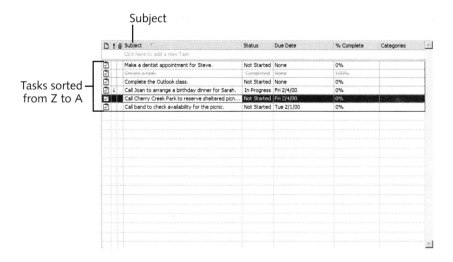

Tasks sorted from A to Z →

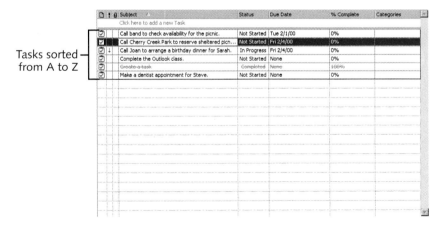

In this exercise, you sort tasks by Due Date and Status.

1 Click the Due Date column heading.

The tasks are sorted by due date. The due date the farthest in the future appears first. Tasks without a due date appear last.

2 Click the Due Date column heading again.

The tasks are re-sorted by due date. The tasks without a due date appear first, and the due date the farthest in the future appears last.

3   Click the Status column heading.

The tasks are sorted by status. The tasks that have the Not Started status appear first, the In Progress task appears next, and the Completed task appears last.

4   Click the Status column heading again.

The tasks are re-sorted by status. The Completed task appears first, the In Progress task appears next, and the Not Started tasks appear last.

> To quickly add or change a due date in the task list, click the task's Due Date box, and click the down arrow that appears to the right of the column. Click a date, or click the Today button to choose the current date.

Printing a Task List

As with the Outlook Calendar, you can also print a task list. For example, if you create a task list to identify the milestones of a project, you probably want to print a copy of the task list and bring it with you to the next project status meeting. To print a task list, click the Print button on the Standard toolbar to display the Print dialog box. Select the print style and, if you want, click the Page Setup button to choose options, such as text formatting, and different paper sizes and types. When you are finished selecting options, click OK.

Two print styles are available—Table Style and Memo Style. The Table Style option prints the task list in columns, similar to the way it appears in Outlook. The Memo Style option prints selected tasks in a two-column list, with the name of the task in the left column and the due date in the right column. Additional information about the tasks, such as the subject, status, and percent complete—appears in paragraph form underneath the columns. If you've created several columns for a task list and they won't all fit within the page margins, Memo Style might be a better printing option. When you select Memo Style, you can elect to print tasks one after another or each task on a separate page.

Organizing Tasks by Using Folders

For large projects that have multiple subprojects, it might be helpful to organize the tasks in different folders. You can use different folders to easily track the tasks for specific projects. For example, the events coordinator at Lakewood Mountains Resort is planning a banquet. She created a folder called Banquet so that she could have a centralized location for all the planning tasks related to the banquet.

In this exercise, you create a folder and move the picnic tasks into it.

1   On the Standard toolbar, click the Organize button.

The Organize pane appears.

2 Click the Using Folders link.

The Using Folders section of the Organize pane appears.

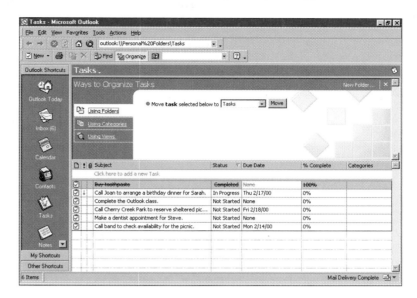

3 In the top-right corner of the Organize pane, click the New Folder button.

The Create New Folder dialog box appears, with the insertion point already in the Name box.

4 Type **Picnic Tasks.**

5 In the Select Where To Place The Folder box, verify that Tasks is selected, and click OK.

The Add Shortcuts To Outlook Bar dialog box appears, asking if you would like to add a shortcut for the folder to the Outlook Bar.

6 Click Yes to place a shortcut on the Outlook Bar.

The My Shortcuts group bar flashes for a few seconds. The Picnic Tasks folder becomes a shortcut in the My Shortcuts group on the Outlook Bar. The text *Picnic Tasks* appears in the Move Task Selected Below To box in the Organize pane.

7 Click the task *Call Cherry Creek Park to reserve sheltered picnic area.*, press and hold the Ctrl key, and then click the task *Call band to check availability for the picnic.*

Both tasks are selected.

8 In the Organize pane, click the Move button.

The tasks are moved to the Picnic Tasks folder.

9 On the Outlook Bar, click the My Shortcuts group bar, and then click the Picnic Tasks shortcut.

The contents of the Picnic Tasks folder appear. The tasks that you moved to the Picnic Tasks folder appear in the task list.

10 On the Outlook Bar, click the Outlook Shortcuts group bar, and then click the Tasks shortcut.

The contents of the Tasks folder appear. The two tasks that you moved to the Picnic Tasks folder no longer appear in the task list.

OL2000.6.3

Organizing Tasks by Using Categories

You can organize tasks by categories just as you can other items in Outlook. Categorizing tasks makes it easier to access just the tasks you need at one time. In the Using Categories section of the Organize pane, you can select one of the existing categories, such as Holiday, Business, or Gifts; or you can create your own category.

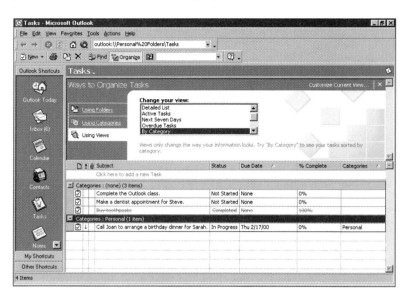

In this exercise, you assign a task to a category and apply the By Category view to your task list.

1   On the Standard toolbar, click the Organize button.

The Using Categories section of the Organize pane appears.

2   Click the Add Tasks Selected Below To down arrow, scroll down, and then click Personal.

3   In the task list, click the task *Call Joan to arrange a birthday dinner for Sarah*.

The task is selected.

4   In the Organize pane, click the Add button.

The task is added to the Personal category. The text Personal appears in the Categories column of the task.

5   In the Organize pane, click the Using Views link.

The Using Views section of the Organize pane appears.

6   In the Change Your View list, click By Category.

The By Category view appears. Notice that there are two gray bars named Categories: (none), and Categories: Personal.

7   On the Personal gray bar, click the plus sign (+).

The task *Call Joan to arrange a birthday dinner for Sarah.* appears.

8   In the Organize pane, in the Change Your View list, scroll up if necessary, and then click Detailed List.

The tasks appear in Detailed List view.

OL2000.6.4

Assigning Tasks to Others

Many projects involve more than one person. Therefore, in addition to setting up tasks for a project, you might also need to assign different tasks to various members of a team. In Outlook, you can easily assign a task to someone else. When you assign a task to someone, you send that person a task request as an e-mail message. The recipient can accept or decline the task.

When you create a task in your task list, you are the **owner** of the task. As the owner, you are the only person who can edit the task. If you assign the task to someone else and the recipient accepts the task, the **ownership** (the ability to make changes to the task) passes to the recipient. If you assign a task to someone and he or she accepts it, you can choose to keep an updated copy in your task list and receive status reports whenever the task is edited or completed.

In this exercise, you create two tasks and assign them to your class partner.

New Task

You can also display a task request by clicking New Task Request on the Actions menu.

1   On the Standard toolbar, click the New Task button.

The task window appears, with the insertion point already in the Subject box.

2   Type **Edit** [your name]**'s brochure.**

3   Click the Priority down arrow, and click High.

4   On the Standard toolbar in the task window, click the Assign Task button.

A task request window, which is similar to the task window, appears. A note at the top of the window indicates that the task request has not been sent yet.

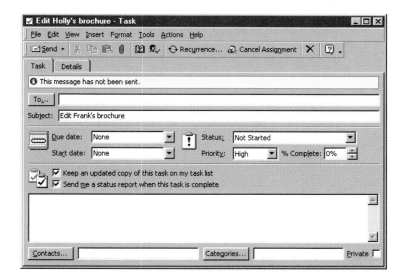

5   Click the To button.

The Select Task Recipient dialog box appears.

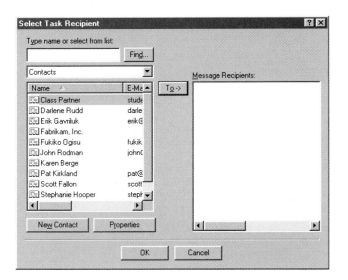

If an alert box appears stating that because you are no longer the owner of the task, the task reminder has been shut off, click OK.

6   In the Select Task Recipient dialog box, click your class partner's name, and click the To button.

Your class partner's name appears in the Message Recipients box.

7   Click OK.

The Select Task Recipient dialog box closes.

You cannot send the task request to yourself. If you are working at home or the office, if possible, ask a coworker or friend to participate as your partner.

8   On the Standard toolbar in the task window, click the Send button.

The task is sent to your class partner.

New Task

9   On the Standard toolbar, click the New Task button.

The task window appears.

10   In the Subject box, type **Water** [your name]**'s plant**.

11   Click the Due Date down arrow, and click Tuesday of next week.

12   On the Standard toolbar in the task window, click the Assign Task button.

A task request window appears. A note at the top of the window indicates that the task request has not been sent yet and that the task is due in eight days.

13   Click the To button.

The Select Task Recipient dialog box appears.

14   In the Select Task Recipient dialog box, click your class partner's name, and click the To button.

Your class partner's name appears in the Message Recipients box.

15   Click OK.

The Select Task Recipient dialog box closes.

16   On the Standard toolbar in the task window, click the Send button.

The task is sent to your class partner.

If an alert box appears stating that because you are no longer the owner of the task, the task reminder has been shut off, click OK.

Depending on when your class partner sends you his or her task requests, you might need to click the Send/Receive button (in the Inbox) again to receive these task request messages. You will accept and decline task requests in the next exercise.

17   On the Outlook Bar, click the Inbox shortcut.

The contents of the Inbox appear.

18   On the Standard toolbar, click the Send/Receive button.

Two task requests from your class partner appear in the Inbox.

OL2000.6.2

Accepting or Declining Tasks

Sending a task request does not mean that the recipient automatically agrees to it. The recipient must respond to the message, either by accepting or declining it. If the recipient declines a task request, the sender can reassign the task to someone else. If the recipient accepts a task request, the recipient receives ownership of the task and the sender receives a message of acceptance. This process prevents task requests from being forgotten. For example, the marketing director at Lakewood Mountains Resort assigned a task related to the picnic to the head chef. Because the chef had prior obligations, he declined the task. After receiving his decline message, the marketing director assigned the task to the head chef's assistant, who accepted the task.

If you receive a task request, you become the temporary owner of the task until you decide what to do with it—to accept or decline the task. If you accept a task, you become the permanent owner of the task. If you decline a task, you return ownership of the task to the person who sent the task request.

A task request appears in your Inbox as an e-mail message. You double-click the message to open the task request. To accept a task request, you click the Accept button. To decline a task request, you click the Decline button. Although it is not necessary to do so, you might want to include a comment with your reply, such as providing a start time, asking questions, or stating a reason for declining the task. To reply without a comment, you click the Send The Response Now option. To enter a comment before sending the reply, you click the Edit The Response Before Sending button. Type your comment, and click the Send button to send the response.

In this exercise, you accept a task request and send a response without comment back to the sender. You also decline a task request, and send a response with a comment to the sender.

1 In the Inbox, double-click the task request *Edit [your class partner]'s brochure*.

The task request window appears.

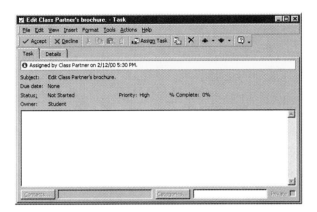

You can also accept a task request by right-clicking its message header in the Inbox and clicking Accept.

2 On the Standard toolbar in the task request window, click the Accept button.

An alert box appears with the Send The Response Now option already selected.

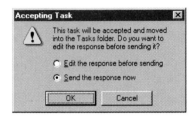

3 Click OK.

The response is sent as an e-mail message.

Close

4 In the top-right corner of the task request window, click the Close button.

The task request window closes.

5 In your Inbox, double-click the task request *Water [your class partner]'s plant*.

The task request window appears.

Notice that the task request, *Edit [your class partner]'s brochure* is no longer in the Inbox.

6 On the Standard toolbar in the task request window, click the Decline button.

An alert box appears with the Send The Response Now option already selected.

7 Click the Edit The Response Before Sending option, and click OK.

A task window appears with the insertion point already in the memo area.

8 In the memo area, type **I'm sorry, but my schedule doesn't allow me to accept this task.**

9 On the Standard toolbar in the task window, click the Send button.

The response to the task request is sent as an e-mail message.

Close

10 If necessary, in the top-right corner of the task request window, click the Close button.

11 On the Standard toolbar, click the Send/Receive button.

Two responses to the task requests appear in your inbox. The first states that you decline the task *Water [your name]'s plant*, and the second states that you accept the task *Edit [your name]'s brochure*.

Tasks

12 On the Outlook Bar, click the Tasks shortcut.

The contents of the Tasks folder appear. Notice that the task *Edit [your class partner]'s brochure* appears in the task list. The other task *Water [your class partner]'s plant* does not appear in the task list because you declined to do it.

Marking Tasks as Complete

In Outlook, if you mark a task as complete, the task appears with a strikeout line through it, and the task no longer appears in Active Tasks view. New tasks marked as complete remain in the task list, and you can make a completed task active again by changing its status. You can mark a task as complete by double-clicking the task to display the task window, clicking the Status down arrow, and clicking Completed. If you click the Details tab, you can also enter a different completion date (other than the current date) and additional completion information (such as total number of hours worked).

In the task list, you can mark a task as complete by right-clicking the task and clicking Mark Complete on the shortcut menu that appears. If the task list is displayed in Detailed List view, you can also type **100** in the % Complete column for the task.

In this exercise, you mark a task as complete using the Details tab of the task window, mark a task as complete using the Status box of the task window, and mark a task as complete in the task list.

1   Double-click the task *Make a dentist appointment for Steve*.

The task window appears.

2   Click the Details tab, and click the Date Completed down arrow.

A mini-calendar appears.

3   Click the date for yesterday.

Yesterday's date appears in the Date Completed column.

> Any date previous to, and including, today's date completes the task. You cannot use a date in the future.

4   On the Standard toolbar in the task window, click the Save And Close button.

The task *Make a dentist appointment for Steve.* appears with a line through it.

5   On the Outlook Bar, click the My Shortcuts group bar, and click the Picnic Tasks shortcut.

The contents of the Picnic Tasks folder appear.

6   Double-click the task *Call band to check availability for the picnic.*

The task window opens.

7   Click the Status down arrow.

The Status list appears.

8   Click Completed.

The task is marked as complete.

9   On the Standard toolbar in the task window, click the Save And Close button.

The task appears with a line through it.

10   Right-click the task *Call Cherry Creek Park to reserve sheltered picnic area.*, and click Mark Complete.

The task appears with a line through it.

OL2000.5.4

Manually Recording a Task in the Journal

The **Journal** is folder in Outlook that appears in a timeline format. The Journal can record when you create, use, and modify Microsoft Office documents (such as Microsoft Excel, Access, Word, and PowerPoint). When the Journal tracks an Office document, the following information is displayed for each document (as shown on the facing page): the document's type, name, and date, the amount of time the document was open, and the path in which the document is stored on your computer. Being able to view a document path is useful if you can't remember where you stored a document.

To set the Journal to automatically track Office documents, click Options on the Tools menu, and click the Journal Options button in the Options dialog box. In the Journal Options dialog box, select the check boxes next to the Office applications on which you want document activities recorded, and click OK twice.

You can open any Office documents and Outlook items recorded in the Journal, by double-clicking the file or item.

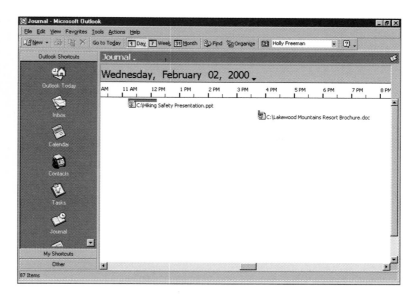

You can also use the Journal to track various Outlook activities, such as e-mails, and tasks. If you want to track an Outlook item, such as a task, you need to manually record it in the Journal.

For example, the marketing director at Lakewood Mountain Resort likes to record tasks in the Journal so that she can have a record of when she starts working on a task so that she can better plan her schedule for future projects and have a clear picture of where her time goes each week.

In this exercise, you create a task and record it in the Journal. Then you access the task from within the Journal and update it.

1 On the Folder Banner, click the folder name *Picnic Tasks*.

The Folder List appears.

Push Pin

2 In the top-right corner of the Folder List, click the Push Pin button to keep the Folder List open.

3 In the Folder List, click the Tasks folder.

The contents of the Tasks folder appear.

You can also drag a task onto the Journal shortcut on the Outlook Bar.

4 In the task list, click in the box that contains the text *Click here to add a new Task*.

5 Type **Create brochures,**, and press Enter.

6   Drag the task *Create brochures* to the Journal folder in the Folder list.

A journal entry window appears.

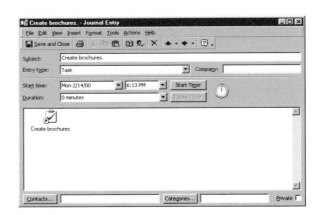

You might need to drag the horizontal scroll bar to the right to see the task.

7   On the Standard toolbar in the journal entry window, click the Save And Close button.

The task will now also appear in the Journal.

8   In the Folder List, click the Journal folder.

The contents of the Journal appear.

9   If necessary, on the Standard toolbar, click the Day button.

The current day appears in the Journal.

10   On the left side of the Task gray bar, click the plus sign (+).

The task appears in the Journal under the time at which you created the task.

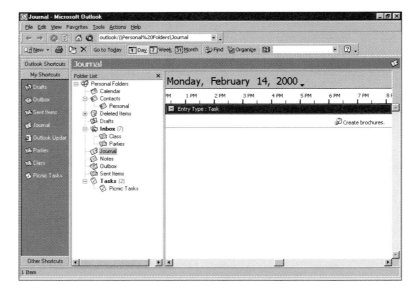

11   Right-click the task, and click Open Item Referred To.

The task appears in a task window.

12   In the % Complete box, select the *0%*, and type **100**.

13 On the Standard toolbar in the task window, click the Save And Close button.

The task is updated.

14 Click the Tasks folder in the Folder List.

Notice that the task has been updated in the task list and is now marked as completed with a line through it.

Deleting Tasks

If you complete a task and mark it as complete, the task still remains as an entry in your task list. Because completed tasks appear with a strikeout line, you can easily identify which tasks have been completed and which tasks are still in progress or have not yet begun. But when you know a task has been completed and don't want the task to clutter your task list, you can delete it. If you delete a task, it's moved to the Deleted Items folder, just as with other Outlook items. The deleted tasks remain in the Deleted Items folder until you empty the Deleted Items folder or restore the task.

In this exercise, you delete a completed task.

1 On the Outlook Bar, click the Picnic Tasks shortcut.

The contents of the Picnic Tasks folder appear.

2 Click the completed task *Call band to check availability for the picnic.*

Delete

3 On the Standard toolbar, click the Delete button.

The appointment moves to the Deleted Items folder.

> You can also delete a task by right-clicking it, and then clicking Delete.

4 On the Outlook Bar, click the Outlook Shortcuts group bar, scroll down, and then click the Deleted Items shortcut.

The task *Call band to check availability for the picnic.* appears in the Deleted Items folder.

Lesson Wrap-Up

This lesson explained how to use the Outlook task list—a tool that you can use to record basic daily tasks, set goals and priorities, and manage projects. In this lesson, you learned how to create and add details to a task, sort tasks, and organize tasks by using folders and categories. You also learned to assign tasks to others and accept or decline tasks sent to you. Finally, you learned how to mark tasks as complete, how to manually record a task in the Journal, and how to delete tasks from the task list.

If you are continuing to the next lesson:

Close

1 In the top-right corner of the Folder List, click the Close button.

The Folder List closes.

2 On the Outlook Bar, click the Tasks shortcut.

The contents of the Tasks folder appear.

If you are not continuing to other lessons:

Close

1   In the top-right corner of the Folder List, click the Close button.
The Folder List closes.

Close

2   In the top-right corner of the Outlook window, click the Close button
Oultook closes.

Lesson Glossary

Journal A folder in Outlook in a timeline format that records when you create, use, and modify Microsoft Office documents and Outlook items.

owner The only person who can edit a task.

ownership The ability to edit a task. Ownership can be assigned to others. Ownership indicates that the owner is responsible for completing the task.

task A personal or work item to be completed. You can assign a task to other network users.

task list The area in the Tasks folder that displays tasks that you created, and that you can use to create and update tasks.

Tasks An Outlook folder that you use to create, edit, and organize tasks.

Quick Quiz

1   What columns appear in the Detailed List view of the task list but do not appear in the Simple List view?

2   How does a completed task appear in a task list?

3   Describe one way to enter a task.

4   If you receive a task request from somebody else, how do you respond to the request?

5   How can you organize tasks?

6   What happens to deleted tasks?

7   Can you assign a task to someone else? Explain your answer.

8   What is a task?

9   What is the Journal?

10   If you send a task request to someone, how and where does it show up?

Putting It All Together

Exercise 1: The events coordinator at Lakewood Mountains Resort must begin to plan the company's holiday party. She wants to put all the tasks into Outlook and store them in a folder called Holiday Party. The tasks are as follows: *Find a location, Plan the food, Buy gifts, Book a band or DJ, Create invitations, Send invitations,* and *Buy decorations.* All the tasks should also be grouped under the category Holiday. The events coordinator will handle most of the tasks; however, she wants to assign the task *Create invitations* to the graphic designer and the task *Buy decorations* to her assistant (your class partner). Create the tasks and organize as specified above. Your instructor will tell you whom you should assign the *Create invitations* task to.

Exercise 2: The following week, the events coordinator needs to update the task list for Holiday Party. So far, she has completed finding a location and booking a band. She is halfway through planning the food. She realized that to get all the gifts she is going to need, she will have to take care of buying the gifts quickly. Update the task list.

LESSON 7

Using Notes

Many people use sticky notes to jot down phone numbers, comments, and other reminders to themselves throughout the day. These small notes can be temporarily placed on desks or computer monitors, or in other locations where they can't be easily overlooked. Sticky notes are a great invention, but if you use them, you might already have discovered that they can create clutter, especially when you have several sticky notes attached to your monitor or around your work area.

Microsoft Outlook has electronic **notes**, which look just like their paper counterparts, except that they appear on the screen. These notes offer you the convenience of sticky notes, but because they are stored on your computer, you won't have to worry about further cluttering your desk. Typically, a note is a brief text entry that you can save, edit, and move independently of the Outlook window. You can even create notes in different colors. Notes can help you keep track of bits of information, such as an airline reservation number, a reminder to pick up your dry cleaning, or the name of someone you just met.

You use the Notes folder in Outlook to create, store, and organize notes. You can copy notes from the Notes folder to the Microsoft Windows desktop (the screen view that appears when you start Windows) so that you can see your notes even when Outlook is closed or minimized. You can also convert a note to another Outlook item, such as a task or an appointment.

For example, suppose that a coworker asks you to review a report she has written. You quickly use Outlook to create a note reminding yourself to review the report. As your day becomes busier, you realize you might not have time to review the report by the end of the day. So you might decide to convert the note to a task so that it appears in your task list of things to do tomorrow. When you convert the note to a task, you can also set a high-priority flag to remind yourself to perform this task as soon as possible tomorrow.

In this lesson, you will learn how to create, edit, copy, and move notes. You will also learn how to forward and delete notes, and how to organize notes by using folders, views, and colors.

Practice files for the lesson

No practice files are required to complete the exercises in this lesson.

important

To complete one of the exercises in this lesson, you will need to exchange an e-mail message with a class partner. If you don't have a class partner or are performing the exercises alone, you can enter your own e-mail address instead of your class partner's and send the message to yourself.

OL2000.8.1

Creating Notes

Notes are easier to create than many other items in Outlook because you don't have to fill in boxes or select options. A note consists of a small window containing a single area for text. Although notes can be any length and size, notes don't provide most of the capabilities of a word processing program. For instance, you can't make text in a note bold or italic, nor can you apply most other formatting. But you probably won't need to because notes are intended to be fast and easy to use. Notes are best for short bits of information. For example, because the head chef at Lakewood Mountains Resort has a tendency to forget his e-mail password, he created a note that contains a clue to remind himself of his password.

To display the Notes window, you click the Notes shortcut on the Outlook Bar. You'll see a window similar to the one shown below.

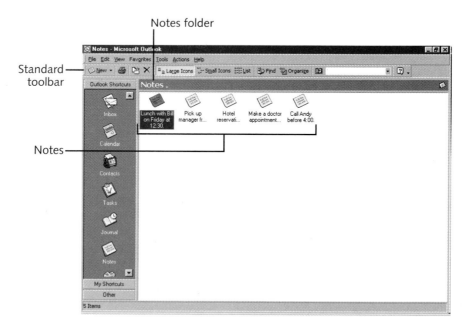

New Note

To create a note, on the Standard toolbar, you click the New Note button, and a blank note appears.

A note icon appears in the top-left corner of a note. When you click the note icon, a menu appears, containing commands for customizing and organizing the note. A Close button appears in the top-right corner of a note. Clicking the Close button saves and closes the note. When you close a note, it is stored in the Notes window.

Along the bottom of the note, the date and time that the note was created appears. If you click and drag the hash marks in the bottom-right corner of the note, you can resize the note horizontally and diagonally at the same time. If you just want to resize a note horizontally, click and drag either the right or left edge of the note. If you just want to resize the note vertically, click and drag the bottom edge of the note

You can also double-click the empty, white area of the Notes window to create a new note.

After a new note appears, you then type the text you want the note to display. You can type more text than will fit into the note as it appears on the screen; however, notes do not have a scroll bar, so to read the text that is not visible, you must scroll through the text using the up and down arrow keys; or, you can make the note larger.

tip

You don't need to display the Notes window to create a note. From any Outlook window, you can click the down arrow to the right of the New button, and click Note. When you use this approach, the note is placed on the Windows desktop and is treated as the active window until you click a different window or close the note. You can also press Ctrl+Shift+N to create a note. If you are already in the Notes window, you can create a note by right-clicking in the window and clicking New Note.

In this exercise, you create three notes.

1   On the Outlook Bar, scroll down if necessary, and click the Notes shortcut.

    The contents of the Notes folder appear.

New Note

2   On the Standard toolbar, click the New Note button.

    A new note appears with the insertion point in the top of the note.

10   Click the plus sign (+) on the left side of each of the gray bars.

The notes are categorized by color.

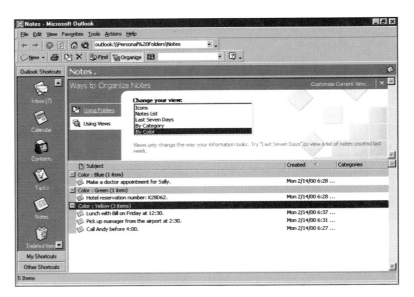

You can also change the view of the Notes folder by pointing to Current View on the View menu, and clicking a view.

11   In the Change Your View list, click Icons.

The notes appear again as icons in the Notes window.

12   In the Organize pane, click the Using Folders link.

The Using Folder section of the Organize pane appears.

13   In the top-right corner of the Organize pane, click the New Folder button.

The Create New Folder dialog box appears with the insertion point already in the Name box.

14   In the Name box, type **Personal Notes**.

15 Verify that Notes is selected, and click OK.

The Add Shortcut To Outlook Bar dialog box appears, asking whether you would like to save the folder as a shortcut on the Outlook Bar.

16 Click Yes to place a shortcut on the Outlook Bar.

The My Shortcuts group bar flashes for a few seconds. The Personal Notes folder becomes a shortcut in the My Shortcuts group on the Outlook Bar. The text *Personal Notes* appears in the Move Note Selected Below To box in the Organize pane.

17 Click the note *Lunch with Bill on Friday at 12:30.*

18 In the Organize pane, click the Move button.

The note is moved to the Personal Notes folder.

19 On the Outlook Bar, click the My Shortcuts group bar, and click the Personal Notes shortcut.

The note *Lunch with Bill on Friday at 12:30.* appears in the Notes window.

20 On the Outlook Bar, click the Outlook Shortcuts group bar, and then, if necessary, scroll down and click the Notes shortcut.

The contents of the Notes folder appear. The note *Lunch with Bill on Friday at 12:30.* no longer appears.

Deleting Notes

When you no longer need a note, you can delete it to remove the item from your Notes window or your Windows desktop. Just as with e-mail messages, contacts, tasks, and appointments, when you delete a note, it is moved to the Deleted Items folder. Deleted notes remain there until you empty the Deleted Items folder. You can also restore a note by opening the Deleted Items folder and dragging the note to the Notes shortcut on the Outlook Bar.

In this exercise, you delete a note.

1 In the Notes window, click the note *Call Andy before 4:00.*

Delete

2 On the Standard toolbar, click the Delete button.

The note moves to the Deleted Items folder.

You can also delete a note by right-clicking it, and clicking Delete.

3 On the Outlook Bar, if necessary, scroll down and click the Deleted Items shortcut to view the deleted note.

Lesson Wrap-Up

In this lesson, you learned how to use notes in Outlook. You learned how to create and edit notes in the Notes folder and to copy and move them to your desktop so that you can see the reminder even when you are not in Outlook. You also learned how to convert a note to another Outlook item, such as a task or message, and you learned how to forward a note as an e-mail attachment. You learned that you can organize notes by views, folders, and colors. Finally, you learned how to delete notes.

This concludes the Microsoft Outlook Core Skills course.

If you are going to review other lessons:

● On the Outlook Bar, click the Notes shortcut.
   The contents of the Notes folder appear.

If you are not going to review other lessons:

Close

● In the top-right corner of the Outlook window, click the Close button.
   Outlook closes.

Lesson Glossary

notes Brief text items that can be saved, edited, and moved independently of the Outlook window.

Quick Quiz

1 What are two ways in which you can organize notes?
2 How do you move a note to another folder?
3 How do you delete a note?
4 What is a note?
5 How do you copy a note?
6 How do you copy a note to the desktop?
7 How do you create a note?
8 What does a note become when you forward it?

Putting It All Together

Exercise 1: Create the following notes: *Make dentist appointment, Call car repair shop for tune-up appointment, Follow up on picnic activities,* and *Set up luncheon meeting for the President of Lakewood Mountains Resort.* The first two notes are the most important, so copy them to your desktop.

Exercise 2: Move the note *Set up luncheon meeting for the President of Lakewood Mountains Resort* to the Tasks folder. Then forward the note *Follow up on picnic activities* to your class partner.

APPENDIX

Setting Up Outlook

When you install Microsoft Outlook on a computer and then run it for the first time, the Outlook 2000 Startup Wizard prompts you for information about yourself and asks whether you want to set up an e-mail account. If you supply all the required information, you might not have to change your user or e-mail information in the future. However, you can add to this information or change settings later if you enter any of the information in your user or e-mail profile incorrectly, or if you don't know which information to provide. This appendix explains how to use the Outlook 2000 Startup Wizard; how to create a user profile; how to add, change, modify, and remove information services for a particular user; and how to specify which profile Outlook should use when it starts.

Using the Outlook 2000 Startup Wizard

The Outlook 2000 Startup Wizard can now detect and import e-mail account information and address book information from more e-mail programs so that it's easier for you to keep your e-mail accounts and contact records in one program.

If you are upgrading from an earlier version of Outlook, you will not have to specify your e-mail address, e-mail server, or other information about yourself. The Outlook Startup Wizard will use the previously installed version's settings to configure the settings for Outlook 2000.

If Outlook has been installed on your computer but has never been started, the Outlook 2000 Startup Wizard will appear automatically when you first start Outlook. This wizard guides you through the installation step by step as you specify your e-mail address, e-mail server, and information about yourself. You must enter the required information into the wizard before you will be able to send and receive e-mail messages in Outlook.

Scenario 1: Installing Outlook Over a Previous Version

Follow these steps if you have an earlier version of Outlook installed on your computer.

When the Outlook 2000 Startup Wizard appears:

1 In the first Outlook 2000 Startup Wizard dialog box, click Next.

The Outlook Mail Usage dialog box appears with a message stating that if you used another version of Outlook, selecting Yes will allow Outlook to use the previously installed version's configuration for Outlook 2000. The Yes option is already selected.

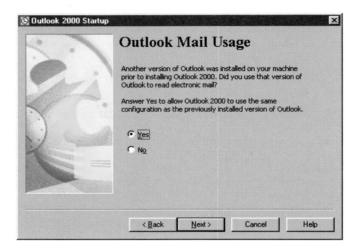

2 Click Next.

The E-Mail Upgrade Options dialog box appears. You can use this dialog box to transfer addresses created in a previous version of Outlook to Outlook 2000.

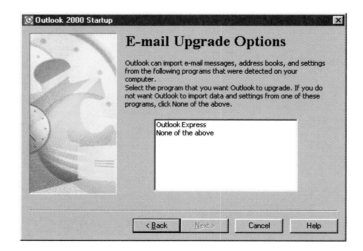

3   Click None Of The Above, and click Next.

The E-Mail Service Options dialog box appears.

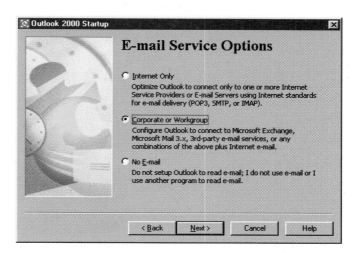

4   Select the Internet Only (if the only e-mail connection you have is with an Internet service provider) or Corporate Or Workgroup (if your e-mail system works with a network) option, and click Next.

If you click Internet Only, an alert box appears notifying you that you can't use the Exchange Server e-mail or other workgroup services, because you selected the Internet Only option.

5   If necessary, click Yes.

Outlook starts. The Outlook window appears with the Office Assistant turned on. The Office 2000 Registration Wizard appears, asking if you want to register your copy of Microsoft Office 2000.

6   Click No to register later.

Scenario 2: Installing Outlook Over a Different E-Mail Program

Follow the steps in this section if your computer has one or more e-mail programs (Microsoft Outlook Express, Eudora, or Netscape Messenger, for example) already installed. If you do not have any other e-mail programs on your computer, and this is the first time you've installed any version of Outlook on your computer, you should see the dialog boxes as specified on the following page; some settings may vary, depending on the options you choose and the way your computer was set up.

The Office Assistant is discussed later in this lesson.

If an alert box appears asking if you want Outlook to resolve any conflicts between Microsoft Office and other e-mail–enabled programs, click Yes. If asked, restart your computer.

The steps in this section also apply if you are installing Outlook on a computer that does not have another e-mail program installed.

Before you begin, you will need to find out your e-mail address, the address for your incoming mail server, and the address for your outgoing mail server. You can get this information from your instructor or your Internet service provider (ISP).

When the Outlook 2000 Startup Wizard appears:

1   In the first Outlook 2000 Startup Wizard dialog box, click Next.

The E-Mail Upgrade Options dialog box appears. You can use this dialog box to transfer addresses created in other applications to Outlook.

2   Click None Of The Above, and click Next.

The E-Mail Service Options dialog box appears.

3   Select the Internet Only (if the only e-mail connection you have is with an ISP) or Corporate Or Workgroup (if your e-mail system works with a network) option, and click Next.

If you click Internet Only, an alert box appears notifying you that you can't use the Microsoft Exchange Server e-mail or other workgroup services because you selected the Internet Only option.

4   If necessary, click Yes.

The Internet Connection Wizard appears.

5   Type your name, and click Next.

The next Internet Connection Wizard dialog box appears.

6   Type your e-mail address, and click Next.

The next Internet Connection Wizard dialog box appears, with the insertion point already in the Incoming Mail Server box.

7   Type the address for your incoming mail server, and press Tab.

The insertion point moves to the Outgoing Mail Server box.

8   Type the address for your outgoing mail server, and click Next.

The next Internet Connection Wizard dialog box appears, with the insertion point already in the Account Name box.

9   Type your e-mail account name (if it is different than the one Outlook inserts), and press Tab. Your e-mail account name is usually the portion of your e-mail address that precedes the @ symbol.

The insertion point moves to the E-mail Account Password box.

10   Type your e-mail account password, verify that the Remember Password check box is selected, and then click Next.

The next Internet Connection Wizard dialog box appears, asking you to specify how you connect to the network.

11   Verify that the Connect Through My Local Area Network (LAN) option is selected, and click Next.

The next Internet Connection Wizard dialog box appears, congratulating you on successfully setting up Outlook.

12   Click Finish.

13   If the Internet Accounts dialog box appears, click the Close button.

An alert box might appear, warning you that Outlook is not the default e-mail manager on your computer, meaning that other programs on your computer that can send and receive e-mail will not use Outlook to do so.

Sidebar notes:

If you do not have any other e-mail programs on your computer, you will not see the E-Mail Upgrade Options dialog box.

In step 9, you can enter an e-mail account name that's different from the one that the computer inserts in the Account Name box.

In step 10, you do not have to enter your password or select the Remember Password check box if you want to enter your password every time you start Outlook.

⊠

Close

If you say no in step 13, you can change the default manager later by clicking Start on the Windows taskbar, pointing to Settings, and clicking Control Panel. Double-click Internet Options, click the Programs tab, and use the E-Mail down arrow to select your default manager.

14   To use Outlook as the default e-mail manager, click Yes.

The Outlook window appears with the Office Assistant turned on. The Office 2000 Registration Wizard appears, asking if you want to register your copy of Microsoft Office 2000.

15   Click No to register later.

Creating a User Profile

Microsoft Outlook 2000 allows you to establish e-mail accounts and other services for different people who use the same computer. When you run Outlook for the first time and respond to the prompts by entering information about yourself, Outlook creates a **user profile**—a collection of Outlook settings that describes the information services, e-mail accounts, and settings for a particular person.

Outlook will either detect existing **information services**—collections of settings that tells Outlook how to send, receive, and store messages for a user—or will prompt you for the information services that you want to set up for your user profile. Whether Outlook detects the information or prompts you for it depends on how Outlook was installed on your computer.

If you use Outlook at work, you might use more than one information service. For example, Lakewood Mountains Resort has both an interoffice network and access to the Internet. On each computer, the network administrator sets up one information service to use Internet mail (for e-mail), and another information service to access e-mail from his or her interoffice network post office.

If you rarely use a particular information service, you might want to set up a separate user profile so that the service and its folders only appear in Outlook when you log on under a different user name. If you share a computer with others, you will need to set up a user profile for yourself. Doing so allows you to send and receive your own e-mail messages, and prevents others who use the computer from viewing your messages. Creating a separate user profile also prevents you from receiving another user's messages.

important

The user profile that you set up in Outlook is not the same as the user profile that you set up in Microsoft Windows. A user profile in Windows identifies personalized startup and desktop settings that take effect when you log on to Windows using the name and password for the user profile. By contrast, a user profile in Outlook sets you up to send, receive, and store e-mail messages.

important

You must set up your e-mail services using the Corporate or Workgroup configuration before you can add a user profile. Start Outlook, and on the Tools menu, click Options, click the Mail Delivery tab, and then click the Reconfigure Mail Support button. In the dialog box, click the Corporate Or Workgroup option, click the Next button, and then follow the screen prompts.

To create a user profile:

1   On the Windows taskbar, click the Start button, point to Settings, and then click Control Panel.

The Control Panel appears.

Mail

2   Double-click the Mail icon, and click the Show Profiles button in the dialog box.

The Mail dialog box appears.

3   In the Mail dialog box, click the Add button.

The first Inbox Setup Wizard dialog box appears.

4   Select the information services that you want to use with the profile, and click Next.

The next wizard dialog box appears.

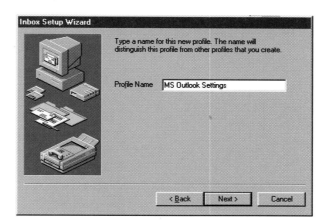

5   In the Profile Name box, type a name, and click Next.

The screen that you see next varies depending on which services you specified. If you select Microsoft Exchange Server, you will be prompted for the name of your server and your mailbox name. Exchange Server is a network program designed to run on a Microsoft Windows NT or Microsoft Windows 2000 server. If you select Microsoft Mail, you will be prompted for the name of your post office. Microsoft Mail is an interoffice e-mail program that can be used on networks that do not use Exchange Server. If you selected Internet E-mail, you will be prompted to set up your e-mail account by specifying your e-mail name and incoming and outgoing mail server addresses.

important

If you need to set up the Microsoft Exchange Server or Microsoft Mail services but you don't know the names of the items you are supposed to specify, check with your network administrator. If you need to set up an Internet e-mail account and need help, either your network administrator or your Internet service provider (ISP) should be able to help.

6   If necessary, in the next wizard dialog box, click Next.

7   In the last wizard dialog box, click Finish.

8   Click the Close button to close the Mail dialog box.

Close

9   In the top-right corner of the Control Panel, click the Close button to close it.

Whenever you start Outlook, the program will prompt you for the User Profile to use.

tip

If you use one telephone line to connect to your mail server and to send faxes from your computer, you can make faxing easier by setting up a new profile using only the Microsoft Fax service.

Understanding, Adding, Changing, and Removing Information Services

Over time, you might need to change the information services that are set up for your user profile in Outlook. Internet changes, updated e-mail addresses, and switching to a different Internet service provider can require a change in your information services.

Outlook allows you to add new services, change the properties of an existing service (such as specifying a new e-mail address or a new mail server), or remove a service that you no longer use.

important

You must set up your e-mail services using the Corporate or Workgroup configuration before you can add an information service. Start Outlook, and on the Tools menu, click Options, click the Mail Delivery tab, and then click the Reconfigure Mail Support button. In the dialog box, click the Corporate Or Workgroup option, click the Next button, and then follow the screen prompts.

To add an information service:

1   On the Tools menu, click Services.

The Services dialog box appears.

2   Click the Add button.

The Add Service To Profile dialog box appears.

3   Select the service that you want to add, and click OK.

Outlook will prompt you for the CD-ROM that contains the service that you want to install.

4   Insert the CD-ROM, and click OK.

5   Click OK to close the Services dialog box.

Outlook will notify you that the changes you specified will not be applied until the next time you start Outlook or the service that you installed.

To modify an information service:

1   On the Tools menu, click Services.

The Services dialog box appears.

2   Click the name of the service that you want to change, and then click the Properties button. The dialog box that appears next will depend on which service you selected.

3   Change the properties as needed, and click OK.

4   Click OK to close the Services dialog box.

Outlook will notify you that the changes you specified will not be applied until the next time you start Outlook or the service that you installed.

To remove an information service:

1   On the Tools menu, click Services

The Services dialog box appears.

2   Click the name of the service that you no longer want, and click the Remove button.

3   Click Yes to confirm that you want that service removed, and click OK to close the Services dialog box.

Selecting a User Profile When Outlook Starts

If more than one user profile is set up on a computer, you must select which profile to use when Outlook starts. You can set up the profiles so that you use a specific profile each time Outlook starts, or you can have Outlook prompt you to select a user profile each time.

To select a user profile when Outlook starts:

1   On the Tools menu, click Options, and click the Mail Services tab in the Options dialog box.

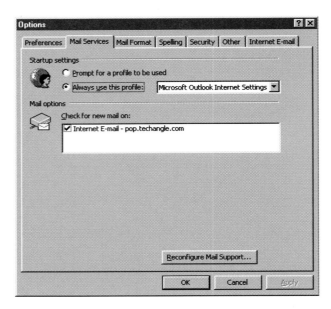

2   In the Startup Settings section of the dialog box, click either the Prompt For A Profile To Be Used option or the Always Use This Profile option. If you select the Always Use This Profile option, you must select a profile from the list that appears.

3   Click OK.

The new settings will take effect the next time you start Outlook.

Glossary

information services Collections of Outlook settings used to determine how to send, receive, and organize messages for a user.

user profile A collection of Outlook settings that describes the information services and e-mail capabilities for a particular person.

Quick Reference

Lesson 1: Introduction to Outlook

To start Outlook

1   On the Windows taskbar, click the Start button, point to Programs, and then click Microsoft Outlook.
2   If necessary, click the Maximize button.

Maximize

To scroll through the contents of the Outlook Bar

●   Click the up arrow to scroll up through the Outlook Bar.
    Or
    Click the down arrow to scroll down through the Outlook Bar.

To expand a short menu

1   Click the desired menu.
2   Click the down arrows at the bottom of the menu.
    Or
    Wait a few seconds for the menu to expand on its own.

To use the Outlook Bar

●   On the Outlook Bar, click a shortcut.

To display a different group on the Outlook Bar

●   On the Outlook Bar, click the Outlook Shortcuts, My Shortcuts or Other Shortcuts (or Other) group bar.

To add a Web site to the list of Favorites

1   On the Windows taskbar, click the Start button, point to Programs, and then click Internet Explorer.
2   Type the address of the Web site you want to add, and press Enter.
3   Click Add To Favorites on the Favorites menu.
4   Click OK to accept the default title line as the name of the Favorite.
    Or
    Type a new name, and click OK.

To add a folder to the list of Favorites

1   On the Windows taskbar, click the Start button, point to Programs, and then click Windows Explorer.

2   Click the folder you want to add, click Add To Favorites on the Favorites menu, and then click OK to accept the default title line as the name of the Favorite.

To access a favorite Web site or folder from Outlook

1   On the Outlook bar, click the Other Shortcuts group bar (or Other group bar).

2   Click the Favorites folder, and double-click the name of the Web site or folder that you want to open.

To display a folder using the Folder List

1   If the Folder List is not already open, click the folder name that appears on the Folder Banner.

2   Click the name of the Outlook folder that you want to display.

Or

1   If the Folder List is already open, click the name of the Outlook folder that you want to display.

To keep the Folder List open

1   Click the Folder Banner.

 2   Click the Push Pin button.

Push Pin

Or

1   On the View menu, click Folder List.

To close the Folder List

 ●   In the Folder List, click the Close button in the top-right corner.

Close

To use the Office Assistant

 1   On the Standard toolbar, click the Microsoft Outlook Help button.

Microsoft Outlook Help **2**   Type a question, and click the Search button.

3   In the list of topics that appears, click the topic that most closely matches your help request.

To hide the Office Assistant

1   Right-click the Office Assistant.

2   Click Hide.

Lesson 2: Using E-Mail in Outlook

To compose, address, and send a message

New Mail Message

1   In the Inbox, click the New Mail Message button on the Standard toolbar.

2   In the To text box, type an e-mail address.

3   Press Tab, and type another e-mail address in the Cc box, if necessary.

4   Press Tab, type the message description in the Subject text box, and then press Enter.

5   Type your message, and click the Send button.

To flag a message

Flag

1   Create an e-mail message.

2   On the Standard toolbar in the message window, click the Flag button.

3   Select your options, and click OK.

To save a message as a template

1   Create the e-mail message that you want to use as a template.

2   On the File menu in the message window, click Save As.

3   In the Save As dialog box, click the Save As Type down arrow, click Outlook Template (.oft), and then click the Save button.

To open a template

1   On the Tools menu, point to Forms, and click Choose Form.

2   In the Choose Form dialog box, click the Look In down arrow, click User Templates In File System, and then double-click the name of the template.

To attach a file to a message

Insert File

1   Follow the steps for composing and addressing a message.

2   On the Standard toolbar in the message window, click the Insert File button.

3   Click the Look In down arrow, and navigate to your file.

4   Double-click the file to attach it to the e-mail message.

5   On the Standard toolbar in the message window, click the Send button.

To set message priority

Importance High

Importance Low

●   On the Standard toolbar in the message window, click the Importance: High button.

Or

On the Standard toolbar in the message window, click the Importance: Low button.

To check for e-mail messages

1   If necessary, on the Outlook Bar, click the Outlook Shortcuts group bar, and click the Inbox shortcut.

2   On the Standard toolbar, click the Send/Receive button.

To read e-mail messages and messages with attachments

1   In the Inbox, double-click the message header of the message you want to read.

2   Double-click the attachment icon in the message (if one is included) to read the attachment.

To turn AutoPreview on or off

●   On the View menu, click AutoPreview.

To turn the Preview Pane on or off

●   On the View menu, click Preview Pane.

To reply to a message

1   Click the message header for the message to which you want to reply.

2   On the Standard toolbar, click the Reply button.

3   Type your message.

4   On the Standard toolbar in the message window, click the Send button.

To forward a message

1   In the Inbox, click the message header for the message that you want to forward.

2   On the Standard toolbar, click the Forward button.

3   In the To box, type an e-mail address.

4   On the Standard toolbar in the message window, click the Send button.

To print a message

1   In the Inbox, click the message header for the message that you want to print.

2   On the Standard toolbar, click the Print button.

Print

To print a message with an attachment

1   In the Inbox, click the message header for the message that you want to print.

2   On the File menu, click Print.

3   In the Print Options section in the Print dialog box, select the Print Attached Files With Item(s) check box, and click OK.

To find a message

1   On the Standard toolbar, click the Find button.
2   In the Look For box, type the search criteria.
3   Click the Find Now button.

To recall a message

Push Pin

1   If necessary, click the folder name Inbox on the Folder Banner, and click the Push Pin button in the top-right corner of the Folder List.
2   Click Sent Items.
3   Double-click the message header for the message that you want to recall.
4   On the Actions menu, click Recall This Message.
5   Click OK.

To delete a message

1   In the Inbox, click the message header for the message that you want to delete.

Delete

2   On the Standard toolbar, click the Delete button.

To empty the Deleted Items folder

1   In the Folder List, click Deleted Items.
2   Select the message or messages that you want to delete.
3   Press Delete, and click Yes.
    Or
1   On the Tools menu, click Empty "Deleted Items" Folder, and click Yes.

To save drafts

Close

●   In the top-right corner of the message window, click the Close button, and click Yes.
    Or

Save

On the Standard toolbar in the message window, click the Save button, and click the Close button in the top-right corner of the message window.

To retrieve a draft

1   Display the Folder List, and click the Drafts folder.
2   Double-click the desired message to open it.
3   Complete or edit the message, and send it just as you normally would.

Lesson 3: Customizing E-Mail

To specify e-mail options

New Mail Message

1   On the Standard toolbar, click the New Mail Message button.

2   On the Standard toolbar in the message window, click Options.

3   Select the options you want.

4   Click the Close button.

To change message format

1   On the Tools menu, click Options.

2   Click the Mail Format tab.

3   In the Message Format section, click the Send In This Message Format down arrow, select the desired format, and then click OK.

To use stationery

1   On the Actions menu, point to New Mail Message Using, and click More Stationery.

2   Select the stationery you want, and click OK.

To add a signature to an e-mail message

1   On the Tools menu, click Options.

2   Click the Mail Format tab.

3   Click the Signature Picker button.

4   Click the New button.

5   Type the name of your signature, and select the method you want to use to create the signature.

6   Click the Next button.

7   Type the text you want to include in your signature.

8   Click Finish, and click OK twice.

To set viewing options

1   On the Standard toolbar, click the Organize button.

2   Click the Using Views link.

3   Select the view option you want.

4   On the Standard toolbar, click the Organize button.

To sort messages

1   On the View menu, point to Current View.

2   Click Customize Current View.

3   Click the Sort button.

4   Select your options, and click OK twice.

To filter a view

1   On the View menu, point to Current View.

2   Click Customize Current View.

3   Click the Filter button.

4   Select the filter options that you want, and click OK twice.

To create folders

1   On the Standard toolbar, click the Organize button.

2   Click the Using Folders link.

3   In the top of the Organize pane, click the New Folder button.

4   In the Name box, type a folder name.

5   In the Select Where To Place The Folder list, select where to place the folder, and click OK.

To move messages between folders

1   Highlight the desired message.

2   On the Standard toolbar, click the Organize button.

3   Click the Using Folders link.

4   In the first line, select the folder to which you want to move the message.

5   Click the Move button.

To color-code message headers

1   On the Standard toolbar, click the Organize button.

2   In the Organize pane, click the Using Colors link.

3   Click or type an e-mail address.

4   Select your color options.

5   Click the Apply Colors button.

To filter junk e-mail

1   On the Standard toolbar, click the Organize button.

2   In the Organize pane, click the Junk E-Mail link.

3   Select the desired filter options.

4   Click the Turn On button.

To archive messages

1   On the File menu, click Archive.

2   Select your options, and click OK twice.

Lesson 4: Using the Contacts Folder

To view a contact

Contacts

1   On the Outlook Bar, click the Contacts shortcut.

2   In the Contacts pane, double-click the title bar for the desired contact.

To create or edit a contact

New Contact

1   On the Standard toolbar, click the New Contact button.

2   Type the information that you have about the person and/or company.

3   On the Standard toolbar, click the Save And New button.

To enter multiple contacts for the same company

1   In the Contacts folder, click the existing contact from the same company.

2   On the Actions menu, click New Contact From Same Company.

3   Type the information that you have about the new contact.

4   On the Standard toolbar in the Contact window, click the Save And Close button.

To use the Office Clipboard

1   Double-click a contact.

2   On the View menu, click Toolbars, and click Clipboard.

3   Highlight the items you want to copy.

Copy

4   On the Clipboard toolbar, click the Copy button.

5   Start the application to which you want to copy the information.

6   Click either the Paste All icon or the icon containing the specific information you want to copy.

To delete a contact

1   Click the contact record you want to delete.

Delete

2   On the Standard toolbar, click the Delete button.

To restore a contact

●   Drag the contact record from the Deleted Items folder to the Contacts shortcut on the Outlook Bar.

To create folders

1   On the Standard toolbar, click the Organize button.

2   In the Organize pane, click the Using Folders link.

3   In the top-right corner of the Organize pane, click the New Folder button.

4   In the Name box, type a name for the new folder.

5   Select the desired folder options, and click OK.

To move contacts into a folder

1   On the Standard toolbar, click the Organize button.

2   In the Organize pane, Click the Using Folders link.

3   Click the contact you want to move.

4   In the Organize pane, click the Move button.

To display the Contacts folder using views

1   On the Standard toolbar, click the Organize button.

2   In the Organize pane, click the Using Views link.

3   In the Change Your View list, choose the view you want from the Change Your View list.

To create a new category

1   On the Standard toolbar, click the Organize button.

2   Click the Using Categories link.

3   In the Create New Category Called box, type the name of the new category.

4   Click the Create button.

To assign a contact to a category

1   In the Contacts folder, click the desired contact.

2   In the Organize pane, select the desired category, and click the Add button.

To sort information by using categories

1   On the Standard toolbar, click the Organize button.

2   In the Organize pane, click the Using Views link.

3   In the Change Your View list, click By Category.

To assign a contact to multiple categories

1   In the Contacts folder, double-click the desired contact.

2   In the Contact window, click the Categories button.

3   In the Categories dialog box, select the desired categories, and click OK.

To add a category to the Master Category List

1   On the Edit menu, click Categories.

2   Click the Master Category List button.

3   In the New Category box, type the new category name.

4   Click the Add button.

To delete a category from the Master Category List

1   On the Edit menu, click Categories.

2   Click the Master Category List button.

3   In the Master Category List, click the desired contact.

4   Click the Delete button.

To reset the Master Category List

1   On the Edit menu, click Categories.

2   Click the Master Category List button.

3   In the Master Category List, click the Reset button.

4   Click OK.

To sort contacts

1   On the Standard toolbar, click Organize.

2   Click the Using Views link.

3   In the Change Your View list, click the desired view.

4   At the top of the Organize pane, click the Customize Current View button.

5   Click the Sort button.

6   In the Sort Items By section, select the desired options.

7   Click OK twice.

To use the Address Book to send e-mail

Address Book

1   On the Standard toolbar, click the Address Book button.

2   Select a recipient.

3   On the toolbar, click the Action button, and click Send Mail.

4   Compose and send an e-mail message as you normally would.

To use contacts to send e-mail

1   In the Contacts folder, double-click the desired contact.

2   On the Standard toolbar in the message window, click the New Message To Contact button.

3   Compose and send an e-mail message as you normally would.

To send contact information via e-mail

1   If your computer is set to Internet Only, right-click the desired contact record in the Contacts folder, and click Forward As vCard on the shortcut menu that appears.

Or

If your computer is set to Corporate or Workgroup, click Forward as vCard on the Actions menu.

2   In the To text box, type the address of the recipient.

3   Click the Send button.

To insert a vCard into a signature

1   On the Tools menu, click Options.

2   Click the Mail Format tab, and click the Signature Picker button.

3   Select an existing signature, and click the Edit button.

4   At the bottom of the dialog box, click the New vCard From Contact button.

5   Click a desired vCard, click the Add button, and then click OK.

To receive contact information via e-mail

1   On the Outlook Bar, click the Inbox shortcut.

2   Double-click the message containing the vCard.

3   Double click the vCard.

4   In the contact window, click the Save And Close button.

To create a letter by using the Letter Wizard

1   In the Contacts folder, click the desired contact.

2   On the Actions menu, click New Letter To Contact.

3   In the Letter Wizard dialog boxes, fill in the information as requested in Microsoft Word.

4   Click the Finish button.

5   Complete the letter and save and/or print it.

Lesson 5: Using the Calendar

To navigate within the Calendar

Calendar

1   On the Outlook Bar, click the Calendar shortcut.

2   In the Appointment Area, drag the scroll bar up or down to display the times of the day you wish to view.

3   Click the desired date in the Date Navigator.

4   At the top of the Date Navigator, click the arrows to display previous and future months.

5   In the Date Navigator, click and hold the name of the current month to display a menu of months.

6   On the Standard toolbar, click the Go To Today button to display the current day.

To change the Calendar view

1   On the Standard toolbar, click the Work Week button to display the work week.

2   On the Standard toolbar, click the Week button to display the week.

3   On the Standard toolbar, click the Month button to display the month.

4   On the View menu, click Preview Pane to split the window and display the Preview Pane.

5   On the View menu, click Preview Pane to close the Preview Pane.

6   On the Standard toolbar, click the Day button to display the day view.

To schedule an appointment

1   In the Date Navigator, click the date for which you want to make the appointment.

2   In the Appointment Area, click the time slot for which you want to schedule the appointment.

3   Type the name of the appointment, and press Enter.

To schedule an event

1   In the Date Navigator, click the first day of the event you want to schedule.

2   On the Standard toolbar, click the New Appointment button.

3   In the Subject box, type the name of the event, and press Tab.

4   In the Location box, type the location of the event.

5   Select the All Day Event check box.

6   Click the End Time down arrow.

7   In the mini-calendar, click the end date for the event.

8   Click the Show Time As down arrow, and click the option that suits your event.

9   On the Standard toolbar in the event window, click the Save And Close button.

To create recurring appointments

1   In the Date Navigator, click the date of the recurring appointment.

2   In the Appointment Area, click the time slot in which you want the appointment to occur.

3   Type the name of the appointment, and press Enter.

4   Double-click the appointment.

5   On the Standard toolbar, click the Recurrence button.

6   In the Recurrence Pattern section, click the option that suits the appointment.

7   Select the check box of the day on which you want the appointment to occur.

8   In the Range Of Recurrence section, click the End After option.

9   In the End After box, type the number of weeks you want the appointment to recur.

10   Click OK.

To set reminders

1   In the Date Navigator, click the date on which you want to remind yourself of an appointment.

2   Double-click the appointment for which you want a reminder.

3   If necessary, click the Reminder check box.

4   Click the Reminder down arrow, scroll up, and click the time at which you want to remind yourself of the appointment.

5   Click the Reminder button.

6   Click OK.

7   On the Standard toolbar in the appointment window, click the Save And Close button.

To edit appointments

1   Double-click the appointment that you want to edit.

2   Click the Location box to change the location of the appointment.

3   Click the first Start Time down arrow.

4   In the mini-calendar, click another date to change the date of the appointment.

5   Click the Show Time As down arrow, and select the option that best suits your appointment.

6   On the Standard toolbar, in the appointment window, click to change the importance of the appointment.

7   In the bottom-right corner of the window, select the Private check box to make the appointment private.

8   On the Standard toolbar, in the appointment window, click the Save And Close button.

To delete normal appointments

1   Click the appointment that you want to delete.

2   On the Standard toolbar, click the Delete button.

Delete

To delete recurring appointments

1   Click the recurring appointment that you want delete.

2   On the Standard toolbar, click the Delete button.

3   In the alert box that appears, click OK.

To restore a deleted appointment

1   On the Outlook Bar, scroll to the Deleted Items shortcut.

2   Drag the appointment that you want to restore onto the Calendar shortcut on the Outlook Bar.

Deleted Items

3   On the Outlook Bar, click the Calendar shortcut.

4   On the Date Navigator, click the date to which you want to restore the appointment.

Calendar

To organize appointments by using categories

1   On the Standard toolbar, click the Organize button.

2   In the Organize pane, type a category name in the Create A New Category Called box.

3   Click the Create button.

4   In the Date Navigator, click a date, and in the Appointment window, scroll down and click an appointment.

5   In the Organize pane, click the Add button.

To organize appointments by using views

1   In the Organize pane, click the Using Views link.

2   In the Change Your View list, scroll to the bottom, and click By Category.

3   If necessary, click the plus sign (+) on the Planning gray bar.

4   In the Organize pane, click Recurring Appointments in the Change Your View list.

5   In the Change Your View list, click Active Appointments.

6   In the Change Your View list, scroll up to the top, and click Day/Week/Month.

7   On the Standard toolbar, click the Organize button.

To plan meetings

1   On the Navigation Bar, click a future date.

2   Click the time at which you want to have the meeting.

3   On the Standard toolbar, click the down arrow to the left of the New Appointment button, and click Meeting Request.

4   Click the To button.

5   Scroll down if necessary, and click the names of the people you want to attend the meeting, and click the Required button.

6   Click OK.

7   Click the Subject box, type the subject of the meeting, and press Tab.

8   In the Location box, type the location of the meeting.

9   Click the Memo box, and type a memo.

10   On the Standard toolbar in the meeting window, click the Send button.

To accept an invitation to a meeting

1   On the Outlook Bar, scroll up if necessary, and click the Inbox shortcut.

2   On the Standard toolbar, click the Send/Receive button.

3   Double-click the meeting request.

4   On the Standard toolbar in the meeting request window, click the Accept button.

5   In the alert box that appears, click OK.

6   On the Standard toolbar, click the Send/Receive button.

To print a Calendar

Print

1   On the Standard toolbar, click the Print button.

2   In the Print Style section, scroll down, and click a style.

3   In the Print Range section, click the Start down arrow.

4   Click the first day of the month you want to print.

5   In the Print Range section, click the End down arrow.

6   Click the last day on the calendar that you want to print.

7   Click OK.

To save a Calendar as a Web page

1   On the File menu, click Save As Web Page.

2   In the Duration section, click the Start Date down arrow, and click the first day of the month you want to save.

3   In the Duration section, click the End Date down arrow, and click the last day of the month you want to save.

4   In the Calendar Title box, type your name (if necessary), press the Spacebar, and type the title of the calendar.

5   Click the Browse button.

6   Click the Save In down arrow, and navigate to the folder in which you want to save the Web page.

7   In the File Name box, type the name of the page.

8   Click the Select button.

9   Click the Save button.

To integrate the Calendar with other Outlook components

1   In the Calendar, click the box that contains the text *Click Here To Add A New Task* in the TaskPad.

2   Type the task, and press Enter.

Lesson 6: Using Tasks

To create a task

Tasks

1   On the Outlook Bar, click the Tasks shortcut.

2   Click the box that contains the text *Click Here To Add A New Task*, and type the name of the new task.

3   To the right of the task that you just created, click the Due Date column.

4   Click the down arrow.

5   Click a due date for the task.

6   Press Enter.

To change task views

●   On the View menu, point to Current View, and click the desired view.

To add task details

1   Double-click the task to which you want to add details.

2   Enter information in the Task and Details tabs.

3   On the Standard toolbar in the task window, click the Save And Close button.

To sort tasks

● Click the column heading by which you want to sort.

To print a task list

Print

1 On the Standard toolbar, click the Print button.

2 Select the print style and, if you want, click the Page Setup button to choose options, such as text formatting, and different paper sizes and types.

3 When you are finished selecting options, click OK.

To organize tasks by using folders

1 On the Standard toolbar, click the Organize button.

2 Click the Using Folders link.

3 In the task list, select the task(s) that you want to move.

4 In the Organize pane, click the Move Task Selected Below To down arrow, and select the desired folder.

5 Click the Move button.

To organize tasks by using categories

1 On the Standard toolbar, click the Organize button.

2 Click the Using Categories link.

3 In the task list, select the task(s) that you want to move.

4 In the Organize pane, click the Add Tasks Selected Below To down arrow, and select the desired category.

5 In the Organize pane, click the Add button.

To assign a task

1 Select the task that you want to assign.

2 On the Standard toolbar in the task window, click the Assign Task button.

3 Click the To button.

4 In the Select Task Recipient dialog box, click the name of the person you're assigning the task to, and click the To button.

5 Click OK.

6 On the Standard toolbar in the task window, click the Send button.

To accept or decline a task

1 In the Inbox, double-click the task request that you want to accept or decline.

2 On the Standard toolbar in the task request window, click the Accept button or the Decline button.

Close

3 Click OK to send the response now, and in the top-right corner of the task request window, click the Close button.

Or

Click the Edit The Response Before Sending option, click OK to edit the response, type comments in the memo area, and then click the Send button.

To mark a task as complete

1   Open the task that you want to mark as complete.
2   Click the Details tab, and click the Date Completed down arrow.
3   Click the date on which the task was completed.
    Or
    Click the Status down arrow, and click Completed.
4   On the Standard toolbar in the task window, click the Save And Close button.

To manually record a task in the Journal

1   Drag the task that you want to record to the Journal folder in the Folder List or to the Journal shortcut on the Outlook Bar.
2   Enter the desired information in the Journal Entry window.
3   On the Standard toolbar in the journal entry window, click the Save And Close button.

To delete a task

1   Select the task that you want to delete.
2   On the Standard toolbar, click the Delete button.

Delete

Lesson 7: Using Notes

To create notes

1   On the Outlook Bar, click the Notes shortcut.

2   On the Standard toolbar, click the New Note button.
New Note
3   Type the text for the note.
4   In the top-right corner of the note, click the Close button.

To edit notes

1   In the Notes window, double-click the note.
2   Change the text in the note.

3   In the top-right corner of the note, click the Close button.
Close

To copy a note to a folder or to the desktop

1   Click the note that you want to copy.
2   Drag it to a folder or to the Windows desktop.

To move notes

1   On the Standard toolbar, click the Organize button.

2   Click the Move Note Selected Below To down arrow, and click the name of the folder to which you want to move the note. (Verify that the folder contains note items.)

3   Click the note that you want to move, and click the Move button.

To forward notes

1   Right-click the note that you want to forward.

2   On the shortcut menu that appears, click Forward.

3   In the To box, type an e-mail address, and complete the message as necessary.

4   Click the Send button.

To change the Notes view

1   On the Standard toolbar, click the Organize button.

2   In the Organize pane, click the Using Views link.

3   In the Change Your View list, click the desired view.

To change the color of notes

1   Right-click the desired note.

2   On the shortcut menu that appears, click Color.

3   Click the color that you want the note to appear.

To delete a note

1   Click the note that you want to delete.

Delete

2   On the Standard toolbar, click the Delete button.

Appendix

To install Outlook over a previous version

1   In the first Outlook 2000 Startup Wizard dialog box, click Next.

2   Click Next.

3   Click None Of The Above, and click Next.

4   Select the Internet Only (if the only e-mail connection you have is with an ISP) or Corporate Or Workgroup (if your e-mail system works with a network) option, and click Next.

5   If necessary, click Yes.

6   Click No to register later.

To install Outlook over a different e-mail program

1   In the first Outlook 2000 Startup Wizard dialog box, click Next.

2   Click None Of The Above, and click Next.

3   Select the Internet Only (if the only e-mail connection you have is with an ISP) or Corporate Or Workgroup (if your e-mail system works with a network) option, and click Next.

4   If necessary, click Yes.

5   Type your name, and click Next.

6   Type your e-mail address, and click Next.

7   Type the address for your incoming mail server, and press Tab.

8   Type the address for your outgoing mail server, and click Next.

9   Type your e-mail account name (if it is different than the one Outlook inserts), and press Tab. Your e-mail account name is usually the portion of your e-mail address that precedes the @ symbol.

10 Type your e-mail account password, verify that the Remember Password check box is selected, and then click Next.

11 Verify that the Connect Through My Local Area Network (LAN) option is selected, and click Next.

12 Click Finish.

13 If the Internet Accounts dialog box appears, click the Close button.

Close

14 To use Outlook as the default e-mail manager, click Yes.

15 Click No to register later.

To create a user profile

1   On the Windows taskbar, click the Start button, point to Settings, and then click Control Panel.

2   Double-click the Mail icon, and click the Show Profiles button in the dialog box.

Mail

3   In the Mail dialog box, click the Add button.

4   Select the information services that you want to use with the profile, and click Next.

5   In the Profile Name box, type a name, and click Next.

6   If necessary, in the next wizard dialog box, click Next.

7   In the last wizard dialog box, click Finish.

8   Click the Close button to close the Mail dialog box.

Close

9   In the top-right corner of the Control Panel, click the Close button.

To add an information service

1   On the Tools menu, click Services.

2   Click the Add button.

3   Select the service that you want to add, and click OK.

4   Insert the Outlook 2000 or Office 2000 CD-ROM, and click OK.

5   Click OK to close the Services dialog box.

To modify an information service

1   On the Tools menu, click Services.

2   Click the name of the service that you want to change, and then click the Properties button. The dialog box that appears next will depend on which service you selected.

3   Change the properties as needed, and click OK.

4   Click OK to close the Services dialog box.

To remove an information service

1   On the Tools menu, click Services.

2   Click the name of the service that you no longer want, and click the Remove button.

3   Click Yes to confirm the removal of the service, and click OK to close the Services dialog box.

To select a user profile when Outlook starts

1   On the Tools menu, click Options, and click the Mail Services tab.

2   In the Startup Settings section of the Options dialog box, click either the Prompt For A Profile To Be Used option or the Always Use This Profile option. If you select the Always Use This Profile option, you must select a profile from the list that appears.

3   Click OK.

Index

A

accepting
invitations to meetings, C.14
tasks, 6.13–6.15, C.16
accessing Favorites, 1.13, C.2
adding
categories to the Master Category
List, C.9
folders to Favorites, 1.12, C.2
information services, A.8–A.9,
C.19–C.20
Outlook Bar shortcut to Web
pages, 5.25
signatures to messages,
3.12–3.14, C.6
task details, 6.4–6.6, C.15
Web sites to Favorites, 1.12, C.1
Address Book
button, 4.21
defined, 4.21, 4.34
sending e-mail with, 4.21–4.23,
C.10
window, 4.22
Address Cards
defined, 4.2, 4.34
view, 4.14
addressing messages, 2.2–2.4, C.3
Appointment area, 5.3, 5.4, 5.27
appointments
about, 5.2–5.3
creating recurring, 5.11–5.13,
C.12
defined, 5.1, 5.27
deleting, 5.16–5.17, C.13
editing, 5.14–5.15, C.13
organizing with categories, 5.17,
C.13
organizing with views,
5.18–5.19, C.13–C.14
restoring, C.13
scheduling, 5.8–5.11, C.11
viewing with Exchange Server,
5.19

appointments, *continued*
window components, 5.9
Archive dialog box, 3.32
archiving messages, 3.31–3.32, C.7
assigning
items to multiple categories,
4.17–4.18, C.9
tasks to others, 6.11–6.13, C.16
attaching
files to messages, 2.5–2.7, C.3
notes to e-mail, 7.7
attachments
defined, 2.5, 2.17
file size, 2.7
icons, 2.5
opening in Preview Pane, 2.9
printing, 2.5, 2.13, C.3
AutoPreview
defined, 2.17
turning on or off, C.4
using, 2.10

B

Bell icon, 5.10
buttons
Address Book, 4.21
Cc, 2.2
Close, 1.14
Copy, 4.9
Delete, 2.16
Display Map Of Address, 4.4
down arrow, 1.5
Flag For Follow Up, 2.3
Font Color, 3.9
Importance: High, 2.6
Importance: Low, 2.6
Insert File, 2.7
Maximize, 7.5
Microsoft Outlook Help, 1.15
Minimize, 1.2, 7.5
Move To Folder, 3.24
New Appointment, 5.10
New Contact, 4.5

buttons, *continued*
New Mail Message, 2.3
New Message To Contact, 4.23
New Note, 7.3
New Task, 6.2
Paste All, 4.9
Print, 2.12, 5.23
Push Pin, 1.14
Reminder, 5.14
Restore, 7.5
Save, 2.17
Save And New, 4.7
Send, 2.2
Send/Receive, 2.8
Tasks, 5.25
To, 2.2
up arrow, 1.5
By Category view, 4.14, 7.8
By Color view, 7.8
By Company view, 4.14
By Conversation Topic view, 3.15
By Follow-Up Flag view, 3.15, 4.14
By Location view, 4.14
By Sender view, 3.15

C

Calendar
about, 1.7, 1.8
changing views, 5.5–5.7, C.11
defined, 5.1, 5.27
displaying dates in, 5.5
icon, 5.3
integrating with Outlook
    components, 5.25–5.27, C.15
navigating in, 5.3–5.5, C.11
printing, 5.22–5.23, C.14
saving as Web page, 5.23–5.25,
    C.15
sections, 5.4
sending via e-mail, 5.24
categories
assigning items to multiple,
    4.17–4.18, C.9
creating, C.9
defined, 4.15, 4.34
options, 3.4
organizing appointments with,
    5.17, C.13
organizing contacts with,
    4.15–4.16, C.9

categories, *continued*
organizing tasks with, 6.10, C.16
sorting with, C.9
Cc button, 2.2
Change Your View list, 3.16
changing
Calendar views, 5.5–5.7, C.11
color of notes, 7.8–7.11, C.18
information services, A.8–A.9
Tasks view, 6.4, C.15
views, 4.15
checking e-mail messages, 2.7–2.8,
    C.4
choosing Office Assistant, 1.14
Clipboard, 4.8–4.11, C.8
Clipboard toolbar, defined, 4.9,
    4.34
Close button, 1.14
closing
Folder List, 1.5
notes, 7.4
Office Assistant, 1.2
Outlook, 1.2
color, changing in notes, 7.8–7.11,
    C.18
color-coding, message headers,
    3.27–3.28, C.7
composing
messages, 2.2–2.4, C.3
messages with templates, 2.5
conditions, filtering, 3.20
contact information. *See* vCard
contact record, 4.5, 4.34
contacts
creating letters for, 4.29–4.33,
    C.11
creating, 4.5–4.7, C.7
defined, 4.1, 4.34
deleting, 4.11–4.12, C.8
editing, 4.5–4.7, C.7
entering multiple for one
    company, 4.8, C.8
icon, 4.12
linking, 4.7
mapping, 4.4
moving into folders, C.8
opening Web browsers in, 4.7
options, 3.4
organizing with categories,
    4.15–4.16, C.9

contacts, *continued*
organizing with views, 4.13–4.15
pane, 4.2
restoring, 4.11–4.12, C.8
sending e-mail with, 4.23–4.24,
    C.10
sending via e-mail, 4.24–4.28,
    C.10
sorting, 4.19–4.21, C.10
viewing, 4.2–4.4, C.7
window, 4.3
Contacts folder
about, 1.7, 1.9
defined, 4.1, 4.34
Copy button, 4.9
copying, notes, 7.5–7.6, C.17
Corporate Or Workgroup mail
    configuration, A.6
creating
appointments, 5.10–5.11
categories, C.9
contacts, 4.5–4.7, C.7
drafts, 2.17
events, 5.10–5.11
folders, 3.21–3.23, C.7, C.8
letters with Letter Wizard,
    4.29–4.33, C.11
notes, 7.2–7.4, C.17
recurring appointments,
    5.11–5.13, C.12
tasks, 6.2–6.3, C.15
user profiles, A.5–A.8, C.19
customizing
forwarding, 3.7
menus, 5.7
message appearance, 3.6–3.10,
    C.5–C.6
recurring appointment days, 5.13
replying, 3.7
toolbars, 5.7
views, 3.14–3.16
Work Week, 5.5

D

Date Navigator, 5.3
defined, 5.4, 5.27
declining, tasks, 6.13–6.15, C.16
Delete button, 2.16
Deleted Items folder
about, 1.7, 1.10
defined, 2.16, 2.17

Deleted Items folder, *continued*
   emptying, C.5
   icon, 4.11
deleted messages, restoring, 2.16
deleting
   appointments, 5.16–5.17, C.13
   categories from Master Category
     List, C.9
   contacts, 4.11–4.12, C.8
   messages, 2.16–2.17, C.5
   notes, 7.11, C.18
   tasks, 6.19, C.17
Detailed Address Cards view, 4.14
displaying
   dates in Calendar, 5.5
   events, 5.11
   folders with Folders List,
     1.13–1.14, C.2
   groups in Outlook Bar, C.1
   new message window, 2.3
   Office Assistant, 1.15, C.2
Display Map Of Address button,
   4.4
down arrow button, 1.5
downloading junk e-mail filters,
   3.29
drafts
   creating, 2.17
   defined, 2.18
   retrieving, 2.17, C.5
   saving, 2.17, C.5
Drafts folder, about, 1.7

E

editing
   appointments, 5.14–5.15, C.13
   contacts, 4.5–4.7, C.7
   notes, 7.4, C.17
e-mail. *See also* **messages**
   attaching notes, 7.7
   defined, 2.1, 2.18
   formatting, 3.6–3.10, C.6
   junk, 3.2, 3.33
   messages, checking, 2.7–2.8, C.4
   receiving vCards via, 4.28–4.29,
     C.10–C.11
   sending Calendar via, 5.24
   sending contacts via, 4.24–4.28,
     C.10
   sending with Address Book,
     4.21–4.23, C.10

e-mail, *continued*
   sending with contacts, 4.23–4.24,
     C.10
   specifying options, 3.2–3.6,
     C.5–C.6
emptying
   Deleted Items folder, 4.11, C.5
entering multiple contacts, 4.8, C.8
events
   defined, 5.1, 5.27
   scheduling, 5.8–5.11, C.12
Exchange Server, viewing
   appointments with, 5.19
expanding menus, 1.5, C.1

F

Favorites folder
   about, 1.7
   accessing folders and Web sites
     in, 1.13, C.2
   adding folders to, 1.12, C.2
   adding Web sites to, 1.12, C.1
   using, 1.12–1.13
files
   attaching to messages, 2.5–2.7,
     C.3
   defined, 2.5, 2.18
Filter dialog box, 3.21
filtering
   conditions, 3.20
   defined, 3.2, 3.33
   junk e-mail, 3.29–3.31, C.7
   views, 3.19–3.21, C.6
finding messages, 2.13–2.14, C.5
Flag For Follow Up button, 2.3
flagging
   defined, 2.3, 2.18
   messages, 2.3, C.3
Folder Banner, 1.3, 1.4, 1.16
Folder List
   about, 1.3, 1.4
   closing, 1.5
   defined, 1.13, 1.16
   using, 1.13–1.14, C.2
folders
   accessing in Favorites, 1.13, C.2
   adding to Favorites, 1.12, C.2
   creating, 3.21–3.23, C.7, C.8
   defined, 1.16
   moving contacts into, C.8

folders, *continued*
   moving messages between,
     3.24–3.26, C.7
   organizing tasks with, 6.8–6.9,
     C.16
Font Color button, 3.9
Format menu, using, 3.7
formatted text, defined, 3.6, 3.33
formatting
   e-mail, 3.6–3.10, C.6
   signatures, 3.12
forwarding
   defined, 2.10, 2.18
   messages, 2.10–2.11, C.4
   notes, 7.6–7.7, C.18
   options, 3.7

G

glossaries
   Appendix, A.10
   Lesson 1, 1.16
   Lesson 2, 2.17–2.18
   Lesson 3, 3.33
   Lesson 4, 4.34
   Lesson 5, 5.27–5.28
   Lesson 6, 6.20
   Lesson 7, 7.12

H

Help. *See* **Office Assistant**
hiding Office Assistant, 1.15, C.2
High Priority flag in task lists, 7.6
HTML, message format, 3.6

I

Icons view, 7.8
icons
   for attachments, 2.5
   Bell, 5.10
   Calendar, 5.3
   Contacts, 4.12
   defined, 2.5, 2.18
   Deleted Items, 4.11
   Mail, A.6
   Page, 4.9
   Tasks, 6.2
Importance: High button, 2.6
Importance: Low button, 2.6
importants
   accessing Office Clipboard, 4.9

importants, *continued*
    Corporate Or Workgroup, and
        Address Book, 4.21
    Corporate Or Workgroup setting,
        2.14
    Exchange Server and
        appointments, 5.19
    folder content requirements, 3.22
    information services
        requirements, A.8
    Internet Explorer and Calendar,
        5.25
    printing attachments, 2.13
    recalling messages and server
        settings, 2.14
    Reminder dialog box, 5.13
    sending e-mail, 2.4
    server types and messages, 2.8
    setting up Corporate Or
        Workgroup mail
        configuration, A.6
    setting up Microsoft Exchange
        Server or Microsoft Mail, A.7
    user profiles in Windows and
        Outlook, A.5
    vCards and VcViewer program,
        4.24
importing, archive files, 3.32
Inbox
    about, 1.7
    defined, 2.7, 2.18
information services
    about, A.8–A.9
    adding C.19–C.20
    defined, A.5, A.10
    removing, C.20
    using, A.8–A.9
Insert File button, 2.7
inserting vCards in signatures,
    4.26–4.27, C.10
installing
    Outlook 2000 over different
        e-mail programs, A.3–A.5,
        C.18–C.19
    Outlook 2000 over previous
        versions, A.2–A.3, C.18
integrating Calendar with Outlook
    components, 5.25–5.27, C.15
interoffice mail, defined, 2.8, 2.18
invitations, accepting, C.14

items, 1.3, 1.4
    assigning to multiple categories,
        4.17–4.18, C.9
    defined, 2.5

J

Journal folder
    about, 1.7
    defined, 6.16, 6.20
    recording tasks in, 6.16–6.19,
        C.17
junk e-mail
    defined, 3.2, 3.33
    filtering, 3.29–3.31, C.7

L

Last Seven Days view, 3.15, 7.8
Lesson Glossaries
    Appendix, A.10
    Lesson 1, 1.16
    Lesson 2, 2.17–2.18
    Lesson 3, 3.33
    Lesson 4, 4.34
    Lesson 5, 5.27–5.28
    Lesson 6, 6.20
    Lesson 7, 7.12
Lesson Wrap-Ups
    Lesson 1, 1.16
    Lesson 2, 2.17
    Lesson 3, 3.33
    Lesson 4, 4.33
    Lesson 5, 5.27
    Lesson 6, 6.19–6.20
    Lesson 7, 7.12
Letter Wizard, creating letters with,
    4.29–4.33, C.11
linking contacts, 4.7

M

Mail icon, A.6
mail queue, defined, 2.8, 2.18
mapping contacts addresses, 4.4
marking tasks complete, 6.15–6.16,
    C.17
Master Categories List
    defined, 4.18, 4.34
    deleting categories, C.9
    modifying, 4.18–4.19, C.9
    resetting, C.9
Maximize button, 7.5

maximizing notes, 7.4
meetings
    about, 5.2–5.3
    defined, 5.1, 5.27
    planning, 5.19–5.21, C.14
    reserving resources for, 5.22
Menu bar, 1.3, 5.3
menus
    customizing, 1.4, 5.7
    expanded and short, 1.5
    expanding, C.1
message area, 2.2
message headers, 2.8
    color-coding, 3.27–3.28, C.7
    selecting multiple, 2.16
Message Options dialog box,
    3.3–3.4
message priority, setting, 2.6, C.3
messages
    adding signatures to, 3.12–3.14,
        C.6
    addressing, 2.2–2.4, C.3
    archiving, 3.31–3.32, C.7
    attaching files to, 2.5–2.7, C.3
    checking, 2.7–2.8, C.3
    color-coding headers, 3.27–3.28,
        C.7
    composing, 2.2–2.4, C.3
    composing with templates, 2.5
    customizing appearance,
        3.6–3.10
    defined, 2.18
    deleting, 2.16–2.17, C.5
    expiring, 3.4
    filtering junk e-mail, 3.29–3.31
    finding, 2.13–2.14, C.5
    flagging, 2.3, C.3
    HTML, 3.6
    moving between folders,
        3.24–3.26, C.7
    Plain Text, 3.7
    printing, 2.11–2.12, C.4
    reading, 2.9, C.4
    recalling, 2.14–2.16, C.5
    receiving vCards via, 4.28–4.29,
        C.10–C.11
    replying and forwarding,
        2.10–2.11, C.4
    saving as templates, 2.5, C.3
    saving drafts of, 2.17, C.5
    sending, 2.2–2.4, C.3

messages, *continued*
sending contacts via, 4.24–4.28, C.10
sending to other e-mail applications, 3.5
sending with Address Book, 4.21–4.23, C.10
sending with contacts, 4.23–4.24, C.10
sorting, 3.17–3.18, C.6
with Web site addresses, 2.3
Messages view, 3.15
Messages With view, 3.15
Message Timeline view, 3.15
Microsoft Exchange Server
defined, 2.8, 2.18
setting up, A.7
Microsoft Fax, A.8
Microsoft Mail, setting up, A.7
Microsoft Outlook Help button, 1.15
Microsoft Outlook Rich Text, 3.6
Minimize button, 1.2
modifying the Master Category List, 4.18–4.19
MOUS objectives
accept and decline tasks, 6.13
add and remove meeting attendees, 5.20
add a signature to mail, 3.12
address mail by entering text, 2.2
archive mail messages, 3.31
assign items to a category, 4.17
assign tasks to others, 6.11
book office resources directly, 5.22
change the view for tasks, 6.4
compose mail by entering text, 2.2
configure basic mail print options, 2.11
configure Calendar print option, 5.22
create, edit, and delete contacts, 4.5, 4.11
create and edit notes, 7.2, 7.4
create and update one-time tasks, 6.2
create and use Office documents inside Outlook 2000, 4.29
create folders, 3.21

MOUS objectives, *continued*
create tasks from other Outlook components, 5.25
customize menu and task bars, 5.7
customize notes, 7.8
customize the calendar view, 5.5
customize the look of mail, 3.6
filter a view, 3.19
flag mail messages, 2.3
integrate and use mail with other Outlook components, 4.21, 4.23, 4.24
integrate Calendar with other Outlook components, 5.25
link activities to contacts, 4.7
manually record an activity in the Journal, 6.16–6.19
modify the Outlook Master Categories List, 4.18
move items between Outlook components, 1.3, 1.6
navigate within Calendar, 5.3
navigate within mail, 2.9
organize and view notes, 7.7
organize contacts by category, 4.15
organize tasks using categories, 6.10
plan meetings involving others, 5.19
print in Calendar, 5.22
print mail, 2.11
read mail, 2.9
save a personal or team Calendar as a Web page, 5.23
schedule appointments and events, 5.8
schedule multiday events, 5.11
schedule recurring appointments, 5.11
send contact information via e-mail, 4.24
send mail, 2.2
set reminders, 5.13
set viewing options, 3.14
sort contacts using fields, 4.19
sort information using categories, 4.15
sort mail, 3.17

MOUS objectives, *continued*
use address book to address mail, 4.21
use mail features (forward, reply, recall), 2.10, 2.14
use mail templates to compose mail, 2.5
use Outlook Help and Office Assistant, 1.14
use the Office Clipboard, 4.8
work with attachments, 2.5
Move To Folder button, 3.24
moving
contacts into folders, C.8
messages between folders, 3.24–3.26, C.7
notes, C.18
My Computer folder, about, 1.7
My Shortcuts group, 1.11

N
naming Web pages, 5.24
navigating
in Calendar, 5.3–5.5, C.11
in Outlook, 1.3–1.6
New Appointment button, 5.10
New Contact button, 4.5
New in Outlook 2000
adding Outlook Bar shortcut to Web pages, 5.25
e-mail message formats, 3.7
Favorites folder, 1.12
meeting schedules, 5.19
Office Clipboard, 4.9
saving Calendar as Web page, 5.23
short menus, 1.4
vCard duplicates, 4.28
New Mail Message button, 2.3
New Message To Contact button, 4.23
new message window, displaying, 2.3
New Note button, 7.3
New Task button, 6.2
notes
changing color, 7.8–7.11, C.18
changing views, 7.10, C.18
closing, 7.4
copying, 7.5–7.6, C.17

notes, *continued*
  creating, 7.2–7.4, C.17
  defined, 7.1, 7.12
  deleting, 7.11, C.18
  editing, 7.4, C.17
  forwarding, 7.6–7.7, C.18
  maximizing, 7.4
  moving, C.18
  organizing, 7.7–7.11
Notes List view, 7.8

O

Office Assistant
  choosing, 1.14
  closing, 1.2
  defined, 1.14, 1.16
  using, 1.14–1.15, C.2
Office Clipboard
  defined, 4.9, 4.34
  using, 4.8–4.11, C.8
on/off toggles, 2.10
Open envelope, 2.9
opening
  attachments in Preview Pane, 2.9
  templates, 2.5, C.3
  Web browsers in contacts, 4.7
options
  customizing in e-mail, 3.2–3.6,
    C.5–C.6
  forwarding, 3.7
  replying, 3.7
  setting for views, 3.14–3.16, C.6
  tasks, 6.5
organizing
  appointments with categories,
    5.17, C.13
  appointments with views,
    5.18–5.19, C.13–C.14
  contacts with categories,
    4.15–4.16, C.9
  contacts with views, 4.13–4.15
  notes, 7.7–7.11
  tasks with categories, 6.10, C.16
  tasks with folders, 6.8–6.9, C.16
  Other Shortcuts group, 1.11
Outbox folder
  about, 1.7
  defined, 2.4, 2.18
Outlook 2000
  closing, 1.2
  folders in, 1.7

Outlook 2000, *continued*
  installing over different e-mail
    programs, A.3–A.5,
    C.18–C.19
  installing over previous versions,
    A.2–A.3, C.18
  navigating in, 1.3–1.6
  setting up, A.1–A.10
  starting, 1.6, 1.2, C.1
Outlook 2000 Startup Wizard,
    A.1–A.5
Outlook Bar
  about, 1.3
  adding to Web pages, 5.25
  defined, 1.16
  displaying groups, C.1
  scrolling, C.1
  using, 1.6–1.12, C.1
Outlook Today folder, 1.8
Outlook window, 1.2
owner, defined, 6.11, 6.20
ownership, defined, 6.11, 6.20

P

Page icon, 4.9
Paste All button, 4.9
Phone List view, 4.14
Plain Text, 3.7
planning, meetings, 5.19–5.21, C.14
Preview Pane, 1.3, 1.4, 2.9
  opening attachments in, 2.9
  using, 2.10
Print button, 2.12
Print dialog box, 2.12
printing
  attachments, 2.5, 2.13, C.4
  Calendar, 5.22–5.23, C.14
  messages, 2.11–2.12, C.4
  multiple copies, 2.12
  task lists, 6.8, C.16
Priority. *See* **High Priority flag in**
    task lists; Importance: High
    button; Importance: Low
    button
Push Pin button, 1.14
Putting It All Together
  Lesson 1, 1.17
  Lesson 2, 2.19
  Lesson 3, 3.34
  Lesson 4, 4.35
  Lesson 5, 5.28

Putting It All Together, *continued*
  Lesson 6, 6.21
  Lesson 7, 7.12

Q

Quick Quizzes
  Lesson 1, 1.17
  Lesson 2, 2.19
  Lesson 3, 3.34
  Lesson 4, 4.34–4.35
  Lesson 5, 5.28
  Lesson 6, 6.20
  Lesson 7, 7.12

R

reading messages, 2.9, C.4
recalling
  defined, 2.14, 2.18
  messages, 2.14–2.16, C.5
Recall This Message dialog box,
    2.15
receiving, vCards via e-mail,
    4.28–4.29, C.10–C.11
recording tasks in Journal,
    6.16–6.19, C.17
recurring, defined, 5.11, 5.28
recurring appointments, creating,
    5.11–5.13, C.12
Reminder button, 5.14
reminders, setting, 5.13–5.14, C.12
removing, information services,
    A.8–A.9, C.20
replying
  defined, 2.10, 2.18
  options, 3.7
  to messages, 2.10–2.11, C.4
reserving meeting resources, 5.22
resetting, from Master Category
    List, C.9
Restore button, 7.5
restoring
  contacts, 4.11–4.12, C.8
  deleted appointments, C.13
  deleted messages, 2.16
retrieving drafts, 2.17, C.5
Rules Wizard, 3.24–3.26

S

Save And New button, 4.7
Save button, 2.17

saving
   Calendar as Web page,
      5.23–5.25, C.15
   drafts, 2.17, C.5
   messages as templates, 2.5, C.3
scheduling
   appointments, 5.8–5.11, C.11
   events, 5.8–5.11, C.12
scrolling, Outlook Bar, C.1
selecting
   multiple message headers, 2.16
   user profiles when Outlook
      starts, A.10, C.20
Send button, 2.2
sending
   contact information via e-mail,
      4.24–4.28, C.10
   e-mail with Address Book,
      4.21–4.23, C.10
   e-mail with contacts, 4.23–4.24,
      C.10
   messages, 2.2–2.4, C.3
   messages to other e-mail
      applications, 3.5
   schedules via e-mail, 5.24
   vCards via e-mail, 4.24–4.28,
      C.10
Send/Receive button, 2.8
Sensitivity, 3.3
Sent Items folder
   about, 1.7
   defined, 2.13, 2.18
Sent To view, 3.15
setting
   Journal tracking, 6.16
   message priority, 2.6, C.3
   reminders, 5.13–5.14, C.12
   view options, 3.14–3.16, C.5
setting up
   Corporate Or Workgroup mail
      configuration, A.6
   Microsoft Exchange Server or
      Microsoft Mail, A.7
   Outlook, A.1–A.10
shortcut
   about, 1.3, 1.4
   adding to Web pages, 5.25
   defined, 1.16, 5.25, 5.28
   group, 1.7

signatures
   adding to messages, 3.12–3.14,
      C.6
   defined, 3.2, 3.33
   inserting vCards in, 4.26–4.27,
      C.10
sorting
   with categories, C.9
   contacts, 4.19–4.21, C.10
   messages, 3.17–3.18, C.6
   tasks, 6.6–6.8, C.16
sound cards and reminders, 5.14
Standard toolbar, 1.3
starting Outlook, 1.2, C.1
Startup Wizard, using, A.1–A.5
stationery
   defined, 3.10, 3.33
   using, 3.10–3.12, C.6
Status bar, 1.3, 1.4
student notes
   appointment conflicts, 5.13
   attaching notes to e-mail, 7.7
   attachment icons, 2.5
   Bell icon, 5.10
   changing Notes view, 7.10
   changing task due date, 6.8
   choosing Office Assistant, 1.14
   closing Find Items, 2.14
   closing Folder List, 1.5
   closing notes, 7.4
   closing Office Assistant, 1.2, 4.30
   closing Outlook, 1.2
   customizing Work Week, 5.5
   Delete All Occurrences, 5.16
   Deleted Items folder, 4.11
   displaying events, 5.11
   displaying new message window,
      2.3
   displaying task request, 6.11
   dragging notes onto desktop, 7.5
   filter vs. sort, 3.19
   formatting signatures, 3.12
   including Web addresses in
      messages, 2.3
   maximizing notes, 7.4
   menu size, 1.5
   modem speed and attachments,
      2.7
   on/off toggles, 2.10
   opening Web browsers from a
      contact window, 4.7

student notes, continued
   Outbox capabilities, 2.4
   phone number format, 4.6
   printing attachments, 2.5
   printing multiple copies, 2.12
   restoring deleted messages, 2.16
   selecting multiple message
      headers, 2.16
   sending messages to other e-mail
      applications, 3.5
   sending schedules via e-mail,
      5.24
   Send/Receive, 2.8
   setting Journal tracking, 6.16
   shortcut groups, 1.7
   sound cards for reminders, 5.14
   To box, 2.4
   Undo Move, 3.25
   using To button, 4.23
Subject box, 2.2

T
task lists
   defined, 6.1, 6.20
   printing, 6.8, C.16
Task Pad, 5.3
   defined, 5.4, 5.28
tasks
   accepting, 6.13–6.15, C.16
   adding details, 6.4–6.8, C.15
   assigning to others, 6.11–6.13,
      C.16
   creating, 6.2–6.3, C.15
   declining, 6.13–6.15, C.16
   defined, 6.1, 6.20
   deleting, 6.19, C.17
   marking complete, 6.15–6.16,
      C.17
   options, 6.5
   organizing with categories, 6.10,
      C.16
   organizing with folders, 6.8–6.9,
      C.16
   recording in Journal, 6.16–6.19,
      C.17
   sorting, 6.6–6.8, C.16
Tasks button, 5.25
Tasks folder, 5.26
   about, 1.7, 1.9
   changing views, 6.4, C.15
   defined, 6.2, 6.20

Tasks folder, *continued*
  dialog box, 6.4
  icon, 6.2
  window, 6.2
templates
  composing with, 2.5
  opening, 2.5, C.3
  saving messages as, 2.5, C.3
tips
  Calendar printing format, 5.23
  changing appointment time, 5.15
  changing recurring appointment
    days, 5.13
  creating notes, 7.3
  displaying dates in Calendar, 5.5
  download junk e-mail filters,
    3.29
  importing archive files, 3.32
  linking contacts, 4.7
  mapping contacts, 4.4
  Microsoft Fax service, A.8
  natural language in Outlook, 6.5
  replying to and forwarding
    messages, 2.11
  revising meetings, 5.20
  searching message text, 2.14
  Sent Items folder alternatives,
    3.25
  using Format menu, 3.7
Title bar, 1.3
To box, 2.4

To button, 2.2
  using, 4.23
toolbars
  customizing, 5.7
  Standard, 1.3
Tools menu, 1.5

U

Undo Move, 3.25
Unread Messages view, 3.15
up arrow button, 1.5
user profiles
  creating, A.5–A.8, C.19
  defined, A.5, A.10
  selecting when Outlook starts,
    A.10, C.20

V

vCard
  defined, 4.1, 4.34
  inserting in signatures,
    4.26–4.27, C.10
  receiving via e-mail, 4.28–4.29,
    C.10–C.11
  sending via e-mail, 4.24–4.28,
    C.10
viewing
  appointments with Exchange
    Server, 5.19
  contacts, 4.2–4.4, C.7
  with Folders List, 1.13–1.14, C.2

views
  changing, 4.15
  changing in Calendar, 5.5–5.7,
    C.11
  changing Notes, 7.10, C.18
  changing Tasks, 6.4, C.15
  customizing, 3.16
  defined, 3.14, 3.33
  filtering, 3.19–3.21, C.6
  lists, 4.14
  options, 3.14–3.16
  organizing appointments with,
    5.18–5.19, C.13
  organizing contacts with,
    4.13–4.15, C.8

W

**Web browsers, opening from a
  contact window, 4.7**
Web pages
  adding Outlook Bar shortcut to,
    5.25
  naming, 5.24
  saving Calendar as, 5.23–5.25,
    C.15
Web site addresses, in e-mail, 2.3
Web sites
  accessing in Favorites, 1.13, C.2
  adding to Favorites, 1.12, C.1
Work Week
  customizing, 5.5
  defined, 5.5, 5.28

ActiveEducation and Microsoft Press

Microsoft Outlook 2000 Step by Step Courseware has been created by the professional trainers and writers at ActiveEducation, Inc., to the exacting standards you've come to expect from Microsoft Press. Together, we are pleased to present this training guide.

ActiveEducation creates top-quality information technology training content that teaches essential computer skills for today's workplace. ActiveEducation courses are designed to provide the most effective training available and to help people become more productive computer users. Each ActiveEducation course, including this book, undergoes rigorous quality control, instructional design, and technical review procedures to ensure that the course is instructionally and technically superior in content and approach.

ActiveEducation (*www.activeeducation.com*) courses are available in book form and on the Internet.

Microsoft Press is the book publishing division of Microsoft Corporation, the leading publisher of information about Microsoft products and services. Microsoft Press is dedicated to providing the highest quality computer books and multimedia training and reference tools that make using Microsoft software easier, more enjoyable, and more productive.

See clearly—
now!

Here's the remarkable, *visual* way to quickly find answers about the powerfully integrated features of the Microsoft Office 2000 applications. Microsoft Press® AT A GLANCE books let you focus on particular tasks and show you, with clear, numbered steps, the easiest way to get them done right now. Put Office 2000 to work today with AT A GLANCE learning solutions, made by Microsoft.

- MICROSOFT OFFICE 2000 PROFESSIONAL AT A GLANCE
- MICROSOFT WORD 2000 AT A GLANCE
- MICROSOFT EXCEL 2000 AT A GLANCE
- MICROSOFT POWERPOINT® 2000 AT A GLANCE
- MICROSOFT ACCESS 2000 AT A GLANCE
- MICROSOFT FRONTPAGE® 2000 AT A GLANCE
- MICROSOFT PUBLISHER 2000 AT A GLANCE
- MICROSOFT OFFICE 2000 SMALL BUSINESS AT A GLANCE
- MICROSOFT PHOTODRAW™ 2000 AT A GLANCE
- MICROSOFT OUTLOOK® 2000 AT A GLANCE

mspress.microsoft.com

up! Step Step

STEP BY STEP books provide quick and easy self-training—to help you learn to use the powerful word processing, spreadsheet, database, presentation, communication, and Internet components of Microsoft Office 2000—both individually and together. The easy-to-follow lessons present clear objectives and real-world business examples, with numerous screen shots and illustrations. Put Office 2000 to work today with STEP BY STEP learning solutions, made by Microsoft.

- MICROSOFT® OFFICE 2000 8-IN-1 STEP BY STEP
- MICROSOFT WORD 2000 STEP BY STEP
- MICROSOFT EXCEL 2000 STEP BY STEP
- MICROSOFT POWERPOINT® 2000 STEP BY STEP
- MICROSOFT PUBLISHER 2000 STEP BY STEP
- MICROSOFT ACCESS 2000 STEP BY STEP
- MICROSOFT FRONTPAGE® 2000 STEP BY STEP
- MICROSOFT OUTLOOK® 2000 STEP BY STEP

mspress.microsoft.com

MICROSOFT LICENSE AGREEMENT

Book Companion CD

IMPORTANT—READ CAREFULLY: This Microsoft End-User License Agreement ("EULA") is a legal agreement between you (either an individual or an entity) and Microsoft Corporation for the Microsoft product identified above, which includes computer software and may include associated media, printed materials, and "online" or electronic documentation ("SOFTWARE PRODUCT"). Any component included within the SOFTWARE PRODUCT that is accompanied by a separate End-User License Agreement shall be governed by such agreement and not the terms set forth below. By installing, copying, or otherwise using the SOFTWARE PRODUCT, you agree to be bound by the terms of this EULA. If you do not agree to the terms of this EULA, you are not authorized to install, copy, or otherwise use the SOFT-WARE PRODUCT; you may, however, return the SOFTWARE PRODUCT, along with all printed materials and other items that form a part of the Microsoft product that includes the SOFTWARE PRODUCT, to the place you obtained them for a full refund.

SOFTWARE PRODUCT LICENSE

The SOFTWARE PRODUCT is protected by United States copyright laws and international copyright treaties, as well as other intellectual property laws and treaties. The SOFTWARE PRODUCT is licensed, not sold.

1. **GRANT OF LICENSE.** This EULA grants you the following rights:

   a. **Software Product.** You may install and use one copy of the SOFTWARE PRODUCT on a single computer. The primary user of the computer on which the SOFTWARE PRODUCT is installed may make a second copy for his or her exclusive use on a portable computer.

   b. **Storage/Network Use.** You may also store or install a copy of the SOFTWARE PRODUCT on a storage device, such as a network server, used only to install or run the SOFTWARE PRODUCT on your other computers over an internal network; however, you must acquire and dedicate a license for each separate computer on which the SOFTWARE PRODUCT is installed or run from the storage device. A license for the SOFTWARE PRODUCT may not be shared or used concurrently on different computers.

   c. **License Pak.** If you have acquired this EULA in a Microsoft License Pak, you may make the number of additional copies of the computer software portion of the SOFTWARE PRODUCT authorized on the printed copy of this EULA, and you may use each copy in the manner specified above. You are also entitled to make a corresponding number of secondary copies for portable computer use as specified above.

   d. **Sample Code.** Solely with respect to portions, if any, of the SOFTWARE PRODUCT that are identified within the SOFTWARE PRODUCT as sample code (the "SAMPLE CODE"):

      i. **Use and Modification.** Microsoft grants you the right to use and modify the source code version of the SAMPLE CODE, *provided* you comply with subsection (d)(iii) below. You may not distribute the SAMPLE CODE, or any modified version of the SAMPLE CODE, in source code form.

      ii. **Redistributable Files.** Provided you comply with subsection (d)(iii) below, Microsoft grants you a nonexclusive, royalty-free right to reproduce and distribute the object code version of the SAMPLE CODE and of any modified SAMPLE CODE, other than SAMPLE CODE, or any modified version thereof, designated as not redistributable in the Readme file that forms a part of the SOFTWARE PRODUCT (the "Non-Redistributable Sample Code"). All SAMPLE CODE other than the Non-Redistributable Sample Code is collectively referred to as the "REDISTRIBUTABLES."

      iii. **Redistribution Requirements.** If you redistribute the REDISTRIBUTABLES, you agree to: (i) distribute the REDISTRIBUTABLES in object code form only in conjunction with and as a part of your software application product; (ii) not use Microsoft's name, logo, or trademarks to market your software application product; (iii) include a valid copyright notice on your software application product; (iv) indemnify, hold harmless, and defend Microsoft from and against any claims or lawsuits, including attorney's fees, that arise or result from the use or distribution of your software application product; and (v) not permit further distribution of the REDISTRIBUTABLES by your end user. Contact Microsoft for the applicable royalties due and other licensing terms for all other uses and/or distribution of the REDISTRIBUTABLES.

2. **DESCRIPTION OF OTHER RIGHTS AND LIMITATIONS.**

   - **Limitations on Reverse Engineering, Decompilation, and Disassembly.** You may not reverse engineer, decompile, or disassemble the SOFTWARE PRODUCT, except and only to the extent that such activity is expressly permitted by applicable law notwithstanding this limitation.

   - **Separation of Components.** The SOFTWARE PRODUCT is licensed as a single product. Its component parts may not be separated for use on more than one computer.

   - **Rental.** You may not rent, lease, or lend the SOFTWARE PRODUCT.

   - **Support Services.** Microsoft may, but is not obligated to, provide you with support services related to the SOFTWARE PRODUCT ("Support Services"). Use of Support Services is governed by the Microsoft policies and programs described in the user manual, in "online" documentation, and/or in other Microsoft-provided materials. Any supplemental software code provided to you as part of the Support Services shall be considered part of the SOFTWARE PRODUCT and subject to the terms and conditions of this EULA. With respect to technical information you provide to Microsoft as part of the Support Services, Microsoft may use such information for its business purposes, including for product support and development. Microsoft will not utilize such technical information in a form that personally identifies you.

   - **Software Transfer.** You may permanently transfer all of your rights under this EULA, provided you retain no copies, you transfer all of the SOFTWARE PRODUCT (including all component parts, the media and printed materials, any upgrades, this EULA, and, if applicable, the Certificate of Authenticity), **and** the recipient agrees to the terms of this EULA.

   - **Termination.** Without prejudice to any other rights, Microsoft may terminate this EULA if you fail to comply with the terms and conditions of this EULA. In such event, you must destroy all copies of the SOFTWARE PRODUCT and all of its component parts.

3. **COPYRIGHT.** All title and copyrights in and to the SOFTWARE PRODUCT (including but not limited to any images, photographs, animations, video, audio, music, text, SAMPLE CODE, REDISTRIBUTABLES, and "applets" incorporated into the SOFTWARE PRODUCT) and any copies of the SOFTWARE PRODUCT are owned by Microsoft or its suppliers. The SOFTWARE PRODUCT is protected by copyright laws and international treaty provisions. Therefore, you must treat the SOFTWARE PRODUCT like any other copyrighted material **except** that you may install the SOFTWARE PRODUCT on a single computer provided you keep the original solely for backup or archival purposes. You may not copy the printed materials accompanying the SOFTWARE PRODUCT.

4. **U.S. GOVERNMENT RESTRICTED RIGHTS.** The SOFTWARE PRODUCT and documentation are provided with RESTRICTED RIGHTS. Use, duplication, or disclosure by the Government is subject to restrictions as set forth in subparagraph (c)(1)(ii) of the Rights in Technical Data and Computer Software clause at DFARS 252.227-7013 or subparagraphs (c)(1) and (2) of the Commercial Computer Software—Restricted Rights at 48 CFR 52.227-19, as applicable. Manufacturer is Microsoft Corporation/One Microsoft Way/Redmond, WA 98052-6399.

5. **EXPORT RESTRICTIONS.** You agree that you will not export or re-export the SOFTWARE PRODUCT, any part thereof, or any process or service that is the direct product of the SOFTWARE PRODUCT (the foregoing collectively referred to as the "Restricted Components"), to any country, person, entity, or end user subject to U.S. export restrictions. You specifically agree not to export or re-export any of the Restricted Components (i) to any country to which the U.S. has embargoed or restricted the export of goods or services, which currently include, but are not necessarily limited to, Cuba, Iran, Iraq, Libya, North Korea, Sudan, and Syria, or to any national of any such country, wherever located, who intends to transmit or transport the Restricted Components back to such country; (ii) to any end user who you know or have reason to know will utilize the Restricted Components in the design, development, or production of nuclear, chemical, or biological weapons; or (iii) to any end user who has been prohibited from participating in U.S. export transactions by any federal agency of the U.S. government. You warrant and represent that neither the BXA nor any other U.S. federal agency has suspended, revoked, or denied your export privileges.

DISCLAIMER OF WARRANTY

NO WARRANTIES OR CONDITIONS. MICROSOFT EXPRESSLY DISCLAIMS ANY WARRANTY OR CONDITION FOR THE SOFT-WARE PRODUCT. THE SOFTWARE PRODUCT AND ANY RELATED DOCUMENTATION ARE PROVIDED "AS IS" WITHOUT WARRANTY OR CONDITION OF ANY KIND, EITHER EXPRESS OR IMPLIED, INCLUDING, WITHOUT LIMITATION, THE IMPLIED WARRANTIES OF MERCHANTABILITY, FITNESS FOR A PARTICULAR PURPOSE, OR NONINFRINGEMENT. THE ENTIRE RISK ARISING OUT OF USE OR PERFORMANCE OF THE SOFTWARE PRODUCT REMAINS WITH YOU.

LIMITATION OF LIABILITY. TO THE MAXIMUM EXTENT PERMITTED BY APPLICABLE LAW, IN NO EVENT SHALL MICROSOFT OR ITS SUPPLIERS BE LIABLE FOR ANY SPECIAL, INCIDENTAL, INDIRECT, OR CONSEQUENTIAL DAMAGES WHATSOEVER (INCLUDING, WITHOUT LIMITATION, DAMAGES FOR LOSS OF BUSINESS PROFITS, BUSINESS INTERRUPTION, LOSS OF BUSINESS INFORMATION, OR ANY OTHER PECUNIARY LOSS) ARISING OUT OF THE USE OF OR INABILITY TO USE THE SOFTWARE PRODUCT OR THE PROVISION OF OR FAILURE TO PROVIDE SUPPORT SERVICES, EVEN IF MICROSOFT HAS BEEN ADVISED OF THE POSSIBILITY OF SUCH DAMAGES. IN ANY CASE, MICROSOFT'S ENTIRE LIABILITY UNDER ANY PROVISION OF THIS EULA SHALL BE LIMITED TO THE GREATER OF THE AMOUNT ACTUALLY PAID BY YOU FOR THE SOFTWARE PRODUCT OR US$5.00; PROVIDED, HOWEVER, IF YOU HAVE ENTERED INTO A MICROSOFT SUPPORT SERVICES AGREEMENT, MICROSOFT'S ENTIRE LIABILITY REGARDING SUPPORT SERVICES SHALL BE GOVERNED BY THE TERMS OF THAT AGREE-MENT. BECAUSE SOME STATES AND JURISDICTIONS DO NOT ALLOW THE EXCLUSION OR LIMITATION OF LIABILITY, THE ABOVE LIMITATION MAY NOT APPLY TO YOU.

MISCELLANEOUS

This EULA is governed by the laws of the State of Washington USA, except and only to the extent that applicable law mandates governing law of a different jurisdiction.

Should you have any questions concerning this EULA, or if you desire to contact Microsoft for any reason, please contact the Microsoft subsidiary serving your country, or write: Microsoft Sales Information Center/One Microsoft Way/Redmond, WA 98052-6399.

PN 097-0002296

Proof of Purchase

Do not send this card with your registration.
Use this card as proof of purchase if participating in a promotion or
rebate offer on *Microsoft® Outlook® 2000 Step by Step Courseware
Core Skills Student Guide*. Card must be used in conjunction with
other proof(s) of payment such as your dated sales receipt—see offer details.

Microsoft® Outlook® 2000 Step by Step Courseware Core Skills Student Guide

WHERE DID YOU PURCHASE THIS PRODUCT?

CUSTOMER NAME

Microsoft®

mspress.microsoft.com

Microsoft Press, PO Box 97017, Redmond, WA 98073-9830

OWNER REGISTRATION CARD   ## Register Today!   0-7356-0706-0

Return the bottom portion of this card to register today.

Microsoft® Outlook® 2000 Step by Step Courseware Core Skills Student Guide

FIRST NAME   **MIDDLE INITIAL**   **LAST NAME**

INSTITUTION OR COMPANY NAME

ADDRESS

CITY   **STATE**   **ZIP**

( )

E-MAIL ADDRESS   **PHONE NUMBER**

U.S. and Canada addresses only. Fill in information above and mail postage-free.
Please mail only the bottom half of this page.

For information about Microsoft Press®
products, visit our Web site at
mspress.microsoft.com

Microsoft®

NO POSTAGE
NECESSARY
IF MAILED
IN THE
UNITED STATES

BUSINESS REPLY MAIL
FIRST-CLASS MAIL   PERMIT NO. 108   REDMOND WA

POSTAGE WILL BE PAID BY ADDRESSEE

MICROSOFT PRESS
PO BOX 97017
REDMOND, WA 98073-9830